Pistols, Politics
and the Press

Pistols, Politics and the Press

Dueling in 19th Century American Journalism

RYAN CHAMBERLAIN

McFarland & Company, Inc., Publishers
Jefferson, North Carolina, and London

LIBRARY OF CONGRESS CATALOGUING-IN-PUBLICATION DATA

Chamberlain, Ryan, 1973–
    Pistols, politics and the press : dueling in 19th century
American journalism / Ryan Chamberlain.
        p.   cm.
    Includes bibliographical references and index.

    ISBN 978-0-7864-3829-7
    softcover : 50# alkaline paper ∞

    1. Dueling — United States — History —19th century.   2. Journalism —
Social aspects — United States — History —19th entury.   I. Title.
CR4595.U5C43   2009
394'.80973 — dc22   2008037814

British Library cataloguing data are available

Cover art: E.W. Kemble, *The Duel,* ink on paper, 1887
(Cabinet of American Illustration, Library of Congress)

Manufactured in the United States of America

McFarland & Company, Inc., Publishers
  Box 611, Jefferson, North Carolina 28640
  www.mcfarlandpub.com

To my parents, family, friends and wife, Kristen Chamberlain, whose unconditional love and support made this research possible, and to the brave American journalists of the nineteenth century, who continually risked their lives for the press freedoms we hold dear over a century later. May this work contribute to your immortality.

Acknowledgments

Much of the research that created the foundation for this book was borne out of work done while I was a graduate student at the E.W. Scripps School of Journalism at Ohio University. I would like to thank faculty members Dr. Douglass Daniel, Dr. Bernhard Debatin and especially Dr. Patrick Washburn for their encouragement on this topic and their thoughtful advice. I would also like to thank Bertram Wyatt-Brown for his encouraging correspondences via e-mail during the initial stages of this research. I would also like to acknowledge the wonderful assistance I received from many of the staff at libraries and state archives across the country. Among these people, I would particularly like to recognize Ara Kaye, State Historical Society of Missouri; Joyce M. Cox, Nevada State Library and Archives; Gregory H. Stoner, Virginia Historical Society; Nicholas Graham, Massachusetts Historical Society; Margaret Humberston, Springfield Library and Museum; Sharon Bennett and Julia Logan, the Charleston Museum; and Greg King for his assistance at the California State Library. I would also like to recognize the Mississippi Department of Archives and History for their helpful efforts and expertise in fulfilling my research requests. Thanks should also go to Megan White and Bonnie Gruttadauria for their editorial guidance and wisdom. Finally, I would like to express my heartfelt gratitude to my parents, Larry and Mary Lou Chamberlain, who were enormous patrons of this research.

Table of Contents

Preface

This book is intended as a call to action for journalism scholars and historians. Among both groups the influence of dueling and honor rituals has been considered a novelty, an interesting footnote within the discipline. Instead, it should be treated as more of a fundamental building block of mass communication, one that greatly influenced the development of American journalism throughout the nineteenth century and beyond.

The nucleus of this premise formed quite innocently. I don't remember the exact time or date, but I remember as a Denver Place Elementary School student in my hometown of Wilmington, Ohio, reaching for *Denver, the Man*, by George C. Barnes, in the school library. I was curious to find out if many of the places in Wilmington, such as the General Denver Hotel and my school, were somehow related to the capital of Colorado and Barnes' book. Much to my surprise, they were!

It turned out that *Denver, the Man* was a wonderful introduction into the life of General James W. Denver, a career statesmen and soldier who was at the center of many important political events in mid–nineteenth-century America. At various points in political and military career, Denver was a captain in the Mexican War, state senator of California, secretary of state for California, U.S. representative from California, commissioner of Indian affairs and a brigadier general in the Union army during the Civil War. He was also governor of the territory known infamously as "Bleeding Kansas" and helped Colorado gain its statehood. Colorado's capital city, Denver, was so named to court his political favor. All the while, he maintained his permanent residence in Wilmington, as he did for most of his life. Denver's residence was turned into the home of the Clinton County Historical Society, and was located right across the street from my childhood home.

A dramatically pivotal point in Denver's early life was a duel with Edward Gilbert, the founder and editor of the *Alta California*, one of San Francisco's leading newspapers at the time. Gilbert died in the exchange of gunfire. I heard grumblings from Wilmington historians that *Denver, the Man*, which I've been told by some town elders was written on behalf of the family long after General Denver's death, was more archival propaganda than a balanced historical treatment. But the one thing that Barnes did right, and which makes the book extremely valuable as a historical resource, was transcribe many of Denver's letters, including all the correspondences with Gilbert leading up to the duel. Denver, a former journalist himself in Xenia, Ohio, was a prolific and articulate writer.

Obviously, at an elementary school level I couldn't process the social and political complexities of honor rituals in the Denver-Gilbert duel. However, I kept revisiting Denver as a historical topic throughout junior high and high school. As a boy who was raised on syndicated television re-runs of *Gunsmoke, Rawhide, The Lone Ranger* and *The Cisco Kid*, I was naturally drawn to Denver's real-life Western shootout and Civil War battles. I would walk across the street to his house and admire his military uniform with mild hero worship.

I remember being very frustrated and puzzled that there was no special day in Wilmington (or his namesake city) to honor General Denver's legacy. After all, here was an icon of American history in my opinion, one who had ties to my small Ohio town and was buried in the local Sugar Grove cemetery. There was little else exciting to do growing up in Wilmington except wait to attend the outhouse races at the annual Corn Festival, so why not have a "General Denver day?" Whenever I inquired about this, the short answer was always something to the effect of "He never did much for Wilmington gallivanting across the country," or "We feel uncomfortable paying tribute to someone who killed another man." While I could respond to the first answer in enough detail to fill another book, the second answer that I received from Wilmingtonians was the one that sent me on the research path leading to this work.

The town of Wilmington has strong Quaker roots, so I can certainly appreciate the townspeople not wanting to glorify violence. Nevertheless, it was very clear from reading the newspaper articles and correspondences surrounding the event that there was little or no personal malice involved on Denver's part in Gilbert's death. In fact, the two had not even met before they took the field of honor against each other outside Sacramento in 1852. If we are to believe Denver's account, which I do based on my research, he had no desire to see Gilbert die and did everything he felt he could on the dueling grounds to avoid killing him. Unlike Wilmington, however, it seemed as if the mid–nineteenth-century California community did not see anything abnormal in the circumstances surrounding Gilbert's demise. Not only was Denver not convicted in Gilbert's homicide, he was promoted to be California's secretary of state shortly after the affair.

It also seemed clear from reading the correspondences that there was more to the Denver-Gilbert encounter than arriving on the field, drawing guns and shooting each other. This was not like the Wild West shows I grew up watching, with stories of two-dimensional characters. This was not a showdown in the middle of Dodge City. Edward Gilbert was not wearing a black cowboy hat, and Denver was not wearing white. Denver and Gilbert were both prominent, well-respected men in the community, guided by a cultural force that required them to follow a set of almost tediously complex rules known as the *Code Duello*. What was the *Code Duello*? Where did it come from? Why did some people choose to duel while others did not? Was this normal for the time period? The more I read about the Denver-Gilbert affair, these were the logical questions that began to surface. I was determined to prove that Denver was a reluctant participant in Gilbert's demise, in hopes of finally getting my General Denver day in Wilmington. In a sense, I was out to prove that the general's actions and ethics in the duel were honorable for that period.

Of course there has been much written on the subject of dueling and its chivalric origins. As I left Wilmington to pursue my undergraduate degree in English at the University of Cincinnati, I would read stories such as *Beowulf* and many versions of Arthurian romances by Chrétien de Troyes and Mallory, with knights of the roundtable battling Moorish Saracens who mysteriously charged out the forest in full armor on horseback. These knights, like Gilbert and Denver, were fighting for honor. Was there a connection? If we are to believe historians of honor rituals in Judeo-Christian culture, there was. The problem with many of the scholarly books written about chivalry, dueling and the *Code Duello* was that they focused primarily on the military and combat aspect of the duel. They lacked the social and political context to explain why in 1852 it was socially acceptable, even justified, to duel to the death in California, but not in Massachusetts.

Furthermore, it was written into the original 1849 State Constitution of California that dueling was illegal. If caught, the participants were disqualified from public office. From these basic facts, one can start to draw some inferences. First, even as late as 1849, dueling was common enough that state lawmakers believed it needed to be included in the constitution. Second, even though it was mortal combat, apparently dueling was not perceived as murder, manslaughter or even assault by the California courts. This would become acutely apparent when California Supreme Court Justice David S. Terry was acquitted in the death of Senator David C. Broderick in the aftermath of their infamous duel in 1859. Third, the focus of dueling in the California Constitution seemed to revolve around politics. Gilbert, a member of the state constitutional convention, knew that dueling was illegal. Yet, he still felt compelled to issue a challenge to a person he had never even met. Furthermore, even though the California state constitution disqualified duelists from holding public office, Denver was elected to Congress in 1854. These paradoxes defied twenty-first century logic.

I didn't pursue the topic with any academic rigor until my graduate work in the E.W. Scripps School of Journalism at Ohio University. I was required to do an extensive research piece for a journalism history project and was at a loss for a topic. I hadn't forgotten about Denver. Every time I would go home to Wilmington for a visit, there was Denver's house, much as it stood during his lifetime, reminding me there was still no General Denver day in Wilmington. It occurred to me that Denver dueled with a newspaper editor and thus was relative to my journalism studies, so I decided to revisit the topic again.

Because I was now researching dueling from a mass communication perspective, it forced me to see the *Code Duello* in a completely different light. I no longer viewed it as merely combat. By delving into the origins and causes of dueling in America, it began to reveal itself as an intricate nineteenth-century communication process of insult and apology that could go on for weeks or months. Sometimes it ended in violence; sometimes it didn't. However, a violent resolution for libel was always a possibility when the language of the *Code Duello* was referred to by an offended party.

My early research was well-received by professors and my peers, and encouraged by this success, I began to expand my research beyond the Denver-Gilbert affair and track down primary sources for duels involving newspaper editors across nineteenth-century America. Over and over I would read tales of how honor rituals were used to intimidate editors. But I discovered that editors themselves also used honor rituals to their advantage in order to make inroads into a highly stratified political scene in early America. I deemed this to be an extremely important concept when understanding the close relationship between politics and journalism during the Party Press era.

Naturally, I sought out others within the journalism community who shared my opinion. I joined journalism history associations and went to journalism conventions in hopes of finding other journalists researching the effect of honor rituals on the nineteenth-century press. Journalists in America were dueling for at least a century over libel; therefore it seemed common sense that honor rituals must have had a significant impact on the function and development of the press. Much to my consternation, I discovered that many journalism historians did not consider honor rituals as an important factor in understanding the nineteenth-century press. At a conference, I remember asking a well-respected and accomplished historian of nineteenth-century journalism point blank, "What effect do you think dueling and honor rituals had on nineteenth-century journalism?" The historian's reply was, "I don't think it had any effect at all." At that point, I knew this book must be written.

As of this writing, there is still no General Denver day in Wilmington. However, it would be satisfying to me if this book imbues the reader with a deeper sense of the communication challenges that journalists and public figures such as Denver and Gilbert faced throughout the nineteenth century. The contents of these pages are neither the first nor hopefully last words regarding the tangled history of honor rituals and journalism. It is my hope that by showing the connection between nineteenth-century journalism and the ritual of the duel, this book will serve as a platform for a deeper discussion of the pressures and paradoxes faced by those who sacrificed so much in the name of honor, free speech and democracy.

Introduction

What started out as a scathing local editorial exchange between rival Virginia editors turned into a national sensation and one of the last major duels in American history.[1] Richard F. Beirne, editor of the *Richmond State*, accused William C. Elam of being a false advocate of black rights in Virginia for political gain.[2] Elam, editor of the *Richmond Whig*, had been using his newspaper as a central mouthpiece for the emerging Readjuster political party. Personal and political rivalries showcased publicly in a free, but partisan-slanted, press gave the Beirne-Elam encounter all the elements of a classic American duel.

Beirne, who wrote for the political opposition, had made it his editorial mission to discredit Elam's rhetoric as both parties geared up for the 1883 election.[3] In a vicious retort, one paragraph in particular from Elam's June 21 editorial would set a ritualistic chain of events in motion: "Consequently — unintimidated, and not utterly crushed — we laugh at the *State*'s vituperation and vaporing, and beg to remark that not only does the *State* lie, but its editor and owner lies, and the poor creature who may have actually written the article in question also lies — all, jointly and severally — deliberately, knowingly, maliciously and with the inevitable cowardice that is always invoked with insolent bravado."[4] Thanks to the telegraph, news spread quickly across the nation that Elam had announced publicly, and on the record, that Beirne was essentially a liar and a coward. Under the headline, "Appealing To the Code," the *New York Times* wrote, "It is understood that as soon as MR. BEIRNE heard of the offensive editorial in the *Whig* he placed himself [in] communication with MR. ELAM and demanded satisfaction."[5] For Beirne, satisfaction meant a public apology from Elam or a pistol duel, according to the rules of the *Code Duello*.[6]

There would be no apology. On that same day, friends, or "seconds," were appointed to handle the administrative functions of the hostile affair.

Through secret communications, a challenge was delivered and accepted, and then the place and time had to be decided. Finally, they had to agree on the choice of weapons and the distance each man would stand apart from each other at the time of the shot. After much formality, the editors, through their seconds, agreed to meet that night at Cardoso's farm two miles south of Hanover Junction outside of Richmond. The weapons chosen were navy six-shooters, the largest of their kind. It was decided that the distance would be eight paces instead of the usual ten due to Elam's extreme nearsightedness.[7]

Even though the editors were miles apart, both men were there on time ready to duel. However, one of the seconds could not arrive until late that night, and the duel had to be postponed.[8] When the second arrived, it was agreed that both parties would meet at the dueling ground at four o'clock in the afternoon with the exchange taking place at six.[9] Both men retired to separate nearby farmhouses for the night.[10]

Even though it was a felony under Virginia law, neither editor was a stranger to dueling. Beirne had been in a dueling affair with a senator two years previous. No shots were fired because Beirne's second forgot the percussion caps, rendering the pistols useless. Beirne ordered the second to leave and return with the caps, but the senator and his party cried foul and the affair ended in fiasco.[11] Elam's duel in June 1880 with Colonel Tom Smith ended more violently, with Elam being shot in the chin. It was clear to most people in Virginia, and the nation, that both men would rather fight than back down.[12]

It was also clear to the local authorities that Beirne and Elam would not hesitate to kill each other if given the chance. After learning the details of the duel, Alexander Tomilson, a Richmond policeman, took the railroad to Hanover Junction and, disguised in plainclothes, snuck up on the dueling parties by horseback. With everyone attending engrossed in the details of the affair, it was not difficult to surprise them.[13] After both parties had returned to the dueling grounds that day, there had been a heated debate over a breach of protocol by Elam's seconds. Instead of the agreed upon navy six-shooters, Elam's seconds had brought a pair of much smaller five-shooters.[14] As both parties argued, Tomilson announced his presence and immediately arrested Beirne on the charge of being about to engage in a duel.[15] He also tried to take the bystanders into custody as witnesses, but everyone scattered when they realized what was going on. Elam, standing off to the side, was able to flee from the scene and avoided arrest.[16] Tomilson placed Beirne into custody with the sheriff of Hanover Junction. No duel would be fought that day.[17]

The breakup by the police did not stop the determined editors. After dropping Beirne off at Hanover Junction, the Richmond police went searching for Elam, who they suspected was taking refuge in a farmhouse near the dueling grounds. When they arrived, the owner of the house refused to let them in, and without a search warrant, the police decided not to force entry.[18] Elam, who was in the farmhouse, escaped unnoticed back to Richmond, where he remained in hiding. Meanwhile, Beirne escaped from custody and hopped a train bound for West Virginia, which was out of the jurisdiction of Virginia police.[19] The *New York Times* wrote, "The excitement over the expected duel between Beirne and Elam has not abated. All day anxious inquiries have been made as to where the principals are."[20] It was assumed by most people that since both parties were still at large that a duel between Beirne and Elam was only a matter of when and where.[21]

Not everyone was anxious for a fight. Under the headline "Bloodthirsty Babies," a *New York Times* editorial read:

> MR. BEIRNE, it is now declared, has left Virginia with the intention of goading MR. ELAM to come out of his inviolate hole and follow him. It may be that the public curiosity may yet be assuaged upon the question whether MR. ELAM is a corrupt henchman or MR. BEIRNE is a deliberate, knowing, and malicious liar. But in any case the public is distinctly notified that two newspapers in Richmond are edited by grown-up babies, who have been engaged in a performance that will be no less infantile if it ends in a tragedy than it is now that it seems to have ended in a farce.[22]

This view did not keep the *Times* from running almost daily reports in anticipation of a duel under the headlines "No Duel Fought Yet" and "The Duellists Apart." The *Times*, like the rest of the nation, was caught up in the unfolding conflict between Beirne and Elam.[23]

The sensational and national coverage of the rival editors started to have broader political implications. As the excitement of the impending duel increased, the duelists began to represent more than their personal quarrel. Because each editor was a strong advocate for his own political party, they began to symbolize opposing political ideals. In an editorial, the *New York Times* wrote: "This feeling cannot be confined to the personal friends of the duelists. The interest in the duel arises from the feeling that it is not a private quarrel but a public war. It is a survival, in fact of the 'wager of battle.' Elam is the champion of the Readjusters, and Beirne carries the hopes of the Funders. Looked at in this way, the public interest is explained, as combining the interests of 'cause' and of a horse race."[24] Thus, what started out as a personal quarrel was quickly turning into a battle of competing political ideology.[25]

Days after the averted duel, both editors were still at large and in hiding. A railroad official spotted Beirne in West Virginia and another warrant was issued for his arrest. In Lewisburg, a friend of Beirne's warned him of his impending arrest, and he escaped. But he was still stuck in West Virginia, many miles from Elam, who was still in hiding somewhere outside Richmond.[26]

Neither distance nor the police could prevent Beirne and Elam from contacting each other. Elam's second, Page McCarthy, stepped forward as a messenger. However, everyone suspected of being a part of the affair was under heavy surveillance by Richmond detectives. So, McCarthy sent a coded message by telegraph and two messengers to Beirne. One messenger was sent with the navy six-shooters and another messenger was sent with the key to the coded telegram. The police suspected that the messenger with the key code was heading to Beirne and gave chase. But the messenger escaped the chasing lawmen by running into a large cornfield. Beirne received the message: the duel would take place June 30 in Waynesboro at 6 a.m. The passwords would be "Number one" to avoid a reoccurrence of the previous duel.[27]

As messengers were going back and forth, the nation wondered when or if the duel would take place. The *New York Daily Herald* wrote, "Nobody except those concerned know what has been done, but tonight it is rumored that some understanding had at last been reached, and that the fight would soon take place."[28] The *New York Times* echoed similar sentiments when it wrote, "When or where the meeting will take place is more of a mystery now than ever. That it will occur, however, is not doubted. Although the excitement of the past three days has somewhat abated, the anxiety and desire to hear from the principals is still intense."[29] In this way, newspapers helped to build anticipation for the duel.

There were lingering critics who tried to point out the absurdity of both men going to such great lengths just to shoot at each other. An editorial in the *New York Daily Tribune* read: "Let Mr. Beirne ascend a high mountain in the Greenbrier range in West Virginia, and Mr. Elam another high mountain in the Blue Ridge range in Virginia.... As Mr. Beirne is not likely to be content with anything except a very murderous weapon, both men could be furnished with a Gatling gun, and could peg away at each other with great noise and slight danger of harm.... It contains all the elements of a successful modern Southern duel."[30]

In an editorial, the *New York Times* echoed similar sarcasm: "If the Southern politicians mean to keep up the cheerful old custom, they would do well to revive the details, and instead of taking up with new fangled

Derringers and navy revolvers, fight in public with club and buckler [shield] from sunrise to the coming out of the stars in the evening. The combatant who was worsted in this all-day pummeling was then additionally hanged."[31] The idea that this hostile affair was becoming absurd, even by duelists' standards, was not unfounded. In order to throw the police off suspicion, both Elam and Beirne appointed new seconds to handle the final parts of the hostile affair.[32] Each man had to travel a great distance by horse through torrential downpours. Beirne narrowly escaped drowning in a flash flood when his carriage was swept down a swollen mountain stream. Elam had an equally rigorous journey through mountains and across flooded streams. Finally, each man traveled almost 20 miles apiece, by horse, for a chance to meet the other on the field of honor. [33]

At five o'clock in the morning, a courier from Elam's party contacted Beirne and led his party to the dueling grounds. The editors and their entourage met a few minutes before 6 o'clock outside of Philip Killian's farm. One of Elam's friends acted as a mediator, introducing Frank Wright, Beirne's second, to Sheffey Lewis, Elam's second and the son of Virginia's lieutenant governor. [34] Also acting as seconds were W.E. Chalkley for Beirne and John Snelling, a local politician, for Elam.[35] Lewis measured off eight paces and presented the weapons to Wright for Beirne's use. The seconds loaded the guns for the duelists in plain view and then tossed for the choice of positions. Lewis won the toss and the right to give the command to fire.[36] Elam and Beirne appeared calm and unmoved by the impending exchange of fire.[37]

Everyone not involved with the duel was asked to stand aside as Elam and Beirne took their places eight paces apart.[38] Beirne, twenty-seven, weighed nearly 225 pounds, stood six foot, and wore a dark brown moustache and goatee. Elam, much older at forty-seven, was also smaller at 140 pounds and had prematurely gray hair, glasses, and a full, well-trimmed beard. Both were married with children. Neither had met before that day as they stared at one another from across their marks.[39]

Both editors gripped their pistols and stared at each other in preparation for the first shot. The terms agreed upon before the duel were that after the command, "Gentlemen, are you ready! Fire, one, two, three," shots were to be fired after the word "fire"[40] and before the word "three." If neither hit the other after the first round, then Beirne as the challenger was to decide whether or not his honor was satisfied. If Beirne was not content with the results of the first shot, they would repeat the sequence until their six-shooters were empty. Each editor had the choice of advancing after the word "Fire!" But that meant risking not getting the first shot off. At eight paces, distance was not a real factor.[41] Beirne and Elam held a steady gaze at one another with their pistols cocked and aimed. They were devoid of any outward emotion.[42]

The command was given, "Gentlemen, are you ready! Fire, one, two, three!" The shots echoed in the pristine oak grove as both men raised their pistols and fired almost simultaneously at the word "one." Smoke billowed from both pistols as each man stood firmly at his mark.[43] Beirne's shot missed wide, but Elam's shot barely missed its target. Beirne looked down and saw a bullet hole through his oversized sack coat. He demanded another shot.[44]

Both men, still standing on their mark, cocked their pistols as the command was given again: "Gentlemen, are you ready! Fire, one, two, three!"[45] Both men raised their pistols and fired again almost simultaneously on "one." Beirne stood firm, but Elam staggered forward and exclaimed, "I am shot!" His legs started to give way and his second, who was standing near, asked him what was the matter. Elam replied, "Oh,—it! I am shot again. I can't shoot. That is what's the matter." Dr. Lewis Wheat, Elam's attending surgeon and a nephew to Lieutenant Governor John F. Lewis, rushed over to survey the wound.[46] Beirne declared that he was satisfied, tipped his hat to Elam and left in a carriage along with everyone in his party.[47]

Meanwhile, Wheat probed Elam in search of the bullet. Elam, who was now smoking a cigar that someone handed him, insisted that he was shot in both legs.[48] Wheat assured him that he was only having sympathy pains in his other leg. When told this, Elam declared that had he known that, he would have asked for another shot. It was then concluded that Elam had been shot in the right thigh near his groin area, but Wheat couldn't find the bullet.[49] Wheat bandaged Elam as best he could and the party traveled to the lieutenant governor's house nearly twenty miles away.[50]

There was still the matter of the authorities. Many people speculated that the duelists and the spectators would be arrested. Beirne's driver was arrested as a witness even though he had not seen the duel.[51] Since the Civil War, only one person had actually been convicted of dueling, but the situation might escalate if Elam died.[52]

After the duel, Elam's condition steadily deteriorated. Under the headline, "Mr. Elam's Condition Critical," the *New York Times* wrote: "After his removal from the field to the residence of Mr. Lewis, a closer examination disclosed that the ball had entered the right thigh near the junction of the upper third and lower two-thirds of the femur. After striking the bone it ranged backward and upward through the peritoneum and lodged in the left groin, whence it was extracted. It passed between the urethra and the rectum, lacerating the tissues but not seriously injuring either organ."[53] The *New York Tribune* reported virtually the same details under the headline "Elam's Wound Very Serious." Even though Elam had one of the best doctors attending to him, Dr. Wheat speculated that Elam would either be moving around in ten days, or he would be dead.[54]

By July 4, Elam's condition had improved enough that it was evident he would survive. No other arrests or warrants were ever issued as a result of the duel. Even though 1883 Virginia law prohibited persons who engaged as principals or seconds in duels from holding office,[55] there was already speculation that Elam would be a lock for his party's gubernatorial nomination. When asked if he would use his newfound notoriety as a launching pad for political office, Beirne replied that he would rather be an editor than hold political office.[56]

Fortunately Elam survived the event, but what if he had not? Would Beirne have been convicted for murder? The answer is no, and that creates a conundrum: In the nineteenth century under what circumstances was killing a journalist not considered murder? In spite of the laws against participants holding office, according to the *New York Times* many speculated that Elam would win his party's gubernatorial nomination.[57] Politics, after his duel, should not have been an option for him. But apparently dueling made Elam more politically attractive. What was it about the code of honor and dueling that would not only allow this to happen to a journalist but encourage it to happen again?

These questions and more comprise the main theme of this book. The goal is to reveal how influential honor rituals were in manipulating and intimidating the press during the course of the nineteenth century and thereby derive a comprehensive historical picture that has been lacking in journalism studies. Primary sources will reveal that dueling in cases of defamation or libel was far more prevalent than has been previously realized. Of course, how honor rituals fit into journalism history presents a dilemma because of the nature of the press during most of the nineteenth century. Press and politics were not necessarily discrete terms so it is difficult to have a discussion of one divorced from the other. What seems like political history sometimes is also journalism history, and vice versa, because the two were so closely intertwined in their development.

The Beirne-Elam duel illustrates this dilemma of analysis. Clearly their rivalry was rooted in politics. However, the precipitating remark initiating the duel was a personal insult. As such, it was customary for members of the ruling class in nineteenth-century America to handle personal insults by resorting to the code of honor. What journalism did in this case was elevate the personal insult to the public arena. As journalists their political and economic livelihoods depended on public approval and support, thus the two parties were compelled to resolve their personal dispute in a public way. This public resolution of personal disputes was further compounded for editors whose newspapers were connected to political parties through patronage. Thus, what started as a personal quarrel, as in the Beirne-Elam incident, could quickly turn into a battle of competing political ideology.

It cannot be denied that journalism played an integral role, in situations such as the one described. The nature of partisan editorial comment fused with news reporting compelled the personal to become political. In the highly charged partisan atmosphere that existed in America, that often meant resorting to the code of honor to resolve personal rivalries over political issues. But whereas most journalism research has treated this subject as a historical anomaly, this book differs by postulating that honor rituals were, in fact, an epidemic problem for journalists throughout much of the nineteenth century.

The problems caused for journalists by honor rituals were complex, and they will receive a complex analysis in this book. Hazel Dicken-Garcia's *Journalistic Standards in Nineteenth-Century America* is the most recent comprehensive analysis on the dual role of editor and politician during that period.[58] She refers to dueling briefly in her analysis, but she does not examine how dueling and the code of honor influenced and affected these standards. This is the case as well for Frank Luther Mott's *American Journalism*.[59] What are the forces at work that motivated two editors like Beirne and Elam, who had never met before they reached the dueling grounds, to aspire to kill each other over their newspaper columns? Why did not Elam file a libel suit? If dueling was a privilege of the ruling class, what happened if journalists were critical of those in power? Because honor codes were invoked by and against journalists for nearly a century in America, did this have an impact on the way journalism was perceived and produced?

Lambert Wilmer's *Our Press Gang*, one of the first American books devoted to press criticism, dedicated two chapters to the subject of dueling, but that was published in 1859 and was far from complete in its examination.[60] It did illustrate, however, that honor codes were an imposing force upon journalists of the period. But, because it was a product of its time, it lacked the historical depth and clarity that only hindsight can provide.

For the most part, newspapers were not commercially viable until after 1860 and depended on the political establishment for patronage. How did honor rituals impact and affect this relationship? Joanne B. Freeman's *Affairs of Honor: National Politics in the New Republic*[61] does an excellent job of discussing this sociopolitical relationship between honor and journalism in its early stages in the New York area. However, it does not explain how the relationship between honor rituals, politics and journalism evolved to the point where journalists like Beirne and Elam were still dueling in 1883 Virginia defamation.

The research done by Bertram Wyatt-Brown in his books *The Shaping of Southern Culture*[62] and *Southern Honor*[63] is by far the most innovative and complete analysis of honor rituals in nineteenth-century America. But Wyatt-Brown is not a journalism historian and therefore does not approach the effect of honor rituals from that point of view. When he does discuss the effect of honor rituals on journalists, it is confined to primarily the Jacksonian age. That leaves a tremendous gap to be filled. What this book will do is use primary sources to compare and contrast Wyatt-Brown's theories in other regions and points of time beyond the scope of his research. For instance, when a journalist criticized a politician in 1850s California, why would he sometimes receive a challenge from a political subordinate and not the politician? What would each side have to gain or lose? Questions like these are not answered directly by Wyatt-Brown but his rationale can be applied to similar situations. Although dueling and honor rituals were predominant in the South during the nineteenth century, they were not, as Wyatt-Brown readily admitted, a uniquely Southern phenomenon. Thus, this book will examine honor disputes in other regions beyond the South.

Similarly, C.A. Harwell Wells' 2001 article "The End of the Affair? Anti-Dueling Laws and Social Norms in Antebellum America" in the *Vanderbilt Law Review* is compelling from a law perspective but incomplete as journalism history.[64] Wells suggests that the Civil War led to the demise of dueling, but journalists were dueling in various regions of the country into the 1890s. This book also differs from Wells because it argues that the social conformity to, and enforcement of, early anti-dueling laws did not necessarily quell violent, ritualistic responses to perceived libel. In fact, this book posits that by outlawing the ritual arbitration of insult and apology that led to dueling, it may have increased violent reactions towards journalists in incidences of perceived libel.

In some cases, however, honor rituals called for no arbitration. For instance, Patricia Dooley's book, *Taking Their Political Place: Journalists and the Making of an Occupation*, explained how, in the early 1800s, William Coleman of the New York *Evening Post* was often a target of libel suits.[65] But it does not explain why in some instances it was socially acceptable for a defamed person to beat a journalist like Coleman with a walking cane. The man who beat Coleman so severely that it left him paralyzed claimed his reputation was harmed by Coleman's editorials.[66] It was understood that he did not challenge Coleman to a duel because he considered the editor a social inferior. This notion of social hierarchy seems incongruent with the American notion that all men are created equal. It also raises the question of under what circumstances in the nineteenth century was it more socially correct to whip or cane a journalist than to initiate a duel or libel suit?

This book will show that a comprehensive knowledge of honor rituals is essential in order to understand the mindset of the nineteenth-century journalist. To the author's knowledge, this is the first journalism research of that explores the impact of honor rituals upon nineteenth-century journalism, spanning the rise and decline of dueling. Not every editor in the nineteenth century was challenged to a duel, but many felt the pressures of the ritual. How did the threat of this ritual response to defamation help or hinder the nineteenth-century editor? If an editor decided not to participate in ritual affairs, how did this affect the patronage he received from members of the ruling class? Why was a signed letter in a newspaper considered more defamatory than one that was unsigned or signed with a pseudonym? During the party press era, how did the ritual of the duel affect the relationship between the editor and political parties, who endorsed honor rituals as a measure of self-worth? Why were some editors promoted for dueling and others jailed? These are but some of the questions that this book will address.

CHAPTER ONE

Honor's Influence on the Emerging Partisan Press

If we are to believe Benjamin Franklin, then it would seem that defamation was connected to ritualized violence from the earliest days of American journalism. In his seminal autobiography, America's founding father wrote to his son about the state of journalism in 1788, "Now many of our Printers make no scruple of gratifying the Malice of Individuals by false Accusations of the fairest Characters among ourselves, augmenting Animosity even to the producing of Duels, and are moreover so indiscrete as to print scurrilous Reflections on the Government of neighboring States, and even on the Conduct of our best national Allies, which may be attended with the most pernicious Consequences."[1] So it would also seem that this connection between ritualized violence and defamation had not diminished nearly 11 years later when contemporaries of William Duane, the heir to Benjamin Franklin Basche's legacy at the Philadelphia *Aurora*, began to shed their artisan printer moniker and make inroads into the political process as party printer-editors under the leadership of Thomas Jefferson.[2] The May 15, 1799, encounter between Duane and Joseph McKean illustrated this connection. When Duane chastised Philadelphia's volunteer cavalry, led by McKean, for their misconduct in the course of Fries' Rebellion, the response to the criticism was a public beating of the editor by him and 30 fellow troops, followed by a whipping. In the face of this assault, Duane's reaction was to challenge each man to mortal combat in a duel. The challenge was refused because they did not consider him of equal "gentleman" social rank. It was because of this social stratification that McKean and his troops felt it was within the limits of social acceptability to impose their will on those they deemed "less honorable."[3]

The last point bears further examination if we are to derive a deeper understanding of the challenges faced by the nineteenth-century editor in regard to honor rituals. According to cultural historians such as David Hackett Fischer, the social dynamic in the nineteenth-century American community is almost impossible for someone in the twenty-first century to comprehend. In his book, *Albion's Seed: Four British Folkways in America*, Fischer explained, "This is because we no longer understand human relationships in hierarchical terms, and can no longer accept the proposition that a person's status in the world is determined and even justified by his fortune."[4] This was not a social ranking based on materialism as we might conceive it in modern times, but rather an assertion of class ranking based on a combination of such things as birthright and reputations of honor. Because an honorable gentlemen's social rank was determined by the quantity of virtue and valor that his reputation held in eyes of the nineteenth-century community, his rank was often extremely fragile in the face of libel. Shame and humiliation from such things as libel, as Fischer suggested, had an emotional power that is lost today, where loss of honor and reputation was synonymous with social death.[5]

By and large, these were British cultural mores that were inherited and perpetuated in America from the regions which inspired them. As Fischer described in his book, however, these cultural mores did not develop uniformly and varied according to the English cultural streams or "folkways" that flowed into the American territory from largely Puritanical, Cavalier, Quaker and North Britain backgrounds.[6] These cultures carried with them varying degrees of social stratification. For instance, Fischer explained that "New England ... had a truncated system of social orders. The Virginians, on the other hand, extended the full array of English social orders, and reinforced them."[7] In his book, *Southern Honor: Ethics and Behavior in the Old South*, Bertram Wyatt-Brown suggested that although early America had peculiar sectional differences, they shared a common ethical system, based in honor, which simply developed at different rates.[8]

How much of an effect did these honor rituals have on local journalism during the antebellum era? This is a progressively more important question to nineteenth-century journalism research as the status of Jeffersonian Republican printer-editors began to make successful inroads into the sociopolitical hierarchy of Federalism in what Jeffrey L. Pasley described in his book, *The Tyranny of Printers: Newspaper Politics in the Early American Republic*, as "an inversion of necessary and appropriate social hierarchies that was not to be tolerated."[9] But as early editors worked to change their social standing from artisan printers to a new status as "gentlemen," they also had to contend with, in varying degrees, the ethical system of reward and punishment imbedded within these inherited hierarchies. This ethical system was known popularly in nineteenth-century America as the code of honor and its methods for mediating libel often ended in violence.

In the late eighteenth century when there was only one political party, the establishment of John Fenno's *Gazette of the United States* in 1789 as well as the Alien and Sedition Acts might be seen in many ways as an attempt by Federalists to emulate, assert and reinforce an Americanized version of English social hierarchy. Even when party divisions developed, Pasley wrote, "It became apparent that most newspapers, being run by traditional, trade-oriented printers, would continue in their habit of supporting the constituted authorities or shying away from politics altogether. The Federalists saw themselves as the legitimate governing class rather than as a party, and most printers agreed."[10] This classism could help explain, in part, the visceral backlash Federalists faced in early Republican editors' responses to the Sedition Acts, which Pasley described as not only failing to put political opposition out of business, but calling "new men into the field, in greater numbers and with greater intensity than previously." But even when the establishment of Philip Freneau's Republican mouthpiece *National Gazette* in 1791 and Jefferson's presidential election in 1801 helped to rally opposition to the Federalists by organizing the press as it had never been organized before, the anti–Federalists leaders could scarcely conceive of a political alternative in non-hierarchical terms. Thus, even though a network of newspaper support was instrumental in Jefferson's presidential victory, editors for the most part did not carry a gentleman's status and were considered politically inferior because they did not meet what Pasley called "Jefferson's educational and social requirements, and thus were not usually even considered for presidentially appointed offices."[11]

The fact remains that throughout the antebellum period editors strove for, and achieved to some degree, gentleman status in the political world, which included in many cases deference to the code of honor and all its ritualistic trappings. Before reaching this status, printer-editors, as illustrated by the Duane incident, generally only encountered the code of honor peripherally as proxy supporters for the Federalist and anti–Federalist political elite. That is because even the most prominent eighteenth-century political newspaper voices, such as anti–Federalists Duane and Charles Holt, editor of the New London *Bee*, could only be seen as, Pasley wrote, "a tool of others, with no political will of his own, and thus no right to participate in public life."[12] According to Pasley, this idea was reinforced by the practice of prominent politicians arranging for others to edit their

newspapers and thus avoiding any threats to their status and reputation
as gentlemen. Feeding this inequity was the gentlemen's practice of submitting political articles to party newspapers for publication under a pseudonym.[13] Conveniently, this often left the printer-editor bearing the brunt
of any punishment when it occurred, especially during the period of the
Alien and Sedition Acts.

In the context of honor rituals, however, the gentleman's detachment
from the printer-editor adds another dimension to our understanding of
communication patterns during the nineteenth century. Pasley wrote that
gentlemen justified this detachment because, "In the new 'republic of letters,' the disembodiment of the writer and the excision of his or her personal identity focused attention on what was written rather than who wrote
it and theoretically evened the political odds."[14] This may be true, but it
also kept gentlemen from being subjected to ritual violence, which was
extremely sensitive to defamation.

Most anyone familiar with early nineteenth-century American history has heard of the duel between Aaron Burr and Alexander Hamilton.
Why was Hamilton lauded the hero and Burr considered the political vil-
lain, though Burr won the actual fight? That Hamilton died in the duel
was a tragedy, yes, but it wasn't particularly significant by nineteenth-century standards that accepted dueling as a social norm. So if dueling wasn't
a unique phenomenon during this period, what made the Hamilton-Burr
duel more noteworthy than the others? The difference, as this chapter will
argue, was the press reaction to the event.

Very few, if any, journalism historians consider the duel between
Alexander Hamilton and Aaron Burr as significant to the way we understand the nineteenth-century press. But as this chapter will show, the
Hamilton-Burr duel was quite possibly the defining moment for the party
press era. Following a brief examination of how dueling became entrenched
in American culture will be an analysis of the Hamilton-Burr encounter,
comparing and contrasting press coverage of duels before and after Bur-
rand Hamilton's infamous duel. The press reaction to the Hamilton-Burr
duel is important to journalism history because it altered the way party
editors used and manipulated the ritual of honor in furthering their partisan goals. This not only contributed greatly towards politicizing the ritual of honor in the press, but the language party editors used to promote,
attack and defend politicians.

Before the Hamilton-Burr duel, honor and reputation in America
could be restored through the code of honor. After the Hamilton-Burr
duel, however, political survival of a character attack also depended on

the support of a major party newspaper. This in turn strengthened the symbiotic relationship between newspapers and political parties. Newspapers depended on patronage for their economic survival, likewise, politicians depended on press support for their political survival. This symbiotic relationship, defined in large part by the ritual of honor, would impact journalism throughout the nineteenth century.

But how did the ritual of honor become so ingrained in American culture? Modern connotations of the term "duel" imply simply a struggle between two opposing people, forces or ideas. For instance, the sentences "That baseball game last night was a real pitchers' duel" or "The rival companies are to open dueling software labs in Singapore" illustrate this point.[15] For most of the nineteenth century, however, the term "duel" was limited to formal armed combat between two men, with witnesses, along a strict set of rules called the "code of honor." Imbedded in this code was a linguistic strategy of insult and apology. Those familiar with the code, as you will see throughout this book, knew what words triggered the start of this ritual, and what words could end it without conflict. In the emerging structures of the American press system, newspapers and editors were often caught in the middle of this ritual, often politicized, wordplay.[16]

Knowledge of the rules and customs surrounding dueling is vital to understanding the impact, influence and effect of honor on nineteenth-century journalism. In her book *Journalistic Standards in Nineteenth-Century American Journalism*, Hazel Dicken-Garcia wrote, "They [journalists] were having to learn several momentous lessons in the process of doing: how to debate political issues, how to function in a new kind of government, how to use the press in a new kind of political milieu, and how to ensure that public opinion would serve as a check on government, as the new order decreed."[17] The code of honor, which was considered above the laws of man, gave a sense of order in this confusion.[18]

In the early decentralized American government, when laws were still being developed or didn't exist, the code of honor was integral in filling this void. With European immigrants constituting the early American ruling class, the code of honor transcended the cultural differences and was a common denominator among white gentlemen of European descent. Without a blueprint or standard of conduct in American newspaper content, the code of honor was often a mediator between journalists and the public when considering defamation. As a result, victims often turned to the judicial traditions of the code of honor before the infant American legal system.

A brief examination of the history of dueling can shed light on how the culture of honor became so imbedded in early American society. The American traditions of the duel were ancient in origin.[19] In 501 A.D., King Gundeheld, of the East German tribe of Burgundians, established what is termed by scholars as the "judicial duel." In this case, law disputes were decided by combat. This was a ritual that spread in popularity across Europe.[20] With the rise of knighthood across early eleventh-century Europe, the duel evolved with traditions of chivalry. In this case, knights met with great public fanfare in single armed contests to remedy disputes, defend reputations and protect the honor of kings.[21] Most importantly, this combat took place according to a specific code of conduct.[22] In 1410, Italy published the first rules of dueling called the *Flos duellatorum*. Dueling schools in Germany called *Fechtschulen* flourished and helped cement dueling traditions in Europe.[23] In 1527, Francis I of France challenged Charles V of Spain and the Holy Roman Empire to a duel. Even though the contest never took place, it suddenly made it socially acceptable across Europe to participate in the ritual aspects of the duel.[24] As dueling rose in popularity into the next century, there were movements to standardize dueling protocol across cultures, from the issue of a challenge to the choice of weapons.[25]

The *Code Duello* of the Clonmel Summer Assizes (Irish legal proceedings) of 1777 grew out of this desire to standardize the dueling protocol. Most scholars consider this as the basis for all other dueling codes in the English language.[26] The etiquette of the duel was just as important in demonstrating bravery and courage as the actual combat itself. Any deviation from the rules of conduct could turn a calm, cool display of honor into an ordinary fight.[27] The *Code Duello* provided stringent procedural guidelines for dueling conduct and ushered in the modern era of dueling.[28]

The modern duel of honor, according to the *Code Duello*, was detailed in its set of rules. When provoked, the insulted party would have a note delivered that stated the cause of the offense, why it was offensive and a request for a time and place to be set for satisfaction.[29] Once the challenge was accepted, seconds, or assistants, were appointed to handle the rest of the administrative details of the duel. Next, the challenged party chose the weapons.[30] Swords, daggers and pistols were generally acceptable weapons under the *Code Duello*.[31] Under rule 15, the challenged party had the right to choose the weapon unless the challenger swore he could not use a sword. However, the second choice could not be refused under any circumstances.[32] Most American duels were fought with pistols. At the dueling field, the seconds — having loaded the pistols in the presence of one another — as well as surgeons and spectators would take their positions while the principals stood on their marks with pistols.[33] The standard length between principals was ten paces. When the signal was given, both parties were allowed to fire. Under the rules, firing in the air or purposely missing was prohibited, and a misfire was considered equivalent to a shot.[34] From start to finish, an affair of honor might take weeks or even months.[35]

Even though it had appeared in America sporadically since the early 1600s, dueling really took hold in America during the Revolutionary War. The new U.S. army officers adapted French and British Army customs, and the dueling ritual gained popularity in American society. As Americans were trying to prove themselves as equals on the world stage, dueling was one way to communicate courage and honor across cultures.[36] Duels were fought generally between white gentlemen who were perceived to be of the same social rank. If a gentleman was insulted by someone of lower social status, the gentleman would probably give that person a public caning or flogging before ever engaging in a duel.[37]

During the Revolutionary period, pamphleteering and newspapers helped rally the American colonists politically against the British. The opposing Federalists and anti–Federalists values were at the foundation of the emerging American press values.[38] It was a natural progression that journalism played a continuing role in the emerging U.S. political system that included the creation of a new government, the adoption of the federal constitution, the treaty with England and the dismissal of the Articles of the Confederation.[39] In a political system that ideologically considered itself representative of the people, newspapers became the most effective way for politicians to disseminate their political ideals to the masses.[40] This in turn led to an early American press system that was intricately connected to the emerging political system. The press and politics were virtually inseparable until the 1850s.[41]

In early America, printers produced newspapers in the beginning as a way to supplement their printing business. With a demand for the latest shipping news, mercantile newspapers began to prosper in major port cities such as Boston and New York. With strong ties to Europe, these papers contained very little domestic news and instead focused almost entirely on foreign news.[42] Editors also continued a colonial trend of not printing anything offensive enough to threaten their livelihood.[43] If there was domestic news, it usually revolved around shipping. Daily newspapers began to spring up in New York and Boston, but still were designed for the elite.[44] If there was commentary, it was disguised as letters signed with a pseudonym or interspersed throughout shipping reports.[45]

Papers such as the *Pennsylvania Packet* in 1777 were typical of post-revolutionary America. Often, the first pages would emphasize commercial and mercantile information more than actual foreign and domestic news. There were no headlines in the modern sense and no real editorial voice. The *Pennsylvania Packet*, as would its contemporaries, often reprinted news stories or print letters representing similar views or opinions. There were no correspondents, reporters or news exchanges.[46]

The lack of political ideology in the *Pennsylvania Packet* is noteworthy in contrast with the rise of the partisan journals in the late eighteenth century. According to Dicken-Garcia, "Although ideas dominated these early papers, printers did report events. Generally, however, they simply told that an event had occurred."[47] The duel between Button Gwinnett and General Lachlan McIntosh illustrates this point. The encounter happened May 16, 1777, and the report appeared in the *Pennsylvania Packet* in July from information derived by a letter sent from a source in South Carolina. The account read: "A letter from Charlestown, South Carolina, dated May 24 says a duel has been lately fought with pistols in Georgia, between Button Gwinnett, Esq; late Governor of that State, and General Mackintosh [*sic*], who were both dangerously wounded. Gwinnett is since dead of his wounds, and the General is not out of danger."[48] A similar account also was printed in the *Connecticut Courant* six days later. The duel was noteworthy because Gwinnett was a signer of the Declaration of Independence and a member of the Continental Congress. Gwinnett and McIntosh had been rivals for years, but the animosity intensified when Gwinnett lost the 1777 gubernatorial election.[49]

The account of the Gwinnett-McIntosh duel in the *Pennsylvania Packet* is important to note in contrast to news coverage of later political duels such as the Hamilton-Burr affair. There was not a solid two-party political system in the United States, therefore partisan favor did not factor into the coverage as it would during the party press era. Also, since American journalism had not yet rooted itself in party politics, the coverage of the event itself was not politicized.[50]

Intense political rivalry did not begin to materialize in America until George Washington's presidency ended in 1797. As the major political parties began to emerge at the turn of the century, journalism and journalists played an integral part in shaping and communicating political ideology with the voting public. This period was known as the party press era, which lasted in various forms beyond the Civil War. Newspapers were not expected to be objective in the modern journalistic sense. Instead, newspaper commentary fell along party lines in the quest for political dominance.[51]

Even though the emerging American media at the turn of the eighteenth century depended on the government for much of its existence and profitability, the advent of party politics created a climate for a certain kind of free speech. It was not the same as twenty-first century standards of free speech. In contrast to the government-controlled press in countries such as England, however, the American press was certainly more at liberty to express ideas to the public.[52] As is the case today, newspapers in early American journalism struggled between content and profitability. Advertising was not a viable income source for newspapers until the rise of post–Civil War industrialism.[53] Subscriptions, which were sold on a yearly basis, could provide a source of income — if they were paid for (often they were not). So it was, as party politics took shape in America, that editors were dependent on patronage to keep their newspapers alive.[54]

Writing to a mainly political audience, early newspapers could be thought of as almost completely a forum for political discussion emphasizing ideas more than events.[55] In discussing early nineteenth-century journalism, Dicken-Garcia wrote: "Perhaps because of the Enlightenment values emphasized reason, the Founding Fathers intended to quash traditions restricting political content and, in guaranteeing press protection, assured freedom to discuss political affairs, the Constitution's conferring on the press the role of forum for such discussion set the stage for linking the press with the party system."[56] The Constitution took the traditional European press model and turned it upside-down. In the traditional European model, the press were servants to the government. Now, in the new American experiment, the government was the servant of the people, whom the press represented.[57]

In the beginning it was the Federalist and the Jefferson-era Republicans[58] arguing for and against the power and influence over the new government. During John Adams' Federalist presidency from 1797 to 1801, the Alien and Sedition Acts were passed censuring opposing political voices, which sent many Republicans to jail for opposing political views. It also extended residency requirements for citizenship from four to 15 years. This was done, in part, as a response to the looming war with France. There had been a large influx of French immigrants into America since the French Revolution, and the American government saw this as a threat to national security. The laws also threatened deportation of many leading Republican editors. Many of these editors were émigrés from France as well as England and Ireland. If they spoke out against the American government, deportation was a real threat.[59] However, the repeal and dissolution of these acts in the Thomas Jefferson administration reinforced First Amendment protection of free press. Journalists were encouraged by these free-doms to speak out politically.[60]

The tradition of dueling had very little effect on the editor during the early days of American journalism because gentlemen only engaged in honor rituals with their perceived social equals. In the cases where gentle-men believed they were libeled by someone of lower social stature, the tra-dition within the code of honor was to give that person a public caning or flogging.[61]

This dynamic began to change after Alexander Hamilton successfully defended Henry Croswell, of the Hudson *Wasp*, against prosecution for seditious libel, thereby opening the door to greater leeway in political crit-icism and establishing the truth — plus intent as "the basis of most nine-teenth-century state libel statutes."[62] According to Pasley, "In essence, the judge and jury's subjective beliefs about the character and intentions of an author or publisher became the measure of a publication's libelousness."[63] As other cases followed, it seemingly left the door open for greater region-alism when it came to interpretations of libel. As Pasley noted, subsequent legal arguments, such as *Commonwealth v. Clap*, put "more of a burden on the good intentions of the publisher, and this allowed even the most prurient comments and imaginative speculations to be justified in the name of defending the community's faith and morals."[64] In a matter of two decades from the Croswell decision, printer-editors would achieve legiti-macy in the ranks of the gentleman politician and go as far as to become close political advisors in the era of Andrew Jackson.[65]

That legitimizing partisan criticism, even if truthful, might lead to ritualized violence was not lost upon those who argued against Croswell. "In criminal prosecutions," said Ambrose Spencer, arguing for the prose-cution and quoting British common law, "the tendency which all libels have to create animosities and disturb the public, is the whole the law considers ... it is immaterial with respect to the issue of a libel, whether the matter be true or false, since the provocation, and not the falsity, is the thing to be punished criminally."[66] Spencer was arguing from the gen-tleman class perspective, many of whom felt duty-bound to defend such "provocations" as he described by referring to the arbitration honor ritu-als provided. Thus, it is not without some irony that Spencer's opposing counsel would die in a duel only months after the trial ended in a scenario similar to what he described.

With this new sense of freedom to openly criticize, the political storm ushering in early nineteenth-century elections left the infant democracy reeling and turned election propaganda into an all out newspaper war.

According to Dicken-Garcia, "Personal invective and aspersions on individual character permeated most of the writing in both Federalist and Anti-Federalist papers, and it seems that nothing was too gross for publication."[67] The early editorial voice of American newspapers emerged from the personal tone of political rivals trying to undermine each other's views.[68]

This newspaper controversy, coupled with the tie in the 1800 presidential election, created the climate for dueling.[69] In the election, Aaron Burr tied in electoral votes with fellow Republican Thomas Jefferson.[70] With neither man yielding, personal and political accusations were rampant, and it took 36 ballots before Jefferson was finally named president. With so much at stake, political loyalties were questioned and accusations of corruption were widespread from the most influential newspapers.

Leading politicians such as Alexander Hamilton and Jefferson were personally behind the most influential national papers during the party press era. Not only did politicians support newspapers financially, but in some cases they were actually doing the writing themselves. In other cases, commercial mercantile newspapers would take on partisan characteristics depending on the editor's leanings.[71] The emergence of the American editorial voice came with the necessity of writing and creating an articulate, persuasive and attractive political platform.[72]

With Hamilton as the architect, the Federalist Party officially ushered in the party press era with the establishment of the *Gazette of the United States* in 1789.[73] With Washington as president, it was awarded regular subsidies and actually moved with the government when the U.S. capital was switched from New York to Philadelphia in 1790.[74] The *Gazette* remained politically viable until 1798.[75]

With no Federalist paper in New York, Hamilton founded the *Evening Post* to compete with the Republican *American Citizen*, and Federalist partisan leadership began to shift to the *Evening Post* when the capital moved in 1800 from Philadelphia to Washington, D.C. The *Evening Post* produced a daily regional edition, and a weekly edition which was distributed nationally.[76] Hamilton handpicked William Coleman as editor, but the *Evening Post* gained widespread fame as being the authoritative editorial voice of Hamilton.[77] Although Coleman was an able-bodied editor, Hamilton orchestrated a majority of the editorial decisions until his death during the duel with Burr.[78]

The duel itself was not a unique situation to American politics at that time. Boston's *Columbian Centinel* reported in September 1800: "Party spirit and animosity rage in *North Carolina* and *Virginia* to a degree that must excite the regret of every real friend of our Country. Several Duels, which originated from political disputes, have been fought in these States.... Some days ago, even two Brothers, in the State of *Virginia*, had some altercation respecting the approaching election of President, proceeded to blows, when a fatal stroke put an end to the existence of one of them."[79] With politics and journalism considered almost synonymous, many of these disagreements started in the press. These controversies arose from the party press tradition of endeavoring to destroy the credibility and reputation of the political opposition, which was done in order to reinforce the correctness of their own position.[80] Dueling, or engaging in the ritual of honor, was the most effective demonstration to the public at large that these accusations were false, thus restoring credibility to politicians protecting their reputations.

The presidency of Jefferson did little to quell party animosity reflected in the press or dueling. Affairs of honor,[81] such as the September 5, 1802, duel between General Richard Spaight and North Carolina Senator John Stanley, were frequent. The *Evening Post* was one of the first major newspapers to report the Spaight-Stanley duel on September 21:

> *Extract of a letter from a gentleman in New-bern (N.C.) dated Sept. 9th to his friend in Philadelphia.* There was a duel fought in this place on Sunday last, between Mr. Richard D. Spaight and Mr. John Stanly [*sic*]. (both members of congress.) On the fourth fire, Mr. Spaight received a ball under his arm which put a period to his existence the next day.'[82]

The *National Intelligencer*, in Washington, followed on September 22, 1802, with a similarly worded account citing a Norfolk newspaper as its source:

> We are informed by a gentleman from Newbern, North Carolina, that a duel was fought a short distance from that town on a Sunday evening the 5th inst. between Richard Dobbs Spaight, Esq. formerly governor of the State of North Carolina, and John Stanley, Esq. Senator for the district of Newbern. After exchanging three fires each, with effect; at the fourth fire, R.D. Spaight, received a ball directly under his right arm pit, which put a period to his existence four hours afterwards [*sic*]. The case of this unhappy affair preceded from a dispute of a political nature.
>
> *Norfolk paper.*[83]

The report, which was taken from a Virginia paper, was followed two days later by a more detailed account reprinted from the Raleigh *Register*, which included the notes passed between Stanley and Spaight the morning of the duel.[84] The more detailed accounts of the duel followed three days later in major New York newspapers and then in October when Boston's

Columbian Centinel reprinted the New York account.[85] Newspapers, such as the *Newbern Gazette* in North Carolina, reprinted the handbills in full.[86] In their versions, the *Evening Post* and the *American Citizen* reprinted only excerpts of the handbills and the notes between the two duelists. The *American Citizen* emphasized the part of the Spaight's handbill that attacked Stanley's character, calling him a liar and scoundrel, which during those times would have been justification enough for a duel.

By comparing the similarities and differences between the newspaper reports of duels, such as the Spaight-Stanley encounter, the trends of early American newspapers emerge. Editors were doing more than simply reporting events that had occurred. Reports taken from other newspapers were not necessarily re-counted verbatim, but sometimes rewritten in ways that slanted toward the editor's views, such as calling the duel an "unhappy" event or the *American Citizen* emphasizing certain parts of the handbill as justification for dueling. In addition, the reporting of dueling was becoming increasingly politicized.

Because of cost and lack of manpower, editors rarely left the office to gather news. If events were reported, Dicken-Garcia wrote, they "were generally created out of secondhand knowledge, assembled from accounts of one person — who may have been reporting hearsay from several sources — or from several persons, who also may have been reporting from second or third hand."[87] For news outside of their areas, newspapers depended on the mail, which brought news through letters and regional newspapers.

The dependence between newspapers and politics increased as the nation grew, and newspapers were started in different areas around the country. With political parties founding most major newspapers, politicians could exert their influence using this dependence to their advantage. Likewise, new politicians could find inroads to political parties by establishing newspapers. If the party editor was also postmaster, not only could he enjoy free delivery of his newspaper, but he could also slow down or intercept the delivery of rival political papers.[88]

The Spaight-Stanley coverage also illustrates how early newspapers could have contributed to the popularization and politicization of dueling in nineteenth-century America. Newspapers were the chief means of communication between the infant U.S. government and its citizens. Thus, newspapers were an integral part of defining the laws and the roles of legislators, as well as shaping social mores. By justifying the ritual of dueling, or at the very least not condemning it as murder, newspapers were communicating that this was a socially acceptable means of dealing with disputes. For politicians dependant on popular opinion and votes, this meant dueling could be an opportunity to demonstrate character and bravery to a regional, statewide or even national audience. More importantly, by re-printing the duelists' handbills and notes, newspapers transmitted the protocol used by the country's most respected leaders for dealing with these types of disputes. According to Bertram Wyatt-Brown in *The Shaping of Southern Culture*, "By ritualizing violence in a punctilious grammar of honor, as it were, duels were supposed to prevent chaos. That scourge of public and familial order, the blood feud, could be avoided under the problematic idea that a man's sullied reputation would thereby be restored."[89] Newspapers did not necessarily promote killing. Through its ritualistic language, illustrated in newspapers, dueling could be considered a civilized alternative to all-out war.

Although considered by some as a purely southern U.S. phenomenon, the population of the northern states, including New York, was no stranger to dueling. According to Joanne Freeman in *Affairs of Honor*, between 1795 and 1807 in New York City, there were at least 16 near-duels between politicians that never resulted in an actual challenge or exchange of fire. Hamilton himself was involved in 10 affairs of honor,[90] while Burr was involved in four without an exchange and took the field once against Hamilton's brother-in-law, John Michael Church.[91] In fact, Hamilton's son, Philip, died in 1801 as a result of dueling.

Hamilton exemplified the deep connections between press and politics in early America. Not only was he a founding father of the country, but also an integral founder of the partisan press system. His political and editorial choices in his public confrontation with Burr, a sitting vice-president, would reverberate throughout nineteenth-century America in the same way Charles V and Francis I influenced Europe. After all, Burr and Hamilton did not turn to the judicial system to settle their political dispute; they turned to the code of honor.

Hamilton's political life was on shaky grounds in 1804. He had been disgraced politically in the late 1790s by scandal. In what was known as the Reynolds affair, he had been accused by several senior government officials of giving insider information on government securities to John Reynolds. In addition, Hamilton was accused of having an affair with Reynolds' wife. The accusers, led by then-Senator James Monroe, dropped the allegations after Hamilton produced copies of the letters sent to Maria Reynolds that suggested her husband was using the affair to blackmail Hamilton. He claimed that John Reynolds, who was arrested and sent to jail for other offenses, was making false accusations about the insider information.[92] In the late 1790s, the love letters resurfaced and were printed in a pamphlet distributed to the most influential people in the U.S. In a stunning political move, Hamilton, in a rebuttal printed in a publicly distributed pamphlet, admitted having the sexual affair but denied government corruption. This public admission, coupled with the Republican presidential victory in 1800, severely damaged Hamilton's political influence.[93]

It can be understood, to some degree, why Hamilton felt there was so much at stake politically when Burr challenged him to a duel over an account in the Albany *Register*. The article revealed the details of a dinner conversation in which Hamilton referred to Burr as a "dangerous man."[94] Private rumors and gossip, which had provoked animosity between Burr and Hamilton before, could be explained and refuted without harm to public reputations. But when the accusations were printed in a newspaper, the private quarrel became a struggle to control public perception and opinion. Burr, who had been the subject of numerous public attacks indirectly from Hamilton in the *Evening Post*, had used newspapers to get the political upper hand. When Burr set the affair of honor in motion, Hamilton was then forced into one of two decisions. Either he could apologize for the remarks and thus reinforce Burr's political strength and risk further public humiliation, or he could back up his opinions, and his politics, with his life.[95]

Instead of turning to the code of honor, Burr could have filed a libel suit. However, Burr was politically reeling himself from a recent defeat for New York governor and could not afford to lose any political capital by appearing cowardly in the face of Hamilton's vilification.[96] This was a culture of heroics. Ironically, Hamilton was a champion of early defamation laws. According to Ron Chernow in his book *Alexander Hamilton*, when Harry Croswell, editor of the Federalist paper the *Wasp*, was indicted by a New York grand jury in 1803 for seditious libel against then-President Jefferson, Hamilton's defense of Croswell set the stage for modern interpretations of libel.[97] Chernow wrote that Hamilton argued if Croswell's statements were true, then the intent behind his words should be admissible in his defense. During this period in history, those who filed a libel suit only had to prove defamation, not whether the remarks in question were true or false.[98] Chernow wrote, "By spotlighting the issue of intent, Hamilton identified the criteria for libel that still hold sway in America today: that the writing in question must be false, defamatory, and malicious."[99] In other words, intent must be a factor, but not necessarily the only determiner of libel, linking it with the facts.[100]

The Hamilton-Burr duel, and the coverage surrounding it, created a perfect storm of what Dicken-Garcia described in her book as the para-doxical fusion of partisanism and news function.[101] In the month following Hamilton's death, an idea-driven media suddenly turned event-centered largely by the hand of *Evening Post* editor William Coleman. Inserted dra-matically into a story about the arrival of London mail, the *Evening Post* made a striking announcement: "We stop the press to announce the melan-choly tidings that GENERAL HAMILTON IS DEAD!"[102]

This may not seem particularly surprising from a twenty-first cen-tury perspective accustomed to a constant media barrage, but Dicken-Garcia suggested that nineteenth-century readers were easily shocked by dramatic reports like these.[103] From that announcement on July 12, 1804, the duel was the nearly daily focus of every edition of the *Evening Post* until August 20, when Coleman announced:

> I now return to those customary editorial duties which have been, for more than a month, suspended to give place to the most awful and afflict-ing subject that ever occupied my mind and weighed down my heart.— It was my intention to have closed all discussion of the melancholy event, by an attempt to exhibit the character of him [Hamilton] whom I can never cease to mourn as the best of friends, and the greatest and most virtuous of men; but that ground has been so much preoccupied; that the design, though in great part actually executed, is for the present deferred. And unless it should be rendered necessary, by attacks or remarks from a cer-tain quarter, I shall not again be disposed to bring the affair into the paper.[104]

This coverage included the printing of personal correspondences between Hamilton and Burr leading up to the challenge.

As indicated in his August 20 announcement, Coleman actually sus-pended regular newspaper coverage for more than a month to discredit Burr. During this time, Coleman exacerbated the ambiguous line between news coverage and partisan character assassination. He used the platform of the press to declare, among many other things, that Burr was not an honorable man by suggesting he had premeditated the hostilities as polit-ical revenge. Coleman wrote:

> If anything was wanting to lead us to Mr. Burr's true motives, the close of the above sentence is sufficient —"The effect, (says he) is present and pal-pable." In other words, "It is your having told the people that I was a dan-gerous man, that caused me to lose my election, and brought me to that humiliating situation in which I am: it is 'present,' I am deeply sensible of it, it is 'palpable,' all the world bears witness to it. Such is the fair, and we think the only construction of his words."[105]

The ritual of honor created a conundrum in the party press era as illustrated by its treatment of the Hamilton-Burr duel by newspapers. The causes that compelled one to duel were chiefly idea-oriented or perception-related. However, the physical act of the duel was event-centered. In the idea-centered partisan press of the time, Coleman argued the validity of the confrontation on the grounds that Burr's intentions were dishonorable, thereby making him appear politically corrupt to the public at large. Coleman was not arguing that Burr's participation in a duel was dishonorable; that would have also dishonored Hamilton's legacy. He was arguing that the political motive behind the challenge was dishonorable. In an election year, this kind of constant newspaper barrage could be politically devastating.[106]

Journalism, much to that point in history, was considered a definitive historical record. Dicken-Garcia wrote, "A predominant view saw the press as the keeper of the record of humankind and civilization's store of knowledge."[107] To have it entered into printed history for all time that Burr, as suggested by Hamilton, was unfit to be vice-president would be grounds enough for a challenge in the eyes of the majority of the public. When disagreements arose as to how the newspaper record should read in terms of individual character, the two parties in question left it in the hands of divine providence to decide who was right. In its romanticized extreme, by resorting to the ritual of honor that had been accepted by most Western cultures since the beginning of recorded time, God decided who was right.

In a less romanticized view, by submitting to the ritual of the duel gentlemen were demonstrating strength of character and valor in a way that easily communicated to their peers. Chernow wrote, "The mere threat of gunplay concentrated the minds of antagonists forcing them and their seconds into extensive negotiations that often ended with apologies instead of bullets."[108] During this period, gunplay was not necessarily the goal of an affair of honor, but rather a last resort in cases of stalemate of opinion.

Coleman's style reflected the developing trends of popular American journalism. Perceptions, or ideas, were paramount, more than the facts. Journalism during this era did not seek to elevate the facts for the people to decide the truth. When politics and dueling coincided, it drove the partisan nature of the press, which was strongly tied to the political system, into discussing the ramifications of the duel in terms of its political validity. News reporting and editorial comment were fused together. Therefore, as newspapers became increasingly politically relevant, it was not the role of editors to report the facts, but rather the truth as the editors saw it.[109] By comparing Coleman's account of the duel to previously reported duels, attacking dueling motives would resonate loudly throughout America as a political success. With his editorial barrage, Coleman was able to bring down one of the most powerful men in the country.

As party politics solidified, the party that controlled public opinion subsequent to the event often won political duels. Even though Burr won the actual fight, his failure to control public opinion in the aftermath left him politically defeated. The lessons learned from Burr's political demise would encourage politicians to strengthen their ties with newspapers. Politicians needed a partisan paper to dispense their version of the truth to protect themselves against rivals who were doing the same. The language of honor in conjunction with a two-party system set in motion a system of government that was ill-equipped for compromise short of violence.[110] When politicians put forth a political argument in newspapers there was no middle ground: you were either for or against. This style of partisan journalism had many editors looking down the barrel of a gun.[111]

The decidedly anti–Burr campaign in the *Evening Post* was not altogether surprising since Coleman was a close friend of Hamilton and the mouthpiece of the opposing political party. However, the Republican *American Citizen* also denounced Burr. The condemnation of the duel by James Cheetham, editor of the *American Citizen*, was not because he was against dueling. Ironically, Coleman and Cheetham had confronted each other in a duel two years previous.[112] However, Cheetham was a strong supporter of New York Governor George Clinton, a Republican, and might have seen the Hamilton-Burr duel as a way to seize upon Burr's rising political vulnerability.[113] According to Chernow, in hindsight, several Burr confidants blamed Cheetham for goading Burr and Hamilton into the duel.[114]

A closer look at the connection between Cheetham and Jefferson during Burr's campaign for New York governor in 1804, his last political gasp, is worth noting. It suggests a relationship, brokered by Clinton, to which political chiefs manipulated the partisan press to their own personal agenda as illustrated previously with Hamilton's influence over Coleman. Chernow wrote, "After assuring Burr that he never intruded in elections, he [Jefferson] intimated to two New York Congressmen that Burr was officially excommunicated from the Republican Party."[115] That Clinton would become the new vice president in the 1804 election supports this idea and connection.[116] It also should not go unnoticed that Jefferson, who almost lost the 1800 presidential election to Burr, was a subscriber to the *American Citizen* and frequently made patronage to the paper by awarding printing contracts announcing the latest federal laws.[117]

Cheetham, through the *American Citizen*, was able to attack Burr's character and motives without tarnishing the Republican Party image. On July 23, 1804, Cheetham wrote:

> *General Hamilton's Death.*—The association of *Duellests* [*sic*].— the examination of the [New York] Morning Chronicle for something offensive as a pretext for a challenge — the threat of Mr. Burr's confidants, whose names I could mention, that *twelve or 15 of his friends stood ready* to give, as to the Pamphlet "Aristedes" and the paper "Corrector," *personal satisfaction* to gentlemen who complained, or who might with justice complain, of injured reputation: these circumstances, when viewed in connexion with the repeated and sanguinary whisper that GENERAL HAMILTON *must fall*, are evincive, not only of an understanding and preconcert among Mr. Burr and his partisans, but of a *conspiracy* to take away the life of the DECEASED— to make a widow of his wife and orphans of his children — to deprive the city of its first ornament — to rid Mr. Burr of a formidable opposer.[118]

This is an example of how Cheetham was able to discredit Burr without offending his Republican allies. During this time, it was a liability to be perceived as politically aggressive and ambitious. This is not to say that politicians during this time were not ambitious. However, being recognized publicly as desiring political office was a sign of bad character. As with Coleman, Cheetham was not criticizing Burr for the act of dueling. He was attacking the character of his alleged motives. By making Burr and his close associates seem aggressive and conspiring, he was still protecting Jefferson and paving the way for the Clintonian political machine.[119]

New York City Mayor De Witt Clinton, a nephew of the governor who adamantly called for Burr's arrest, was involved in a duel with John Swartout, a Burrite. After five shots, Clinton ended the duel and walked off the field as Swartout, and other Burrites, called him a coward.[120] The Clinton-Swartout duel, like the Burr-Hamilton duel and many other New York duels of that era, took place in New Jersey, which was outside of New York jurisdiction. Most duels during this period did not end in death or even with one of the principals actually being shot. If shot, a duelist often would be maimed in the leg. In cases where one of the duelists was killed, deaths were not treated like other murders and were rarely prosecuted. Although Mayor Clinton was urging for Burr's arrest, these factors made a Burr murder conviction unlikely.[121]

For politicians, it was to their advantage in the partisan press era not to kill their opponent.[122] The 1808 duel between U.S. Representatives Barent Gardenier, from New York, and George Washington Campbell, from Tennessee, is a good example of how a non-fatal duel caused much less partisan controversy. Federalist Gardenier delivered a passionate speech in the House of Representatives denouncing shipping embargos and accusing the Republican majority of being under the influence of the French.[123] Having made such publicly disparaging remarks, which were also transmitted and documented in newspapers, it seemed inevitable that Gardenier would be challenged to a duel.[124] Campbell challenged Gardenier, and the two fought in Bladensburg, outside of Washington, D.C. Delaware Senator Samuel White was Gardenier's second and Samuel Epps, the president's son-in-law, was Campbell's. After Gardenier had been shot, major Federalist newspapers claimed that, like the Hamilton-Burr duel, it was a Republican conspiracy to murder the political opposition.[125] The editor of the *Columbian Centinel* wrote:

> On the Sabbath the conspiracy was formed, and three bullies were selected to insult him in the House, and to give him the LIE [calling him a liar], knowing his spirit would not brook the outrage; and that the consequence would be, he must fight them all; and probably be sacrificed in the contest. One of these he has met; and, such are the mysterious "*ways of Heaven*," the ruffians have shot him; and thus deprived his country, for a session, of his talents, his virtues, and *Independence*. Americans! Think of these things.[126]

Some Republican newspapers countered by printing all of the exchanges between Gardenier and Campbell leading up to the duel.[127] This time, perhaps in response to the flurry of accusations in the Hamilton-Burr duel, there was an account of the duel that included the statement: "Every thing was conducted on the [dueling] ground with the utmost propriety. To prevent misrepresentations this statement is signed by the friends of both the parties."[128] Since it was signed by both seconds, it made it difficult for either side to argue the details of the duel in rival partisan newspapers.

Both sides also could manufacture political capital from the duel in their party organs as neither man was dying. The *Richmond Enquirer* reported: "A meeting took place on the morning of the day before yesteday [*sic*] between Mr. Gardenier of New York and Mr. George W. Campbell of Tennessee, in which Mr. Gardenier was wounded; but we are happy to say that the surgeons have ascertained it to be only a flesh wound, and not likely to be attended by any dangerous consequences. The gentlemen, we understand, both behaved with great bravery and coolness on the ground."[129]

Both men were portrayed as being brave. Dueling in this case would not be politically damaging to either party or politician. Dueling could be used as a propaganda tool for a politician. Campbell could claim victory for the duel, but Gardenier and his partisan-friendly editors could also claim that his political convictions and reputation were as important as life itself.[130]

In Burr's case, he tried to mount a newspaper defense to quell the flurry of accusations, but it wasn't enough. The *New York Morning Chronicle*, which Burr had founded, ran several defenses of him in the aftermath of the duel. His second, William Van Ness, wrote a series of articles for the *Morning Chronicle* under the pseudonym Vindex. The *Evening Post* in turn began to attack Van Ness, claiming he mishandled Burr's challenge and ignored Hamilton's final attempt at an apology. In essence, it claimed the duel was Van Ness's fault.[131]

An eloquent writer, Van Ness issued a pamphlet justifying his reasons for participating in a duel. But the accusations and remarks about the duel became so numerous that the Burrites could not respond fast enough. Burr left New York in a storm of controversy to preside over the Senate in Washington, D.C.[132] Many months later during the impeachment trial of Supreme Court Justice Samuel P. Chase, one of Burr's duties was to announce Jefferson's second term as president and his Republican rival, George Clinton, as the new vice president.[133]

It would have been difficult for Burr to predict the national outrage, considering the reactions to politicians dueling before and after the Hamilton affair. The development of news exchanges could have contributed to this anger. In other cities, Coleman's dramatic tributes to Hamilton, which included such things as images of Hamilton's coffin, made his views that much more influential.[134] With a large amount of information disseminating from New York, dramatic, heated writing trickled down to other cities and towns such as Boston, Philadelphia and finally to rural areas.[135]

Newspapers during this time were distributed primarily to wealthier segments of the population, but newspapers also were available in reading rooms and taverns. Although daily newspapers existed, they could only be purchased through yearly subscriptions.[136] News traveled slowly sometimes in the United States depending on geography. Details about political duels in more remote areas of the country could take months to reach major cities, which might lessen the social and political impact of the duel. Also, reporting timeliness was not a priority for most papers in the early antebellum period.[137] For instance, the New York *Evening Post* reported on March 29, 1808, that a duel had taken place on March 3, in New Orleans: "It is with deep regret we recorded the death of *John Ward Gurley, Esquire*, late Attorney General of this Territory, who fell in a duel with *Phillip L. Jones, Esq.* yesterday afternoon. He was shot dead the first fire, and Mr.

Jones received a flesh wound in his leg.— His death is sincerely regretted by his numerous and respectable acquaintance and friends."[138] The same report was printed verbatim in the *Richmond Enquirer* on April 15.[139] Nothing more was printed about the duel in any major newspaper in the country.[140] Even though the numerous duels in the New Orleans area might have contributed to its lack of newsworthiness, it would have been better documented nationally if the duel had happened in New York. Finally, politicians who controlled the government also controlled the postal service, which could manipulate such things as postage rates and where the mail was sent.[141] All of these influences should be taken into account when considering how the public perceived the Hamilton-Burr duel.[142]

Death before dishonor was a predominant reality in most nineteenth-century social and familial circles. A newspaper report, to some a record of God's word, had the ability to incite violent blood feuds.[143] General Armistead T. Mason, a senator from Virginia, and John McCarthy were cousins and political rivals.[144] In 1819, the two fought a duel in Bladensburg over a previous election's political dispute. The *Columbian Centinel* reported: "The original quarrel was at an election, when Mason charged McCarthy, who is a federalist, with perjury;— M'Carthy resented the charges, and a hot paper war ensued, in which LIAR, SCOUNDREL, and COWARD, were reciprocally arrayed in all the *pith* of capitals. Mason went so far as to have a supplement to a newspaper printed, *posting* his antagonist, and sent with the papers to every part of the Union."[145]

There were subtle differences in this duel that separated it from others. When Mason sent the challenge, according to the *Columbian Centinel*, McCarthy replied that he "would receive no other communication from Gen. M [Mason] than a challenge;— that he was determined there should be no boy's play in the business; ... that as the *challenged* person, he offered three modes of fighting;—1st. That they should stride two barrels of gunpowder, and set fire to it. 2nd. To fight with dirks [a dagger with a long straight blade]; and 3rd. With muskets at *ten feet* distance."[146] The weapons chosen were marine muskets, and they met at 10:00 A.M. on the dueling field with their parties.[147] Many spectators, including members of Congress, watched the event as it unfolded. The two men stood back to back and each stepped off two paces, turned and faced each other. The signal from the second was given, "Are you ready?" Both men stood in silence waiting for the command to fire.[148] The command was given and each man brought his musket to this hip and fired. Mason was hit in the heart and died instantly.[149] Miraculously, Mason's ball hit the butt of McCarthy's musket, leaving him only slightly injured from the splinters.[150]

A shift in dueling philosophy began playing right into the hands of partisan editors. The procedure, from challenge to acceptance, followed the rules of the code of honor. The key difference in this duel was the choice of the weapons, which were muskets. Fired at close range, the likely outcome was death. Thus, the escalation of weapons increased the dramatic effect and enhanced the newsworthiness by nineteenth-century partisan-press standards. This marked a growing trend ideologically. With duels occurring more frequently, the American public was getting desensitized to the violence. Thus, the more violent the duel appeared to be, the braver the politicians appeared to be in newspapers.[151]

Those who won elections would determine political appointments and where government money was distributed. A politician who engaged in a duel was willing to sacrifice his life in order to protect his reputation. This not only made him electable, but it also made him attractive to political parties, as he stood out from his peers. A duel may have ruined Burr politically, but the death of Hamilton marked the decline and fall of the Federalist Party. Also, the duel made Hamilton, a disgraced politician, into a political legend. In addition, the survival of most early major American newspapers depended on government printing subsidies.[152] These factors combined to help intensify political party animosity and partisan editorial rivalry.

From a journalistic perspective, the deterioration of political dueling protocol is important to note because of its general acceptance in the press. The appearance of courage, bravery and honor won elections in the early nineteenth century, so naturally it was in the partisan editor's best interest to exaggerate those qualities in their party representatives. This was in large part because editors viewed politicians as their main audience.[153] When the rural South began to compete politically on a national level, rural editors who vigorously promoted the party's interests with success were promoted into the Washington, D.C., establishment by political appointment or the awarding of lucrative printing contracts. As early as the 1790s, there were at least 30 printers connected with political societies in nine states.[154] Dicken-Garcia wrote, "The political role established a pattern of press evolution and influence, fostering practices and molding expectations that fed on each other well into the twentieth century as journalists pursued active involvement in politics."[155] Although with the rise of corporatism the partisan nature of newspapers diminished, Dicken-Garcia wrote that newspapers were directly connected to political societies well into the 1850s.[156] The language of honor was one effective way the partisan press could mass communicate across regional and cultural barriers.

In the early antebellum years, politicians and political editors were driven by the desire for fame. This was not fame in the modern sense but a notion of status rooted in the philosophy of Sir Francis Bacon's *Essays*, where men governed empires and nations with wise benevolence and honor. Those with political aspirations could not achieve this goal by simply governing the masses. Politicians and rulers would achieve this notion of true fame when they won the adulation and respect of their peers. In this way, a politician's fame depended on the perception of others.[157] As the fledgling U.S. government developed into its unique style of partisan politics, politicians began to modify the European code of honor in order to conform to partisan goals. In these early years, a successful political duel meant winning public opinion and adulation. Newspapers, used as a partisan publicity tool, became the most effective way to win this public approval.[158]

CHAPTER TWO

The Honor Politics of the Jacksonian Press Network

Quite possibly, the rise and dominance of Andrew Jackson in American politics is what might have been for Aaron Burr if he had been more closely connected to the early American press system. Although it is always tricky to draw historical parallels because of the numerous factors involved, Burr and Jackson shared two major similarities: both men had been ostracized in the press after killing their opponents in a duel and both men came very close to being elected president, only to have it taken away from them by the smallest of margins. Also, not only were Jackson and Burr contemporaries, they were business partners as well, so their political worlds were not that different.

Perhaps the biggest difference between the two men was how they approached the ritual of honor. Burr used honor as a way to affirm a type of courtly, aristocratic entitlement given to the white gentleman ruling class. Jackson, on the other hand, used honor rituals to affirm political fidelity, as a general might command the loyalty of his troops. Thus, Jackson was able to organize a strong political party in a way a general might organize a volunteer army.

This militaristic interpretation of honor rituals had a significant impact on journalism during the period, as this chapter will show. In this political scenario, the question becomes, who is loyal and who is not? As such, newspaper editors who publicly defended Jackson's policies and reputation were rewarded with patronage and political appointments. Those editors who did not support Jackson were considered adversaries to his party and administration. Consequently, Jackson was able to create a national network of partisan-friendly newspapers editors who were willing to lay down their lives in order to prove their fidelity to the party. It is well known that the Jacksonian Age coincided with penny press era and new expressions of individuality in the journalism community. But what price did these new editors pay for this new individuality when it came to honor rituals? This chapter will explore that issue.

The paradox during the Jacksonian Age was that dueling was being outlawed in many states even though more editors and politicians than ever were dueling. Why? One theory was because Jacksonian politics facilitated journalism and promoted social mobility for editors on the basis of a patriarchal system mediated by honor rituals. That dueling was still legal in Washington, D.C., throughout much of the Jacksonian era supports this. This wasn't necessarily leadership by assertion of power and show of force. Whig Party leader Henry Clay's troubled relationship with honor rituals and the press, as illustrated in this chapter, suggests that Jackson's success depended on a skillful political maneuvering.

That fact remains, however, that by vigorously defending the honor of the party, and party leaders, journalists could become a Francis P. Blair or a John Rives at the right hand of the president. Party editors were so important to political survival during this period that sitting congressmen, such as William Graves of Kentucky, would risk their lives in defense of an editor's honor and reputation. An editor, let it not be forgotten, who was the mouthpiece for the party chief.

Thus, as the South grew in political dominance during the late antebellum period, dueling in America reached its peak.[1] Under the patronage system, Southern newspapers, such as the *Richmond Enquirer* and *Washington Globe*, commanded the political spotlight as party organs reached a national audience.[2] With the invention of the penny press, technology made it easier and cheaper to produce newspapers. Even though these changes were creating a new audience and market, party politics would still dominate and control the popular press through such things as patronage and political appointments.[3]

Patronage, penny press technology and democratic reform had a tumultuous impact on the structure of the partisan press during the late 1820s and throughout the 1830s. As politics shifted more toward individualism and encouraged a wider breadth of society to participate in the mechanisms of government, partisan newspapers were pulled into this transition caught between ideas and information.[4] In her book, *Journalistic Standards in Nineteenth-Century America*, Hazel Dicken-Garcia wrote of this democratic reform: "In concert with such views, the press's role changed from an orientation to groups — parties, elites, the commercial class — to the individual and the information citizens needed to understand and participate in the community, nation, and world."[5] In this era of new individuality, the ritual of honor became a measuring stick by which the partisan newspapers promoted and detracted emerging politicians. Those editors who were the most vigorous in their support of a politician could usually expect patronage from his administration on a community, state and national level if elected. However, editors who were more dynamic in their character assassination of party rivals often faced an appeal to the code of honor in lieu of defamation suits.

It should not be surprising that during this time Americans elected the only president in history to shoot and kill another man in a duel.[6] A discussion of Andrew Jackson's political ascendance and the influences working for and against him is integral in understanding the forces behind the structural and content changes during the party press era. Because of the partisan nature of editors during this period, the press and politics were not yet mutually exclusive. Thus, it was not surprising that Jackson would turn to the partisan press system after the presidency was stolen from him in 1824.[7] Using an honor-bound patriarchy system of reward and punishment, Jackson and the editors of the *Washington Globe* would build a journalistic dynasty lasting through the Martin Van Buren administration in 1842.[8]

Jackson's early views on defamation are revealed in his duel with Charles Dickinson on May 23, 1806. When Jackson was tipped off that a defamatory article about him was to be printed in the Nashville *Register*, he burst into the newspaper office and demanded information from the editor about the piece. Confirming from the editor the identity of the author, Jackson challenged him to a duel a few hours later.[9]

They met a week later across the state border in Kentucky at 7:00 A.M. and Dickinson was mortally wounded in the exchange. The duel sent shockwaves through Nashville and the surrounding areas. The *Evening Post* revealed: "On Sunday evening last the remains of Mr. Charles Dickinson were committed to the graves at the residence of Mr. Joseph Erwin, attended by a large number of the citizens of Nashville and its neighbourhood [*sic*]. There have been few occasions on which stronger impressions of sorrow or testimonies of greater respect were evidenced, than on the one we have the unwelcome task to record."[10] Of Jackson's foe, the *American Citizen* reported on May 24: "NB. Dickinson paid the debt of nature the first shot."[11]

In the course of the duel, Dickinson shot Jackson in the rib cage, but Jackson hardly flinched and took slow, deliberate aim at Dickinson. When Jackson attempted to shoot, his gun stopped at half-cock. Dickinson stood in his place from threat of being shot by one of the seconds. Jackson pulled the hammer back again, delivering a mortal wound to Dickinson and violating the spirit of the *Code Duello,* but technically not violating any of the terms agreed upon before the duel.[12] Jackson could have walked off the field without shooting Dickinson, but chose to kill him. So it would seem, the resolution for defamation in Jackson's eyes was death before dishonor.

During this time, America was predominantly a culture of heroics and Jackson held the bar almost impossibly high.[13] During his life, Jackson was shot three times on two separate occasions. He was shot twice in a bar fight with Thomas Hart Benton, the influential statesman from Missouri, and his brother Jesse, and once in the aforementioned Dickinson duel. Jackson suffered many complications from two balls lodged in his body as a result of these incidents.[14] According to Bertram Wyatt-Brown in *The Shaping of Southern Culture*: "He also suffered from rheumatism in his right arm, periodic hemorrhaging, amyloidosis, an inflammatory ailment, dysentery, and other stomach troubles for which he took great quantities of mercury and sugar of lead — then mistakenly thought to be efficacious. He fought the Creek War in 1812 when barely able to ride a horse. He had to hang himself between two poles because he could neither sit up nor lie down."[15] Throughout his life, Jackson's will to survive and courage in the most extreme situations made him seem larger than life.[16]

From the tumult of James Madison's presidency through James Monroe's "era of good feeling," Jackson's popularity steadily increased after his major victory against the British at the Battle of New Orleans in 1812. Seizing upon this popularity, Jackson's friends laid the foundation for his presidential bid in the 1820s and the rise of a strong two party system.[17] Having been retired from public office for about 25 years, Jackson entered into the national political spotlight again as senator and front-runner in the impending presidential election.[18] His new political role was not without controversy. Some felt he had abused his power during the war by ordering the executions of Indian opposition and two British subjects.[19] To his supporters, however, the perception of Jackson's honor-bound and honest character was an antidote to the widespread corruption of the James Monroe administration. This corruption led to, among other things, the Panic of 1819 triggered by the Bank of the United States.[20]

Even though America had returned to a certain degree of stability in the years following the War of 1812, there were still undercurrents of turmoil connected with the degree of authority the federal government should have in regulating and constructing government facilities, such as roads and canals.[21] The Federalist political party gradually dissolved into the National Republicans; their political rivals were known as the Democrats. When the National Republican party effectively dissolved in 1824, the Whig party emerged in opposition to Jacksonian politics.[22] Dicken-Garcia wrote: "These opposing values are at the foundation of the emerging and increasingly inseparable roles of the press and political system in the early years of the nation."[23] In the presidential election of 1824, Jackson, John Quincy Adams, William Crawford and Henry Clay all vied for the executive position.

The presidential election was mired in controversy. Since no one candidate held the majority of the electoral votes, the decision for president was to be determined in the House of Representatives.[24] Clay, the great orator who helped broker the Missouri Compromises in 1820 and 1821, used his position as speaker of the House to gain every advantage. Even though Jackson won the popular vote, he lost the election when Clay brokered a secret deal, giving Adams an electoral majority.[25] Some major newspapers, such as the *Richmond Enquirer*, were outraged:

Denouement

The days of *Prophecy* are past. The reality itself is now before us. "The election is over" — and "the governor" is — John Quincy Adams — That candidate is chosen, who is neither best qualified for the office, nor who is the choice of [a] plurality of the people.[26]

The *Vermont Gazette*, like many papers, published an account of the event written as an unsigned letter sent to the *Columbian Observer* blasting Clay. The letter, thought to be from a Pennsylvania state representative, compared Clay's political maneuvering to the Burr conspiracy. Though Clay's credibility had been tarnished, Jackson was praised for not trying to barter the presidency.[27] One newspaper account read, "And the friends of Clay gave this information to the friends of Jackson, and hinted that if the friends of Jackson would offer the same price, they would close with them. But none of the friends of Jackson would descend to such mean barter and sale."[28] The controversy did not stop there.

Henry Clay was outraged and printed a card denouncing the accusations and the editor. The card ran in the *National Intelligencer* and then was reprinted in various news exchanges, stating: "I believe it to be a forgery, but if genuine, I pronounce the member, whoever he may be, a base and infamous calmuniator, a dastard and a liar; and if he dare unveil himself and avow his name, I will hold him responsible, as I here admit myself to be, to all the laws which govern and regulate the conduct of honor."[29] Clay was defending his threatened reputation by using newspapers to start an honor dispute. Since there was no signature or name attached to the account, the accusations claiming Clay's corruption carried little weight.

The techniques of placing cards or inserting broadsides were popular ways gentlemen, especially politicians, used newspapers to initiate the ritual of honor.[30] Newspapers, such as the *Connecticut Courant,* confirmed that Clay was looking for a fight but questioned his resolve: "We supposed that nothing short of powder and ball would satisfy the Hon. Speaker [Clay] whenever the author of the letter should see fit to 'unveil himself.' Mr. Kremer's card, or some other cause, must have had a wonderful effect in cooling passions."[31] The *Connecticut Courant* was referring to a card that George Kremer, a fellow member of the House, placed in the *National Intelligencer* in direct opposition to Clay's card. In his card, Kremer encouraged Clay to ascertain the name of the writer who wrote the inflammatory letter, and in the meantime he would be available to prove the accuracy of the remarks with a duel.[32] The House, sensing an impending conflict over the card exchange, created a select committee to investigate the charges.[33]

There would be no duel that particular time, but tensions during the Adams administration ran high. The Senate tried to introduce legislation to strip the president of his executive powers. Senator John Randolph, known for his lengthy tirades and unusually high, soprano-like voice, delivered a blistering speech on the floor of the Senate in which he, according to the *Vermont Gazette,* "Denounced Mr. Adams as a monarchist ... and declared that from his days to present, there never had been a more corrupt court than this:— declared that every man had his piece — that Senators have been bought — the one as direct supporter of the administration, and the other, hired to wear the mask of neutrality — and all done by the triumvir of the other House."[34] In his attacks, which were documented in newspapers across the country, Randolph levied accusations of corruption against Clay, who had by now been appointed secretary of state by Adams. This position, held by Jefferson, Madison, Monroe and Adams, was considered the stepping-stone to the presidency.[35]

Even though Randolph's actions were considered an embarrassment because of their public candor, his accusations were not unfounded. Newspapers, such as the *National Journal* and *National Intelligencer,* would receive an enormous amount of patronage if they supported the partisan line.[36] While they were under no obligation to write in support of the administration, not doing so risked losing contracts for official government printing. For national papers, that could mean losing upwards of $50,000 or more. Thus, losing party favor meant risking the life of the newspaper.[37]

Randolph's rantings on the Senate floor did not go unchecked; subsequently, he received a challenge from Clay to a duel. The *Richmond Enquirer* printed an extract of a letter in support of Randolph: "The public will not loose [*sic*] sight of the principal involved, by stopping to refine upon the extent of 'personality' in the mode expressionis. They will see it in its counter.—A Senator has been summoned to the field for his remarks in his place upon the character of the administration."[38] For those who agreed with the *Enquirer's* letter, the dueling challenge was further evidence of a coalition of corruption conspiring to threaten and intimidate those who spoke out against the administration.[39]

The duel took place on Saturday, April 8, 1826. Both men met on the field, exchanged salutations and took their marks. As the gun hung by Randolph's side, it accidentally went off. Randolph turned to his second, Col. Edward Tattnal and said, "I told you so." Tattnal claimed that it was his fault for making Randolph use a hair trigger and pleaded with Clay's second, Senator Thomas Jesup, to allow Randolph to reload with another pistol.[40] With Clay's permission, another pistol was handed to Randolph and shots were exchanged. Both men missed.[41]

As Tatnall and Jesup reloaded, the seconds tried to dissuade any further shots and urged reconciliation. Thomas Benton, the influential statesman from Missouri, rode up while the seconds continued to reload and also urged reconciliation, but neither man would back down.[42]

The word was given again, and Clay shot first with the bullet passing through Randolph's coat. According the newspaper reports: "Mr. Randolph reserved his fire—holding his pistol perpendicularly up—said, 'I do not fire at you, Mr. Clay;' and discharged his pistol."[43] He added, "It was not my intention to have fired at you at all: the unfortunate circumstance of my pistol going off accidentally changed my determination."[44] At that point Benton came up and said, "Yes, Mr. Randolph told me expressly, eight days ago."[45] Seeing his out, Randolph offered Clay his hand and the papers reported that the affair came to an honorable end.[46]

Clay's political misfortunes were typical of the pressures that politicians and editors, especially in the South, faced during the years in late-antebellum America.[47] Over the course of the nineteenth century, Dicken-Garcia wrote, "the press changed in response both to the shifts in society and to its own needs, emphatically demonstrating press-society interaction."[48] It is logical to assume that these changes in the press weren't uniform across the country and, like the ritual of honor, were subject to regional pressures. In his book, *Southern Honor: Ethics and Behavior in the Old South*, Bertram Wyatt-Brown suggested that although the North and South had peculiar sectional differences, they shared a common ethical system, based in honor, which simply developed at different rates.[49] Since the press was closely linked to society and politics, it is safe to assume that this development pattern also affected the partisan press in its shift from an idea model to an information model. In his book, Wyatt-Brown also suggested that the societal changes experienced in the North during the 1830s and 1840s did not occur in the South until about a century later.[50]

This uneven development almost surely would have affected the ethical and communication patterns of these regions. In describing America during the age of Jackson, Wyatt-Brown wrote, "The old means of publicly shaming the deviant had disappeared [in the North] and had been replaced by the relative privacy of the penitentiary system, and an almost exclusive reliance upon the legal apparatus rather than community justice."[51] This system of public shaming and retribution persisted, and even flourished, in the South during this period. In cases of libel in the partisan press, the diverging societies handled the same situations differently. The South maintained a large dependence on the public justice that was afforded by the ritual of honor. As a forum for political discussion and debate, the partisan press played an instrumental role in facilitating and dispensing this public justice. From all appearances, early American laws seemed no match for the voracity of the press in a culture of heroics — especially in the South. In the article "The End of the Affair? Anti-Dueling Laws and Social Norms in Antebellum America," C.A. Harwell Wells wrote, "For a man to turn to the legal system to repair his honor, perhaps by filing a libel or slander suit, was akin to a man admitting that he was unable to protect himself. It was an admission of both weakness and cowardice. A libel suit also carried the message that the plaintiff was one who thought his honor could be repaired by monetary damages."[52] Without any clear standards of conduct in American journalism, often the ritual of the duel was the only publicly accepted recourse for cases of libel and slander in a pre–Civil War culture of heroics. Of course, the emphasis on public justice varied across time and region in antebellum America. Just as the North and South developed their own language dialects, so did they develop into separate cultural dialects and notions of the concept of honor. In the increasingly industrial North, honor became associated with domestic and civil virtue. Honor in the South was more militaristic and akin to the ancient codes of honor associated with the military and the chivalric tales of Arthurian romance.[53]

From these ancient hierarchal traditions of the European feudal system sprang the patron-client system that dominated much of antebellum Southern society, press and politics in much the same way it did in the Northern states before the rise of industrialism. In *The Shaping of Southern Honor,* Wyatt-Brown described the patron-client relationship as a system where two parties of unequal power, but mutual interest, agreed to do favors for each other. Clients would look after their patron's interests in exchange for things such as political appointments or access to a patron's wealthy or influential inner circle. But this relationship of service and reward could not become obvious, as honor demanded the appearance of independence.[54] This patron-client interdependence flourished in the largely rural and agrarian South.

A successful example of this patron-client relationship is Jackson's development of the early Democratic press network. To the public, "Rough" Duff Green was handpicked by Jackson supporters to edit the official organ of the Democratic party.[55] Behind the scenes, it was understood that Green was chosen specifically to support Jackson and his administration. In this capacity, the *United States Telegraph* was established in Washington with patronage as directed by Jackson through his supporters.[56] Green not only became editor of the *United States Telegraph,* he became national coordinator of Jackson's successful 1828 election bid and director of the Washington Democratic central committee. Dicken-Garcia wrote, "Those aspiring to a journalistic career in the era of the political press found that the surest route was through political sagacity."[57] Thus, as long as Green supported Jackson unconditionally, as editor he enjoyed both federal patronage upon Jackson's election and financial support from the Democratic party.

In contrast, Clay and Adams were ostracized politically because the political favors exchanged between them were too obvious. It was seen as an abuse of power to use public office for personal gain. According to Wyatt-Brown, "Clay should have thanked Adams for the offer but declined with hints that a later appointment or the advancement of a friend to the cabinet would be welcome. If deftly arranged, no scandal would most likely have ensued. Instead, an inside deal, grossly mishandled as this matter was, suggest a dependency in the relation between patron and client that a majority of voters were likely to judge shameless and venal."[58] It was not the act of favoritism that was considered corrupt; it was the appearance of personal gain at the public's expense, which made politicians politically vulnerable.[59] Once a gentlemen's image or reputation had been tarnished, the very few ways to mend it included demonstrations of bravery through military achievement or by engaging in a duel.[60]

Appearance was critical in the late antebellum Southern society and was multi-layered in its concept.[61] In the South, honor was the mediator between a person's self-worth and community assessment. As Wyatt-Brown puts it, "One's neighbors serve as mirrors that return the image of oneself."[62] The code of honor, along with dueling, provided a uniform set of rules by which appearances could be challenged or protected against verbal or printed insults. In terms of the partisan press, this was especially important because of the shifting political standards and the lack of journalistic code of conduct. Even though the penny press signaled the beginnings of a transition from an idea model to an information model, newspapers in the Jacksonian era emphasized political discussion. Of this period, Dicken-Garcia wrote, "In many respects, this issue represents the press's role in transition: so long as editors took verbal swipes at each other in the party press era, they were engaging in a by-product of debate dominating those years. Although it may have been tasteless and poorly informed, their behavior correlated with the 'personal' style of politics in the earliest years of the nation."[63] Thus, Clay tried to use the honor code to restore his reputation after being politically libeled after the 1824 elections.[64]

The establishment of the *United States Telegraph* was instrumental in Jackson's election, but with the support of the Albany *Argus*, the organ of Martin Van Buren's New York Democratic machine, and the *Richmond Enquirer*, organ of Thomas Ritchie's Virginia political machine, Jackson was able to dominate politics nationally.[65] Tied together through patronage, these regional political machines, or juntos, and their newspapers received support for their absolute loyalty, which the code of honor demanded. Because these relationships demanded the utmost fidelity, dissenting political and editorial opinion was often perceived as a personal insult and produced dramatic resolutions. When he suspected Green was throwing his support to Vice-President James Calhoun, Jackson removed the *United States Telegraph* as the party organ and established the *Washington Globe*.[66] In comparison, when James Watson Webb, editor of the New York *Courier and Enquirer*, was not consulted in political decision making, he left the Jackson Democrats and joined the Whig Party in opposition, taking one of the largest circulations of any newspaper, 4,500 subscriptions, with him.[67] But while the Whig party had more partisan mouthpieces during the Jacksonian Age, Whig newspapers were not as well organized. The major Democratic press honed the news-exchange system to create an integrated party structure. Between the Jacksonian Democrats and the Whig party, which was strongly influenced by Henry Clay, Southern politics and the partisan press would dominate until the mid–1850s.[68]

As political dueling went into a substantial decline in the Northern states, it began to flourish in the Southern states as the region began to dominate partisan-press content.[69] Even though it was illegal in many states, the dueling ritual was still an important way to reconcile democratic equality in a society of political and social elitism. Wells wrote, "Dueling was illegal everywhere, yet it was not in the law that decided whether men dueled, but public sentiment."[70] Thus, as a representative of this public sentiment, newspapers could be seen as playing a critical role in dueling acceptance or rejection in the community.

If done correctly, a duel could allow class mobility, or the possibility of military promotion or political appointment in conjunction with demonstrations of bravery and integrity.[71] That is why, in early American politics, there sometimes was an increase of dueling around election time. On November 23, 1827, the *Richmond Enquirer* reported via news-exchange from North Carolina's *Raleigh Register* that a Congressional election resulted in a duel.[72] On November 5, Samuel P. Carson, a member of Congress from North Carolina, killed his opponent, Dr. Robert B. Vance. They met near the dividing line between North Carolina and South Carolina. The *Richmond Enquirer* reported, "At the first fire, Dr. Vance received the ball of his antagonist between the two ribs, in the central part of the body, and he expired the next day. No attempt was made on the ground to compromise the difference, which, it appears, grew out of their late contest for a seat in Congress."[73] On December 6, 1827, the *Richmond Enquirer* reported, "We grieve to learn that Henry W. Conway, the amiable, honorable, and universally esteemed Delegate from the Territory of Arkansas, has fallen in a duel with a gentleman of the Territory [Robert Crittenden], the result of a quarrel which grew out of the recent election for Delegate."[74] Coupled with the controversial 1824 presidential election, politics were as volatile as ever.

The controversial nature of politics during the Jackson era was due in large part to more people being allowed and even encouraged to participate in government in the developing territories and emerging states. In turn, the nature of journalism changed to meet the needs of this cultural shift. According to Dicken-Garcia, the Jacksonian view that anyone could hold public office coupled with the expansion of democratic principles to encompass the political abilities of all citizens implied a greater public need for information in order to pursue political interests.[75] Dicken-Garcia wrote, "Emerging conceptions of the press competed with its established political role in the 1830s and aggregate changes, especially during that decade and again in the Civil War era, led increasingly away from a strictly partisan function."[76] In a culture of honor, this expansion of roles in journalism and politics, which was still tightly intertwined, had a significant impact on antebellum American society.

In her book, Dicken-Garcia also wrote that Jackson's journalistic views are important in understanding nineteenth-century journalism in its transition from ideas to information. She wrote, "Andrew Jackson surrounded himself with journalists and was closer to the press than perhaps any other U.S. president. Some have said he was the only president to run the country via the newspaper press. For these reasons, and because he appointed so many journalists to office, his views of journalistic conduct are important."[77] Whether overtly or inadvertently, the policies set in place by the Jackson administration de-emphasized the role of political and business groups and promoted a model that provided information to the new emerging class of political participants.[78]

According to biographer Robert Remini, Jackson went to extraordinary lengths to ensure the success of the *Globe* because of the personal significance of having his own paper in Washington.[79] In his book, *Andrew Jackson and the Course of American Freedom*, Remini wrote, "By the close of 1830 Jackson knew that he must run for a second term [he had initially pledged to only run one term], strike Calhoun from the ticket, and flush away the disloyal and disruptive members of his cabinet."[80] With the founding of the *Globe*, Jackson would achieve these goals.[81]

With the assistance of Amos Kendall, Francis Blair and John Rives, Jackson created a network of state and county newspapers that took the policies and politics of Jackson's *Globe* and amplified them across the nation.[82] Blair and Kendall were both editors of the *Argus of Western America* and became close advisors to Jackson himself. According to William David Sloan in *Media in American History*, "It was Kendall and Blair who took Jackson's ideas of government, often expressed in rambling fashion, and gave them cogent written form."[83] With the addition of John Rives, who was business manager of the *Globe*, Blair and Kendall would form an integral part of what was characterized as Jackson's "Kitchen Cabinet."[84]

A brief examination of Benton's 1836 congressional speech condemning the Bank of United States illustrates the influence of the *Globe* under Jackson. After delivering a scorching oratory on the floor of the Senate in an attempt to rally support against the bank, pro-bank forces led by Whig leader Daniel Webster voted to end the debate and in essence snub the pro–Jackson supporters. Even though the resolution passed in favor of the Whig position advocating the bank, when Blair published it in the *Globe,* the speech took on a new dimension. Other Democratic papers in the Jacksonian press network reprinted the speech, which generated support for Benton, who shared Jackson's views. It also served as an initial rallying point for the eventual demise of the bank.[85]

During the Jacksonian period, the press was commonly charged with provoking, aiding and abetting violent outbreaks.[86] Newspapers played up heroic confrontations, such as the duel between political rivals Major Thomas Biddle and Missouri Representative Spencer Pettis. One journalism critic wrote, "These men were not editors, but as their quarrel began with an intemperate newspaper controversy ... I conceive that the case may be properly introduced to exemplify the mischievous tendencies of an ill-conducted and irresponsible press."[87] Considered one of the most desperate and fatal duels the country had experienced, word of the affair spread quickly among news exchanges.[88] The *Richmond Enquirer* reported,

> The St. Louis paper has the following sentence written on the margin: PETTIS IS DEAD.
>
> The *U.S. Telegraph* of Saturday says, that letters had been received of the 28th ult. stating that "both fell at the first fire, mortally wounded, and expired within a few hours" — and that the *St. Louis Times* and *Louisville Focus* confirm the above.[89]

The duel took place on what was known as "Bloody Island," a popular dueling ground because of its ambiguous territorial status.[90] The *Richmond Enquirer* and *Washington Globe* accounts of the duel emphasized the dramatic nature of the encounter: "Nearly a thousand people were believed to be present, waiting in silence, and with intense feeling, the issue of the combat. A few minutes before five the report of the pistols was heard, and every eye was strained to catch the signals of safety which had been concerted between the parties and their friends on the shore."[91] There would be no signal because both had been mortally wounded in a duel that placed them only five feet apart. When the wounded bodies were brought to shore, the newspaper accounts described the reaction of the onlookers: "Then the crowd broke into two great divisions, every one acting upon his own impulses, and proceeding in silence to the points of landing."[92] Both duelists were heralded as acting honorably on the dueling field. The *United States Telegraph* reported that a monument was erected in tribute to Pettis.[93]

It is impossible to calculate the number of duels in the South during the late-antebellum years. However, it is fair to say that with the formation of new political structures on state and local levels in the South, dueling became a cultural stepping-stone for the politically ambitious.[94] Instructional pamphlets, books and brochures, such as South Carolina Governor John L. Wilson's American adaptation of the *Code Duello*, along with newspaper accounts heralding honor in the face of death, helped institutionalize the dueling ritual in Southern society.[95] Wilson's adaptation, printed in 1838, was reprinted several times until the early 1850s.[96]

As was alluded to earlier, it should not be assumed that dueling was condoned in every sector of Southern society, or even legal in the Southern states. Wilson's adaptation illustrated the contradictions of Southern culture during the late-antebellum years. When Wilson wrote his adaptation, dueling had been illegal in North Carolina since 1812.[97] It was the Southern social norms, amid the pressures of the patron-client hierarchy, which compelled many Southern political duels, even under the penalty of law if it was enforced, which was seldom.[98] The Southern partisan press could be considered as aiding in the perpetuation of these social norms.

The confusion of political roles created by the transition from an idea model of the American press, which stressed partisanism, to an information model, which stressed individualism, was one factor that could have contributed greatly to the rise of ritualized violence in the Jacksonian era. Jackson, by both his policy and own example, opened the door for a new segment of the population to participate in government, thus promoting individualism. But this was a kind of individualism forged under the constraints of honor and the patron-client hierarchy. It was not true individualism as interpreted in the twenty-first century. The patron-client system in the political arena, which Jackson exemplified and promoted, depended on the appearance of utmost fidelity and loyalty between the superior and subordinate.

In *The Shaping of Southern Culture*, Wyatt-Brown characterizes these patron-client relationships as brittle, declaring that any arrangement based on intense expressions of mutual affection, between equals or non-equals, had a certain defective quality in American politics.[99] He further suggested that the partisan press exacerbated the conflicts arising from this defect, leading to an increase in dueling. Wyatt-Brown wrote: "Scholars of modern Italy, where thousands of duels took place from 1870 to 1930, would not be surprised to find a close connection between duels and early partisan politics. In that country, as in the antebellum South, members of the political elite set themselves apart from the lower social ranks not only by establishing close connections with the military but also by the fighting of duels."[100] In turn-of-the-century New England, the antebellum South, Risorgimento Italy and eventually the West, lines between the political and personal were not always clear. Add to that mix an inexperienced free press in a transitional society where libelous or defamatory remarks were permitted, and the results often were violent. These societies were idyllic adaptations of ancient chivalric societies where gentlemen, like knights, had to constantly prove their loyalty, bravery and honor to their political chiefs or parties in order to move up the ranks of society and local, state and national political arenas.

What made the political situation unique in America, however, was that it did not have an aristocratic tradition in comparison to the countries from which the culture of honor originated. Wrote Joanne B. Freeman of politics in the early republic, "Political duelists were not isolated aristocrats competing for glory and preferment at court. Instead, they constituted a novel hybrid: they were aristocratic democrats, popular politicians who used the traditional etiquette of honor to influence public opinion and win political power."[101] American politicians and partisan press editors, who were closely intertwined during this era, were appealing to European transplants that brought with them social norms imbued with the ritual of honor. This most likely was the case in the emerging Southern states where political dueling thrived in the Jacksonian age.

In the post–Revolutionary era of American politics, the mechanisms of government could be seen as conforming to many of the social norms that were characteristic of European countries. Accordingly, the early American press system corresponded with this elitism by appealing almost exclusively to a certain economic class by content and cost. But the emergence of the Jacksonian political machine in tandem with the penny press turned communication patterns completely upside-down again. Wrote Dicken-Garcia, "By the 1820s, the traditional belief that leaders must be eloquent orators able to persuade the educated elite had given way to the view that they must appeal directly to the public and be capable of persuading the masses and shaping public opinion." That Jackson also opened the ritual of honor to a new segment of the population could be seen as a consequence.

Because of the ritual of honor's sensitivity to libel and slander, one can start to understand how the changing patterns of communication during the Jacksonian age could contribute to an increase of political dueling. The 1838 duel between Jonathan Cilley, a congressman from Maine, and William Graves, a congressman from Kentucky, illustrated this sensitivity. On February 12, Henry A. Wise, a congressman from Virginia, brought to the House floor a charge of congressional corruption made by editor James Watson Webb in his newspaper, the New York *Courier and Enquirer.*[102] Quoting a letter he received signed "The Spy in Washington," Webb wrote that there was documented evidence that at least one member of Congress was taking bribes. Wise, in his address to the House, demanded that a select committee be appointed to look into Webb's allegations. Speaking next, Cilley responded, "This charge comes from an editor of a newspaper, and we all know that in a country where the press is free, few men can expect to escape abuse and charges of similar description."[103] He continued by saying that Congress should only act when formal, specific charges are made under oath. In reporting Cilley's speech, the *Congressional Globe* recorded,

> He said that he knew nothing about the editor making the charges; but if it was the same editor who had once made grave charges against an institution of this country, and afterwards was said to have received facilities to the amount of some $52,000 from the same institution, and gave it his hearty support, he did not think that his charges were entitled to much credit in an American Congress.... If we look, we will see what had been said by the public press against Washington, Jefferson, Madison, the two Adamses, Jackson, and Van Buren, yet the people passed upon the merits of all these men, and afterwards the press retracted much that it had said against them.[104]

Thus, it was Cilley's opinion that the charges were too vague and undefined to warrant a Congressional inquiry.[105]

On the morning of February 20, Graves approached Cilley with a note from Webb, asking if his remarks had been correctly reported in the *Globe.* Cilley, upon learning the contents of the note from Graves, declined to receive it with no disrespect intended towards Graves.[106] Graves seemed satisfied with Cilley's reasons and departed,[107] only to deliver a note to Cilley later that day asking for his response in writing. An excerpt from his note read:

> In the interview I had with you this morning ... you hoped I would not consider it in any respect disrespectful to me, and that the ground on which you rested your declining to receive the note was distinctly this: That you could not consent to get yourself into personal difficulties with conductors of public journals, for what you might think proper to say in debate upon this floor in discharge of your duties as a representative of the people; and that you did not rest your objection, in our interview, upon any personal objections to Col. Webb as a gentleman.[108]

Cilley returned a note to Graves: "I neither affirmed or denied any thing in regard to his character; but when you remarked that this course on my part might place you in an unpleasant situation, I stated to you, and now repeat, that I intended by the refusal no disrespect to you."[109] On the defensive, Cilley was becoming increasingly outmaneuvered in this battle of words. In Graves' reply, he chose to intensify the controversy: "Your note of yesterday in reply to mine of that date is inexplicit, unsatisfactory and insufficient.... I have, therefore, to inquire *whether you declined to receive his communication, on the ground of any personal exception to him as a gentlemen or man of honor?* A categorical answer is expected."[110] Cilley sent a note back saying that he refused to give a categorical answer.[111] To speculate, if Cilley was to admit that Webb was a gentleman, he would have had to accept the note and be forced to address Webb's challenge. Accordingly, if he declared that Webb was not a gentleman in writing, he risked being challenged from Webb to a duel on the basis that he was insulted by Cilley's remarks.

But then Graves did something unexpected that would mark an important change in American dueling. On the grounds that Cilley refused to exonerate him from all responsibility growing out of the controversy with Webb, Graves demanded satisfaction from Cilley. In essence, Graves was challenging Cilley to a duel in the place of Webb. The seconds were appointed to handle the affairs of the duel: Gen. George W. Jones of Wisconsin for Cilley and Wise for Graves.[112] Cilley accepted the challenge but tried to turn the tables on Graves. Since the challenged party chose the weapons, time and place of the duel, Cilley, in an unorthodox move, chose rifles at eighty paces.[113] Unknown until after the duel, Cilley had made sure to practice at that distance to insure he had an advantage over Graves, who was relatively inexperienced with weapons.[114] Cilley also chose to set the duel for noon the next day, which lowered the risk of the duel being broken up by the authorities and thus added pressure to compel Graves to back down. At Cilley's instruction, Jones wrote in the acceptance letter, "Should Mr. Graves not be able to procure a rifle by the time prescribed, time shall be allowed for that purpose."[115] Graves spent the greater part of the night trying to get a rifle that was loaned to him in disrepair ready for the duel. The next day, Graves had Wise deliver a note two hours before the scheduled time, indicating the duel would have to be postponed because his rifle was still at the armory getting fixed. An hour later, in an effort to intimidate or goad, Cilley had Jones deliver a rifle to Graves with powder and ball. Cilley had borrowed the rifle from John Rives, an editor of the *Globe*. This left Graves no alternative but to arrange the meeting as soon as possible.[116]

Although dueling had become more frequent and more violent in its outcome, the linguistic strategy of honor still maintained its subtleties. Cilley probably felt safe making character remarks about Webb on the House floor because as a sitting congressman the etiquette of honor dictated he could refuse a potential challenge from an editor because they were not social equals. Most surely Webb and other members of the Whig party anticipated this. Because Webb was an important mouthpiece for the Whigs, his credibility and integrity of reputation was of utmost importance to the party. This explains why it was important that Graves delivered the note. Graves represented not only Webb's interests, but the Whig party as well. Thus, when Cilley tried to refuse Webb's challenge, it could be construed by rivals that Cilley did not consider Graves, a representative of the Whig Party, of enough equal status to receive a note delivered by him, which would be a separate insult in and of itself.

Wise notified Cilley and Jones that his principal would be ready between 1:30 and 2:30 P.M. at the appointed place.[117] Shortly after 3:00 P.M., the rifles were loaded in the presence of the seconds, the parties were called together and the instructions for the exchange of shots reviewed twice.[118] The duelists were ordered to their positions, the word was given and both men missed. The seconds met to negotiate a settlement to the hostilities. Since there was no animosity between Graves and Cilley, Wise asked if Cilley could assign some reason for not receiving Webb's note that would relieve Graves of his position. Wise furthermore declared that the challenge was suspended for purpose of explanation.[119] Jones talked to Cilley and came back with an explanation only to have Wise interrupt him, saying that he should put the explanation in writing. Jones replied that Wise also would be compelled to put everything he said, and might say, in writing as well.[120] At this point, Wise said maybe it was best to hear the explanation first before they went to the trouble of writing it down. The *Globe* reported that Jones then proceeded to say, "I am authorized by my friend, Mr. Cilley, to say, that in declining to receive the note from Mr. Graves, purporting to be from Col. Webb, he meant no disrespect to Mr. Graves, because he entertained for him then, as he now does, the highest respect and the most kind feelings; but that he declined to receive the note, because he chose not to be drawn into any controversy with Col. Webb."[121]

But Wise contradicted this, saying that he heard, "I am authorized by my friend, Mr. Cilley, to say, that in declining to receive the note from Mr. Graves, purporting to be from Col. Webb, he meant no disrespect to Mr. Graves, because he entertained for him then, as he does now, the highest respect and the most kind feelings; but my friend refuses to disclaim disrespect for Col. Webb, because he does not choose to be drawn into an expression of opinion as to him."[122]

The two seconds argued the fine points of honor until it was obvious there would be no reconciliation. A second shot was taken and again both men missed their targets. Again Jones declared that Cilley had satisfied the demands of honor and proven his bravery by rendering satisfaction on the dueling field. But Graves insisted it was his duty to defend the honor of his friend, Webb, and he would not carry the note of someone who was not a gentleman. The two faced each other for another shot. Before the principals took their marks, the seconds tried to negotiate an agreement, but neither man would budge. Cilley was killed on the third shot.[123]

Congress was thrown into controversy. Business was suspended in the House to attend Cilley's funeral and a resolution was passed to wear crape, a black band worn as a sign of mourning, on the left arm for 30 days.[124] Dueling was not yet illegal in the District of Columbia, but there were now serious calls to ban its existence.[125] Amid cries of conspiracies, a special committee was appointed to examine the circumstances connected with Cilley's death and report to the House. Some members of the House, such as William Cost Johnson of Maryland, felt that the suppression of dueling was not a matter within the jurisdiction of Congress.[126] However, there was no quelling the public outcry caused by the duel. The *Springfield Republican* in Massachusetts printed, "If it was the intention of the House to put a seal of reprobation upon the practice of dueling, they certainly ought never to have voted a public funeral, and all the customary honors and obsequies to a man who had died in the open violation of the laws; a violation of the laws which there I now evinced so strong a disposition to punish, or at least censure, in the case of the survivors."[127] Other newspapers, such as the *Richmond Enquirer*, called for reforms in the Code of Honor:

1. If A declined the challenge of B, because he does not hold himself responsible as a member of Congress to B, the conductor of a public journal, has his friend C a right to press the enquiry, whether he has not another objection, viz: that B is not a gentleman?

2. When A expressly disclaims, that his refusing to accept the challenge proceeds from no want of respect for C, but on the contrary *declares*, that he has the highest respect for C, has C a right to infer that his refusing to fight B implies a disrespect to himself?

3. If the refusal to accept the challenge is declared to proceed from no want of respect for C, has C or his friend D a right to insist that B is a gentleman?

(To these three propositions everyone must answer "certainly and *most decidedly NOT.*" A fourth proposition is entitled to a consideration which we hope it may receive from Congress at Washington)

4. If these propositions can be answered in the affirmative, *according to the laws of Honor,* are not those laws founded on the grossest violation of common sense? — Is not such a Code any thing else than a true Code of Honor? — And is it not high time to reform, or abolish it altogether? — And with whom can the reform more properly originate than with those who have had one of their own members hurried into eternity by those bloody laws?"[128]

Graves, and the seconds involved with the duel, endured a lengthy investigation that ended with Samuel Prentiss of Maine asking that dueling be outlawed in the district.[129] But members of Congress, many of them from the South, maintained that dueling was still a demonstration of moral courage and not within the jurisdiction of the laws of government.[130]

By the 1820s, most Southern states had laws prohibiting the act of dueling. These laws also extended to those who engaged in ritual activities leading up to the actual combat and even the language provoking an affair of honor.[131] The last point is significant because it recognized that language was a leading precipitator of ritualized combat, as in the Cilley-Graves duel. There were also libel laws in place to give individuals reparation without resorting to combat. However, according to Wells, there was a general prejudice in American society during the Jacksonian age against libel suits. Wells wrote, "In rare cases where suits were brought, juries proved unwilling to convict one gentleman for libeling another, apparently agreeing that a gentleman should defend his honor outside the courtroom. In the state with the most stringent libel law, Virginia, only a handful of statutory libel cases were reported before 1865."[132] The social norms during this period in American society were as such that individuals in the public eye, especially politicians and editors, were often forced to duel or else be faced with public ridicule and humiliation. As those depending on public support for their livelihood, politicians and editors could see their entire career destroyed if they did not resort to the ritual of honor.

As such, Cilley challenged Webb's credibility and character directly with his damaging remarks on the House floor, which was transmitted across the nation upon being printed in the *Globe.* Although Cilley's verbal attack seems tame by twenty-first century political standards, politicians and political parties were extremely sensitive to such printed remarks to the point of being overwhelmed.[133] This sensitivity to defamatory remarks may have led many, especially those in politics, to believe that the press had a tight grip on public opinion. In her book, Dicken-Garcia wrote, "Another implication of the political role, born of the American revolutionary experience, concerned the press's power over public opinion. After the Revolution, Americans believed that the press directly influenced and molded public opinion, a view that dominated into the 1880s, even though some began to question such power as early as the 1830s."[134]

It should not go unnoticed that a large instigator in the Cilley-Graves affair was John Rives of the *Globe*, who was Webb's political and professional rival. In turn, those who were targets of defamatory remarks might draw their attackers into ritual confrontations by narrow interpretations of any written statement short of an outright apology, which would have a devastating effect on the credibility of the attacker.

An examination of events after the Cilley-Graves affair further suggests that the critical remarks sparking the confrontation nearly led to outright party warfare. In 1843, in the middle of his bid for the presidency, it was revealed that Whig party leader Henry Clay had played a key role in the Cilley-Graves deadly turn of events. The *Brooklyn Eagle* printed an excerpt of a Wise speech accusing Clay of being the catalyst:

> He [Wise] said it was a fair duel — but that if censure and odium attached to any one [*sic*], it should be to Henry Clay; for, he was the counsellor and advisor, and dictated the terms of the duel — that he (Mr. W.) protested against the rifles, and the language of the challenge, which closed the door to an adjustment of the difficulty, but was overruled by Mr. Clay — that he expressed an unwillingness to be the bearer of a challenge so uncompromising in its character, but at length yielded to an appeal from Mr. Graves, who reminded him that he had been his friend on a similar occasion.[135]

Wise even went so far as to accuse Graves of copying the challenge verbatim from a suggested draft by Clay.[136] This further suggests that Cilley and Graves were pawns in a political chess match between the Whigs and Democrats.

For his part, Clay denied the extent to which he was involved in the duel. He denied knowing that Graves delivered a note from Webb until after the delivery.[137] Clay said when he heard Graves had received a satisfactory verbal answer that absolved Graves of all obligations, he congratulated him. From this discussion he had with Graves, Clay said they both agreed it would be best to get the answer in writing to avoid any future misunderstanding or misrepresentation.[138] In countering charges that he did not do enough to stop the Cilley-Graves duel, Clay wrote: "On that day, I was confined to my room by illness, and it was altogether accidental that I obtained information as to the plan, or the hour of their meeting. Contrary to the impression ... I did advise the employment of the police to arrest the parties and to prevent the duel. The constables accordingly went out in search of them, but like myself, being ignorant of the time and place of their meeting, they mistook the route, and failed in the accomplishment of the object."[139]

Whig papers also published and republished a letter by Clay in which he addressed the accusations made about him concerning the Cilley-Graves duel. In this letter, he called the practice of dueling pernicious but thought there were other questions in public affairs more important. In an excerpt from his letter, Clay said: "It is certainly one of the most unlikely events that can possibly be imagined, and *I cannot conceive a case in which I should be provoked or tempted to go to the field of combat.—* But, as I cannot forsee all the contingencies which may possibly arise, in the short remnant of my life, and for the reason which I have already stated, of avoiding any exposure of myself to ridicule, *I cannot reconcile it to my sense of propriety to make a declaration one way or the other.*"[140] He denounced dueling and those who engaged in dueling. But, like many Southerners, he could not disavow dueling altogether.[141]

In the end, Jackson's success over his chief rivals, such as Clay, may have been due to his ability to control and manipulate the perception of honor through the *Globe*. Wrote Elbert B. Smith in the book, *Francis Preston Blair*: "The *Globe* had begun as a propaganda instrument for the reelection of Andrew Jackson, and it had faithfully presented the ideas and principles that Old Hickory had found most congenial. It had assumed the role of spokesman for the Democratic party on specific policies, but had spoken only for the party segment that shared the agrarian principles of Jackson and Blair."[142] Chief among those principles was the code of honor, which made Jackson extremely sensitive to honor rituals.[143] Newspapers, perhaps influenced by the *Globe*, also helped perpetuate a collective vision and status quo of social norms through the heroic and harrowing accounts of dueling.

The close relationship between Blair and Jackson epitomized the intertwining of politics, the ritual of honor and the partisan press. Those aspiring to a journalism career used politics to advance their career and vice versa.[144] But the era of Jackson, aided by technological advances, left a society in transition and a young political system ill-equipped to deal with this cultural and communication shift. Dicken-Garcia wrote, "Thus, a crop of aspiring journalists schooled in politics had prepared themselves by the 1840s according to what they understood as the required qualifications."[145] As American politics entered the decades leading to the Civil War, journalism in this era would still be dominated by the editor's personality and political idealism mixed with information. With highly charged party editors, such as Blair, using new technology to attack rivals on a broader scale, the ritual of honor would play a crucial role in many political disputes that spanned across local, state, national and finally sectional differences.

CHAPTER THREE

Ritual Violence and the Frontier Partisan Press

In the Jacksonian Age, America saw the rise of a strong two-party system between the Whigs and the Democrats. This in turn cultivated and trained an army of partisan editors ready to defend the honor and reputation of party leaders with their lives. However, party politics were in an almost constant state of flux during the decade leading up to the Civil War. The next logical question becomes, what happened to the nineteenth-century partisan editor when party discipline lost its potency? As discussed in previous chapters, press and politics were not yet mutually exclusive; therefore, a general examination of the political arena is necessary when discussing the role of honor in mid–nineteenth-century defamation disputes in the partisan press. This chapter theorizes that in the absence of strong party leadership, especially in emerging frontier governments such as California, weaker politicians and partisan editors rallied around stronger regional politicians in a patriarchal style of government, characterized as political juntos. Acting as knight-errant figures, politicians and editors defended their power base against perceived defamation by utilizing the ritual of honor.

As such, a pattern developed, perhaps influenced by duels such as the Cilley-Graves affair, where critical remarks made in a newspaper toward one politician in a junto would solicit a ritualistic response from all members in the group, justified by social norms as a show of loyalty. Partisan newspapers were a key component in organizing and rallying these political juntos, and editors in California were still on the front line of political combat. In addition, partisan criticism still provoked rampant bloodshed in California politics even on the highest level. Even though anti-dueling laws were written into the state constitution of California, newspaper disparagement would be enough provocation for a sitting chief justice of the California state supreme court to kill a sitting U.S. senator in a duel.

Hostile encounters between editors and politicians, such as the one between Edward Gilbert, editor of San Francisco's first daily, the *Alta California*, and James W. Denver, state senator, were not uncommon in frontier cities before the Civil War.[1] In June 1852, the California Legislature appropriated $25,000 to send supplies for the relief of overland emigrants.[2] The controversy started when Gilbert accused Governor John Bigler of using the California relief train to manufacture political capital. In his description of the wagon train leaving Sacramento City, Gilbert wrote:

> Previous to departing on their long journey, the eight wagons were paraded through the principal streets of Sacramento, with a large placard on each, bearing in enormous capitals the words, "The California Relief Train." Governor Bigler was silly enough to make himself ridiculous by riding on horseback at the head of the procession, and it only needed the addition of an air-splitting brass band to have made people believe it a parade of newly-arrived ground and lofty tumblers, or a traveling caravan of wild animals.[3]

That he was criticizing the Bigler administration was not a surprise. That he had specifically, and publicly, called the governor "silly" and "ridiculous" were key signals that Gilbert was triggering an honor dispute by directly assaulting Bigler's character.

Consequently, a response to Gilbert's editorial was printed in a rival paper, the *Democratic State Journal,* in the form of a public letter. The response said that since the expedition was organized under the immediate supervision of the governor, everyone connected desired him to accompany the wagon train on its departure. The closing of the public letter said, "We can have but one opinion of this attack on the Governor — that it could have emanated only from an envious and malicious heart."[4] Eleven people including Denver signed the published letter. Governor Bigler's signature was noticeably absent.[5]

For whatever political reason, it was obvious Gilbert was trying to draw Bigler out. In his response he wrote, "Their 'indignation!' Pshaw! What is their 'indignation' compared with the universal sentiment of pity and pain which filled the heart of the community when they learned that the high and dignified position of Governor of the State of California had been lost sight of by a huckstering politician who was dragging down his office to subserve his personal ends!"[6] In his closing, Gilbert escalated the conflict of words to a point in which neither party could back down without losing credibility. Gilbert wrote: "As to the perversion of the facts, we will add that we are ready to vouch for the truth of every 'fact' we have stated; and if any of the gentlemen attached to the train, or any other friend of the Governor, desire to make any issue upon the matter, they know where to find us."[7] What might have been an attack designed to provoke the governor to speak out publicly turned instead to a declaration of war against anyone politically connected with Bigler.

When Denver took it upon himself to personally address Gilbert's remarks, he was taking a political gamble more than looking for blood.[8] Likewise, having just lost the last election for U.S. representative, Gilbert was probably trying to maintain what little political vitality he had left.[9] This seems logical because Gilbert had been engaged in a similar battle of words with John Nugent, editor of the *San Francisco Herald*, about using underhanded bidding tactics to secure advertising from the local business community. Gilbert had taken his public dispute with Nugent to the brink of exchanging shots, but backed down at the last moment, printing a humiliating apology in the columns of the *Alta California*.[10]

But as Gilbert's political career was coming to an end, Denver's was just beginning. Newspaper controversies such as this one could make or break an up-and-coming politician such as Denver. Two days later, the *Democratic State Journal* published a response by Denver, which said in part: "As to the threat held out at the conclusion of the article, I can only speak for myself, leaving the other members of the train to act as they may think proper. If the editor of the Alta thinks himself aggrieved by anything I may have said or done, it is for *him* to find *me*, and when so found he may rest assured that he can have any 'issue upon the matter' he may desire."[11] In this manner, Denver was positioning himself as a type of knight-errant figure for Bigler.[12]

With the influence of a Southern patron-client hierarchy, the emerging government and power structure of California political juntos emulated many of the qualities of European feudal traditions of power. Thus, when Denver and the relief train participants were responding to Gilbert's newspaper attacks, they were grouping together to protect the key person of their power base.[13] Keeping with the metaphor, Denver could be perceived as acting as a knight figure in defense of his political party, the motives of which were called into question by Gilbert's disparagement.

The newspaper dispute escalated until August 1, 1852, when Gilbert's second, H.F. Teschemaker, delivered a challenge to Denver. The terms of the duel, Smith and Wesson rifles at forty paces, were set, and both men and their parties met the next day in Oak Grove outside of Sacramento.[14] On the field, Denver was wearing a large black cloak, which he soon discarded, and Gilbert was wearing a green suit he had recently purchased in an attempt to blend in with the surrounding foliage.[15] The word was given, and both men fired. Gilbert's shot narrowly missed, but Denver's shot was obviously wide. Denver laid his rifle down and walked back to his carriage, leaving his second, as was custom, to negotiate a peaceful resolution. But Gilbert, perhaps stigmatized by his previous encounter with Nugent, stayed on his mark and insisted, to the protest of his seconds, on a second shot.[16] Before he returned to his mark, Denver remarked, "Now I must defend myself."[17] The word was given, and Denver shot the newspaper editor in the chest. Gilbert died shortly thereafter.[18]

Neither man had met before the encounter. Gilbert, by libeling a political chieftain in his newspaper, had been drawn into a controversy with all of Bigler's political supporters.[19] In the scheme of paternalism, Denver's actions were not necessarily self-serving. The life of political juntos, and the political associations among them, depended on their leaders advancing, or at least maintaining, the status quo.[20] Soon after the duel, Bigler appointed Denver secretary of state with little if any public protest at the obvious patronage.[21] As with the case of many anti-dueling laws around the country, they were only effective if those in power enforced them.[22] Thus, in a community where social norms permitted dueling as a resolution for defamation disputes, Denver was never prosecuted for the death of Gilbert.[23]

Even though they were under constant threats of violence, California newspapers pulled no editorial punches when criticizing the most influential political elite.[24] When another California founding political father and Jackson political protégé,[25] William Gwin, was involved in a duel with J.W. McCorkle, the *Alta California* wrote:

> The duel between Messrs. Gwin and McCorkle of course settles the Senatorial question as to Mr. Gwin. His friend certainly cannot think of preferring his claims for one of the highest offices in the gift of the state, after he has committed an act that, according to the constitution of California, disqualifies him from holding office, even if he himself should prove so destitute of conscience as to become a candidate. Mr. McCorcle. [*sic*] too, with out doubt, will not think of running for governor, after having sworn to support the constitution of the state — as he must have done when a member of the legislature. He cannot, possibly, so far forget himself as to break his oath by accepting office.[26]

But this anti-dueling rhetoric had little effect on California voters and political allies of duelists who advocated dueling as a remedy for the constant string of disparaging remarks found in the frontier papers.[27]

Many California editors, such as Nugent, were on the front lines of California's political combat.[28] Nugent, who was in many confrontations, including the Gilbert affair, once faced Alderman Hayes on the dueling field on June 10, 1853, with rifles at ten paces. On the second fire, Nugent received the shot in his arm, shattering the bone from shoulder to elbow.[29] It was reported that the bold and harsh manner in which Nugent wrote his editorials was "well calculated to tax severely all the powers of endurance of human nature."[30]

Accounts of politically motivated duels filled California newspapers sent back East.[31] California politicians, such as Denver and Gwin, enjoyed political success after dueling, which appalled many Northern editors. A July 12, 1853, New York Times report declared: "Duelling, which, in the East, has been almost entirely repudiated by men of honor and men of sense, seems to have become epidemic in these [California] cities."[32] The article continued: "Ink before blood, and pens before pistols, is the judgment of this enlightened age; and when anyone reverses this judgment, the question is at once opened, whether the duelist or the world is chargeable with folly."[33]

David C. Broderick and William Gwin emerged in the mid–1850s as major power brokers in California politics. Like Bigler, as chieftains in the junto structure of early California politics Broderick and Gwin were afforded some insulation from political attacks. This was because in the court of public opinion, high-ranking politicians were often compelled to duel only when they faced defamation from someone of equal social status. When Broderick and Gwin both became senators, the rivalry became so intense that most thought a duel between the two was imminent. The New York Times wrote: "Senators GWIN and BRODERICK hurled defiance at one another, while expressing their private griefs in a private way, or in the manner usual among gentlemen. A duel was looked for after the election, and the report that they were to fight, therefore, excited no great astonishment, though the result was anticipated with intense interest."[34]

But even the major newspapers could not anticipate the turn of events. Broderick had made it clear publicly that he would not accept a challenge before the elections, but that after it was over he was ready for any of his enemies.[35] The man he would face on the dueling ground would not be Gwin, but Gwin's political ally Chief Justice David S. Terry of the California Supreme Court.[36]

Terry, in June 1859, had failed to receive the renomination for the Supreme Court. As a one-time ally of Broderick, perhaps Terry felt betrayed he did not receive more support from Broderick in his renomination bid.[37] More likely, Terry was swinging his allegiance to the more powerful Gwin faction, backed by the Buchanan administration. By gaining their favor, he might have received an appointment such as the one Denver received. Even though in this case he was acting as a knight-errant for Gwin, Terry's status as chief justice made it very difficult for Broderick to turn down a challenge without losing public esteem.

Whether Terry made a political pact with Gwin to conspire against Broderick was never clear. However, Terry's reasons for wanting to fight seemed slight in comparisons with most duels. When the *San Francisco Daily National* quoted Broderick as making defamatory remarks against Terry's character, Terry felt he was justified by social norms to challenge Broderick to a duel. The honor dispute began when Broderick made an off-color remark to a friend of Terry's during a breakfast conversation in the International Hotel during a state convention of Democrats.[38] Broderick's remarks were in response to the disparaging comments Terry had made about Broderick in a speech during the same convention.[39] But because Broderick's remarks about Terry were quoted publicly in a newspaper, Terry could claim defamation and thus feel justified by honor to seek resolution through the dueling code.

Almost two months later, as soon as the result of the election was ascertained, Terry sent a challenge which Broderick accepted. The first time they met on the dueling ground, the police arrested them. However, they were subsequently released on the grounds that there was no law under which they could be punished for attempting to fight in a duel.[40] They met two days later in a little dell near California's Lake Merced. The terms of the duel, named by Broderick, were pistols at ten paces. The firing would be between the words "fire" and "two." The *New York Times* wrote: "It is stated that Judge Terry's friends were anxious to have these terms modified, so that the firing might be permitted at any time between the words 'fire-one-two-three': but this was declined — Broderick's friends relying upon his quickness of motion."[41] The weapons used would be Terry's own dueling pistols.[42]

At a little before 7:00 A.M., the second pronounced the words, "Are you ready?" "Ready," responded Terry and Broderick.[43] Immediately after "fire-one-two" was counted off, Broderick raised his pistol to fire from its downward position; however, the gun went off prematurely due in part to the gun's hair trigger.[44] Terry fired an instant later, mortally wounding Broderick, who would be the first, and only, U.S. senator to be killed in a duel while in office.[45]

The circumstances of the duel caused a media uproar. Many major newspapers, such as the *New York Times* and *Richmond Enquirer,* printed detailed accounts of the duel that filtered down to smaller papers.[46] Under the front page heading, "Political Aspects of the Killing of Senator Broderick," the *New York Times* printed an open letter to the editor.

> It is alleged that the killing of Mr. Broderick was entirely disconnected with political matters. An assertion of this kind, directly in the teeth of a convincing chain of circumstantial evidence, is not worthy of serious consideration. Mr. BRODERICK was in the way of political aspirants, of the Lecompton candidates, and possessed of information and secrets which disturbed the peace and conscience of his enemies. It was decreed and predetermined that he should fall.[47]

The Lecompton candidates referred to the Lecompton constitution, which called for Kansas to be admitted as a slave state and was backed by Buchanan. This had grown to be the source of antagonism between Broderick and Gwin.[48] In another edition of the *New York Times*, an editorial under the heading "Political Murder" drew comparisons to the Hamilton-Burr duel:

> This story will carry man's minds back half a century in our chronicles, to the branded day on which ALEXANDER HAMILTON fell, slain by the Vice-President of the United States. But the reminisces will be found to be superficial merely. There is as little resemblance between the social significance of the two cases [as] between the personal value of the combatants. HAMILTON and BURR were men who had won their elevated positions by qualities as elevated, and by services to the State which History need not blush to record. And the deed which robbed the nation of one statesman, made the other a vagabond fugitive.[49]

Hamilton's death had helped deter the practice of dueling in the North. But few thought that Broderick's death would do anything to stop the rampant bloodshed in California politics precipitated in large measure by partisan defamation.[50] Like Hamilton, however, the political impact of Broderick's death was felt nationwide.[51]

Some newspapers went as far as to accuse the Buchanan administration of playing a role in Broderick's death. The *Philadelphia Press*, which had helped elect the Democrat Buchanan, now accused him of conspiring to kill Broderick:

> Mr. Broderick was in every respect a representative man, not simply a representative of his class, but of the great principal involved in the struggle between the people and the Federal Administration. Few men have attracted to themselves more devoted friends than David C. Broderick, and the news that he has fallen in the very prime of life, a victim to the

insatiate and insatiable malevolence of the Federal Administration will be received by these gallant men with sad and heavy hearts.[52]

The editor, John Forney, compared the situation to that of Cilley's encounter with Graves. Forney wrote, "Jonathan Cilley fell for an Administration, and in a personal difficulty — David C. Broderick has yielded up his life for a sacred principle. If he had surrendered to the blandishments of the Administration, he might to day be living among his numerous friends."[53] In response, the president notified Forney of his intention to institute legal proceedings against him for an alleged libel contained in the article on the California duel.[54] The action by Buchanan was a far cry from the Southern attitude that honor was not a quality that could be repaired through the legal system.[55]

The political controversies growing out of the Broderick-Terry duel were representative of the growing sectionalism in American politics. In an article that was reprinted in Southern cities, the *New York Herald* wrote:

> The unhappy duel between Senator Broderick, a law-maker, and Chief Justice Terry of the Supreme Court of California, one of the highest dignitaries of connected with the administration of the law, is traced to its true source — the alarming moral condition to which the struggles of political parties have brought the whole country.... It may be readily imagined what elements are invoked to decide such a struggle — that popular rights and sovereignty become mere mockeries as parts of our institutions, and that "Muscle and Money," in the expressive language of a contemporary, become the real arbiters at the polls.... Take the great cities of the North; will an honest man pretend to maintain that their elections are carried by the free, unbought suffrages of the people according to the theory of our government? We apprehend not![56]

As with the Broderick-Terry duel and most political duels in America preceding it, the real winner was the party that could win public sentiment through their partisan organ. The personal turf wars of California juntos, of which the partisan press played an integral role, had national repercussions. In the end, the Democrats may have won the exchange, but the Republicans won the affair of honor. The anti–Democrat sentiment generated by Broderick's death spawned sympathy for Republicans and led to Kansas' admission into the U.S. as a free state. As this junto mentality proliferated on the frontier in the wake of a splintering Democratic Party, subordinates would rally around the keystone of their power; even if it took them to the brink of civil war.

CHAPTER FOUR

The Antebellum Editor, Honor
and the Community Dynamic

Much of this book so far has focused on how political leaders used the ritual of honor combined with the partisan press to their advantage on a state and national basis. Yet, how much of a factor was the code of honor for local journalism during the antebellum era? This is a progressively more important question to nineteenth-century journalism research as newspaper circulation in rural communities increased in tandem with the emergence of more local reporting during the Jacksonian Age. What this chapter will examine is how the culture of honor affected the newspaper editor in the community dynamic from 1800 to 1861.

This chapter theorizes that as the nineteenth century progressed, the ritual of honor was not an anomaly in defamatory situations, but a daunting source of pressure on the local editor in many communities across the U.S., especially the South and West. In many areas of the country during this period, juries did not consider killing a journalist by ritual violence a criminal offense in defamatory situations. This not only included dueling, but also public beatings with a cane, leather strap or similar device. How could this be? Furthermore, how did this affect journalism in those areas? Why was ritual violence more prominent in some communities than others? This chapter will explore those issues.

This is not to suggest that all cases of libel or defamation in the antebellum American community were dealt with by ritual violence or the suggestion of ritual violence. In her book, *Taking Their Political Place: Journalists and the Making of an Occupation*, Patricia Dooley wrote that "throughout the nineteenth century, in both civil and criminal libel suits, American politicians and government officials continually threatened, and imposed financial burdens on, the nation's more outspoken journalists."[1]

Early nineteenth-century examples of this include editors in the New York community, such as James Cheetham of the *American Citizen* and William Coleman of the New York *Evening Post*, discussed in chapter one of this book, who were often the targets of libel lawsuits. Dooley wrote that Cheetham was brought to court 13 times for libel during his first two years as editor of the *American Citizen*.[2] But as Dooley illustrated in her book, many of these lawsuits ended in a mistrial, an acquittal, a hung jury or a deadlock.[3] Between 1803 and 1807, Cheetham admitted to paying at least $4,000 in libel damages, but if he enjoyed the patronage of the government, damages imposed on partisan papers might seem ineffective.[4] In comparison, Allan Nevins wrote in *The Evening Post: A Century of Journalism*, that no suits against that paper ever succeeded, even though many were attempted.[5]

This culture of honor had a devastating effect on editors such as Cheetham and Coleman, who were constantly faced with the ritual of honor in lieu of libel suits.[6] Under the pressure of public approval, editors often used the threat of violence that the affair of honor offered to defend their columns against accusations of libel from their story subjects and rival editors.

To illustrate, when Cheetham suggested in the *American Citizen* that Coleman had fathered a mulatto child, Coleman responded to the defamation by challenging him to a duel.[7] The duel between the two never occurred because the challenge was made public before the encounter could take place, and the affair was thwarted by the local authorities. When the New York harbor master, Captain Jeremiah Thompson, suggested that Coleman let the facts of the duel become public because he was a coward, Coleman challenged Thompson for his slander. Cheetham was Thompson's second.[8] The two faced each other on Love Lane, described by Nevins as "a sequestered road, then well outside the city, which followed the present line of Twenty-first Street between Sixth and Eighth Avenue."[9] One evening in early January 1804, the duelists fired two shots at ten paces, then moved closer and fired two more until Thompson was mortally wounded. As Nevins described in his book, Thompson "was carried to his sister's house in town, was laid on the doorstep, the bell was rung, and the family found him bleeding and near death."[10] Even though Thompson lived 48 hours after being shot, he and the other witnesses kept the affair secret so Coleman would not be accused of murder.[11]

Newspaper editors across the country in the antebellum era were subjected to, and engaged in, ritualized violence as a defense for libel or defamation. Lambert Wilmer, an important nineteenth-century journalism critic, estimated in his book, *Our Press Gang*, that more than two-thirds of the single combats between civilians in the antebellum United States originated in newspaper disputes.[12] Wilmer wrote, "And I think it will appear that more duels have been fought, in this country, by public journalists than by naval and military officers; though fighting is the trade of the latter, and public opinion seems to exact from them a nicer observance of the 'code of honor' than is ever required of men who are engaged in more pacific avocations."[13] It is generally assumed that dueling and ritualized violence disappeared in Northern states after the Hamilton-Burr duel in 1804, but that is an exaggeration. As evident with the Burr-Hamilton duel, however, it did become substantially less politically advantageous to duel in Northern states that had well-developed local and state governments compared to the South, which did not. But the ritual of honor still remained an imposing force in all areas in antebellum America.

For instance, in 1818 when William Coleman published a report detailing the misconduct of Henry B. Hagerman, a Democratic judge advocate, Hagerman's response on April 11 was to sneak up behind Coleman and beat him with the butt of a rawhide whip. Nevins wrote, "The editor was stunned by the first blow, was repeatedly struck and kicked as he lay prostrate, and when he staggered to his feet, half blind with blood, was given a still more savage beating."[14] Although not the same as dueling, the rationale for Hagerman's actions had very much to do with the code of honor. In fact, this type of behavior was not necessarily considered criminal. In his book, *Political Culture and Secession in Mississippi*, Christopher Olsen suggested that these types of confrontations "were not 'random' acts but served a specific, public purpose. Men used several types of stylized contests — dueling was only the most obvious — to resolve conflicts and defend their honor and manliness. The common theme in all of these encounters was their public quality."[15] By beating him on the street, Hagerman was signaling to the public that Coleman, as an editor, was not honorable enough to receive a challenge from him. Barbara Holland, in her book *Gentlemen's Blood*, wrote that editors were especially vulnerable to the code of honor because the perceived defamation could be easily traced back to the source. "You knew where the newspaper office was and stalked into it with a challenge, or perhaps a cane or a horsewhip; those who considered newspaper editors too inferior socially for a proper duel simply beat them," Holland wrote.[16] The tacit public acceptance of this type of honor-bound retribution, even in the North, was reflected in Hagerman's punishment. He was arrested for this encounter but never criminally prosecuted. Two years later, Coleman was awarded $4,000 in civil damages for the attack. It was a huge compensation in 1820 but relatively light, as one of the most popular editors of one of the largest newspapers in the country was beaten so severely that he was permanently paralyzed.[17]

There are other examples of editors being involved in ritualized violence in the North. Besides being involved in the Cilley-Graves affair, Colonel James Watson Webb of the New York *Courier and Enquirer* was shot just below the knee in a June 25, 1842, duel with Thomas F. Marshall, a Congressman from Kentucky, over a newspaper defamation dispute. The *Brooklyn Eagle* reported on this encounter and on dueling: "The newspapers, of course, are not slow to gratify them; and hence the parties engaged generally succeed in obtaining that which they most covet — a little notoriety. They usually succeed, too, in obtaining the presence of one or two respectable individuals on such occasions, which gives a sort of caste to the outrage, and elevates it, as they probably suppose, above an ordinary, though less brutal fight."[18] This account gives insight into the hierarchal structure that existed even in Northern society and suggests that ritualized violence was one way that editors, who were sometimes considered less than honorable, could make inroads into this upper echelon of society.

As a result of the encounter with Marshall, Webb was arrested for violating dueling laws. Lambert Wilmer wrote of Webb's arrest, "While he was in prison, [James] Bennett of the *Herald*, (who had been flogged by Webb once or twice,) magnanimously sent his old enemy a box of the best cigars to comfort him during his incarceration."[19] This quote suggests that not only did antebellum editors accept this ritualized violence, but they also used it, as in Webb's case, to establish a type of hierarchy within their own community ranks. His imprisonment was short lived, as Governor Silas Wright, under enormous political pressure from Webb's influential friends, issued a pardon.[20] According to Wilmer, Bennett was the first to sign Webb's pardon.[21]

What is difficult to reconcile historically is why defamation-related dueling flourished in the South during the latter half of antebellum America while it waned significantly in Northern communities. One reason was the structure of the early nineteenth-century Southern community, which was ill-equipped to deal with a free press. The community dynamic during this period, which closely mirrored the rural Europe that many of the immigrants and their descendents coming to America left behind, would be difficult for someone in twenty-first-century America to comprehend. What might be harder to understand was the caste-like nature of Southern society, which had developed its own unique set of aristocratic ideals. Clement Eaton in *The Growth of Southern Society* wrote, "The majority of planters did not know at first hand how English squires lived, but the tradition had been handed down from the colonial period and strengthened by the reading of English and Scottish novels. This institution had been modified greatly by the Southern environment, particularly by the discarding of its tenantry basis and the exaggeration of certain aspects of the English model, such as carrying the defense of personal honor to ridiculous extremes."[22]

In the era of the partisan newspapers, political warfare was the lifeblood of the Southern press.[23] In this context, editors regarded themselves, as Nevins wrote, "as so many knights errant, roaming the land for battle, no sooner seeing a strange crest than they galloped to shiver lances."[24]

That there were few libel suits in the South during the antebellum years did not mean harsh political attacks in Southern newspapers did not carry weight. Quite the opposite, as Christopher Olsen described in *Political Culture and Secession in Mississippi*: "Within the context of honor and in the rural society, words were powerful weapons not used lightly."[25] Furthermore, C. A. Harwell Wells noted in "The End of the Affair?" that laws designed to prohibit dueling in the antebellum era did not work because often in rural areas they were not enforced. "For a man to turn to the legal system to repair his honor, perhaps by filing a libel or slander suit, was akin to a man admitting that he was unable to protect himself," Wells wrote.[26] With the press so intertwined in partisan politics during the antebellum era, the survival of a newspaper often depended on the effectiveness of an editor's attack. Vice versa, the political effectiveness of a newspaper also depended on how well editors defended what they wrote. In the heat of partisan political rivalry, for an editor to disavow the code of honor when he was called "liar," "poltroon" or "coward" might suggest that his character and opinion was less than honorable. Remember, the goal of most journalism during the antebellum period was not objectivity but political advantage.[27]

Another factor in the sectional differences between dueling rates might have been the anti-party tradition in much of the lower South, which made it easier for editors to advance politically, but often left them defending accusations of libel on the field of honor instead of courtrooms. As Olsen wrote, this anti-partyism emphasized the patron-client, or personal relationships, over party cliques:

> Predisposed to favor planters, the southern legal system respected their mastery over rural, often isolated plantations. Both contemporaries and

historians detail the weakness of southern institutions, usually focusing on extra legal forms of crime and punishment — the prevalence of lynching and charivari, for example. These social and legal patterns extended to a political philosophy that celebrated the personal, honor-bound connection between a representative and his constituency.[28]

According to Olsen, this anti-party tradition was popular in the lower South in states such as Mississippi, where party politics were only "a grudging necessity in national and most state elections."[29] Thus, newspaper editors in small towns and rural areas in the Deep South were most likely facing a different concept of libel than in the North. This anti-partyism was especially precarious for editors because it depended on constant reinforcement of manliness in an honor-bound patron-client system, which did not lend itself well, to say the least, to public criticism. So, in essence one had many situations in communities throughout the lower and upper South where it applied, where journalism was unrestricted in its use of defamation to assert manliness and honor in order to gain esteem from readers and political constituents who gave patronage. But as Dicken-Garcia wrote in *Journalistic Standards in Nineteenth-Century America*, "As long as the press was tied to the party system, one rationale for partiality was that it served a higher purpose — that of advancing the 'best' or 'right' policies (in the printer's and his party's views)."[30] This created a vicious cycle of ritualized violence in the Deep South between editors and public officials who were constantly having to prove their manliness and honor to the community in response to their utter public denigration by their rivals.

One such example of the heightened ritualized violence editors faced in the Deep South was when the *Vicksburg Sentinel* was introduced to the Mississippi community in 1837 by Dr. James Hagan and Dr. Willis E. Green, brother of editor and Calhounite "Rough" Duff Green.[31] According to the Mississippi Archives, Green was not long connected with the paper and Hagan, an Irish immigrant, soon took sole editorship.[32] Henry S. Foote, a resident of Vicksburg and an acquaintance of Hagan, wrote in his book *Casket of Reminiscences*:

> No such editorial writer as Doctor Hagan had ever before appeared in the State of Mississippi, and Governor McNutt was shrewd enough to discern at once that it might facilitate the accomplishment of his own views of individual ambition very much if he could in some way manage to conciliate this rising genius. What he did for this purpose I have never precisely ascertained, but it is certain that Dr. Hagan, despite some noted differences between himself and Governor McNutt, upon several political ques-

tions of great importance, became in process of time completely devoted
to that personage, and the Sentinel was by all recognized as Governor
McNutt's veritable political organ.[33]

It was not long before Hagan's caustic editorials brought him into conflict
with area politicians and rival editors. According to the Mississippi
Archives, late in 1838 Hugh C. Stewart, a Mississippi congressman from
nearby Hinds county, slapped the unsuspecting Hagan in the barroom of
a local hotel in Jackson called the Mansion House. When Hagan recovered, he suggested that they settle the dispute with pistols in a duel. Stewart declined on the grounds that his position in the House prevented him
from doing so.[34]

Some months later, Stewart made unflattering remarks about
Hagan on the floor of the Mississippi House. This brought a swift rebuttal and the beginning of an honor dispute from Hagan in the form of a
card that was published in the *Tri-Weekly Mississippian*: "Mr. Hugh C.
Stewart, a member of the House, availed himself of his privilege, and made
an attack on me in his place [the House], a few days since. Some months
ago I pronounced this same Hugh C. Stewart, to his face, in a public
house in Jackson, a cowardly poltroon, and dared him to resent it. He
took the opportunity which only a poltroon would take to retaliate."[35]
Stewart's reply came in the following week in the same Jackson newspaper:

> Now let the facts be known. This infamous coward, scoundrel, villain, and
> slanderer, James Hagan, did last fall, (in the barroom of the Mansion
> House, in this city,) deny, in my presence, being a liar, of which I had
> charged him; and, for the insolence of the puppy, I caught him by the col-
> lar, and slapped his jaws — which *he has never dared to resent.*
> It is false that I took advantage of my privilege as a member of the
> House, to retaliate: for I certainly had nothing to resent, after his taking
> my slaps on his jaws so kindly. I also stated, in prefacing my remarks, out
> of the House, as I had said more of it publicly than my own views of pro-
> priety and decorum would permit me to say in the House.[36]

Hagan's reply came in the next issue in the form of a card:

> Mr. Hugh C. Stewart's courage seems to have evaporated in vulgar epithets;
> but he has not had the impudence to deny that I pronounced him a "cow-
> ardly poltroon." His statement that he "slapped my jaws" because "I denied
> being a liar" is so absurd as to carry its own refutation with it; and none
> but an ignorant and dastardly booby of his size would boast, if it had
> been the fact, that he used personal violence to me, in defence of his repu-
> tation as a man of courage. Though he has proved himself to be a poltroon,
> yet I will put him on the footing of a gentleman, and waiving all advantage

of position, meet him on the equal terms which I proposed at the first difficulty.[37]

There would be no duel fought between these men. But this was but one of the first of many incidences of ritualized violence that early *Sentinel* editors would face.

According to his subject file in the Mississippi Archives, Hagan had no difficulty in getting into controversies with members of the legislature and other public officials in Jackson. His sharp writing in the *Sentinel* was indicative of the financial problems that many antebellum newspapers faced. Dicken-Garcia wrote that advertising at this point could not support a newspaper because rates were too low and did not create a solid base.[38] Thus, many editors, as in Hagan's case, depended on political patronage for their newspaper. When Foote suggested to Hagan that his abilities "were of so high a cast that he could have no difficulty whatever in reaching the loftiest position of civil dignity if he would but pay more regard to the rules of social decorum and the laws of a high bred courtesy," Hagan replied, according to Foote, "that he had found the outside pressure upon him for the preparation of articles of a fiercely denunciatory character too strong to be resisted."[39] And although he may have received patronage from his supporters such as McNutt, he often found himself on the receiving end of canings and slappings in addition to dueling.

This ritualized violence came not only from public figures, which Hagan frequently reported on, but from rival editors in the community as well. On April 26, 1839, the *Mississippian* reported a duel between Hagan and William H. McCardle, editor of the *Vicksburg Register*. The report said, "The latter [McCardle] was shot through the side, and believed to be dangerously wounded. Dr. Hagan was uninjured. Both parties are said to have carried themselves with coolness and courage."[40] There was no description in the report of what incited the honor dispute.

In early 1840, when Hagan criticized W.G. Kendall, a member of the House from Yalobusha County, Kendall went, as the *Mississippian* described, "post-haste to Vicksburg to chastise the editor, Dr. Hagan."[41] The article quoted Hagan's description of the encounter:

> While we were engaged in taking our letters out of the post office yesterday, Kendall, like a cowardly scoundrel, came behind us, and struck us three times with a hickory stick on the back of the head; like a base dog, as he is, he made his escape without giving us a fair fight.
>
> The dastard dare not give us fair warning, meet us like a gentleman, face to face, and give us a fair fight. He not only took the advantage of his

great physical strength, but came behind us when stooped, taking out our letters, and without saying a word, felled us with his club, and then made his excape [*sic*], leaving his stick, before we recovered from the blows. It is just what might be expected from so cowardly an imbecile as Kendall is known to be.[42]

The *Mississippian* reported that Kendall, making the attack at 4:00 P.M., immediately traveled the 56 miles back to Jackson by 10:00 A.M. the next day.[43]

When he recovered from the beating, Hagan immediately traveled to Jackson and had his second, named only as Col. Labauve, deliver a note, which was subsequently published in the *Mississippian*. It read:

You made a cowardly attack on me at Vicksburg last Sunday evening, and left your club without giving me an opportunity for redress. I will not send you a challenge, because you are a member of the legislature; but if you possess any of the feelings of a man, you will come down State-Street, opposite the Mansion House, between the hours of one and two o'clock this day, to receive your club, which I have brought along. I will be prepared to deliver it to you, armed with a pair of dueling and a pair of belt pistols.[44]

After delivering the note, the *Mississippian* reported that Labauve struck Kendall with his walking cane "but was prevented from the further chastisement of Mr. K. by the interference of his friends."[45] When the time came for the two to meet, Hagan discovered that Kendall had notified the local authorities. Hagan was subsequently arrested and bound in the penalty of $3,000 to appear at the next term of the Circuit Court of Hinds County.[46] For his part, Kendall replied in the *Mississippian* six days after the encounter saying that he deemed Hagan unworthy of any further notice or treatment than the beating he gave him. He also indicated that he would not pay attention to Hagan further except with another beating.[47] In other words, Hagan was not gentlemen enough for Kendall to duel with him.

Kendall's response outraged the editor of the *Mississippian*, who printed extracts from a letter written from Hagan in Jackson to the editor of the *Columbus Democrat* containing an account of the affair.[48] The *Mississippian* editor wrote, "There is but one opinion entertained here of the conduct of Kendall — that of unmitigated contempt. The baseness of his attack is only surpassed by the cowardly act of his shielding himself under the arm of the law, after violating that law to obtain a mean revenge. Both are without parallel in Mississippi."[49] Wilmer wrote in *Our Press Gang*, "An assault on the reputation of some unfortunate person is often preconcerted by several newspapers; and this mode of operation is much facilitated by means of combinations or associations of editors and reporters."[50] However, the caste-like nature of the Deep South society, which permitted ritual violence in cases of defamation, coupled with weak political parties, most likely left editors, who were often considered social inferiors, no choice but to band together when they were not shooting at each other.

Such was the case in the near duel between L.A. Besancon, editor of the *Mississippi Free Trader and Natchez Gazette*, and P.W. Tompkins, a state representative from Vicksburg and Warren County.[51] It was reported on February 28, 1842, in the *Vicksburg Whig* that Hagan and his partner, James S. Fall, who was also a *Sentinel* editor, were seconds in the affair. The duel never occurred because Tompkins refused to recognize the *Sentinel* editors as seconds for Besancon on the grounds that they were not gentlemen.[52] The Vicksburg *Whig*, which published the formal notes between the two parties, wrote that Tompkins did Besancon too much honor in considering him a respectable adversary, and his conduct throughout the affair was that of a braggadocio and coward.[53] It was reported, incidentally, that in 1838 editor Bescanon gave a caning to F.E. Plummer, president of the Grenada Bank, in the presence of political friends, and that Plummer had "begged like a dog" and "shivered like an aspen."[54]

When James S. Fall took over the *Sentinel's* main editorial duties for Hagan when he was out of the state in the spring of 1842, Fall found himself involved in a duel with T.E. Robbins, a trustee of the Vicksburg Railroad Bank. Robbins took exception to a pointed editorial barrage by the *Sentinel* on April 14. Even though the two had never met, he immediately challenged Fall to a duel.[55] The seconds worked out the strict rules of the encounter, which, according to an eyewitness, stated that "the parties were to stand with a pistol in each hand, and then fire one and then the other in that position, or wheel and advance at pleasure."[56] The duel took place on April 18 on the Louisiana side of the Mississippi river border with no one being shot. After the duel, however, Robbins claimed that Fall had, before the word, slightly elevated his pistol in violation of the rules, which would have required Robbins' seconds to shoot Fall on sight. *The Mississippian* printed an eyewitness account of the affair:

> The time for making this objection, was before, not after, the fight; and it is considered rather extraordinary by the knowing ones, that after the fight was permitted to proceed and two fires take place place [*sic*], that the friends of Mr. Robbins should discover that the terms had been violated. It is unusual on such occasions to notice slight variations from the terms where no advantage was intended or obtained, and in the estimation of the

intelligent, does not accord with any very high notions of chivalry. Besides, as Mr. Fall let his pistol down, there was in truth, no violation of the terms; and what renders this objection still more absurd is, that Mr. Robbins fired first.[57]

Robbins' seconds did not shoot the editor down, and the affair ended without incident.[58]

There was no love lost between the Hagan and the *Whig*. On March 4, 1841, the *Whig* published an article by its editor, Edmund Flagg, stating that Hagan had tried to assassinate him the day before.[59] The argument between the two rival editors had grown from a newspaper dispute to a duel. Although the particulars of the duel are unknown, it was reported on May 14 in the *Whig* that Flagg was acquitted of the charge of dueling and shooting with intent to kill.[60] Subsequently, on May 18, 1841, the *Whig* reported that Hagan was acquitted of the charge of dueling.[61]

Hagan's life met with a violent end on June 7, 1843, as a direct result of an article he published accusing a well-known judge, George W. Adams, of stealing from public funds.[62] On June 8, the *Whig* carried an article with details of a street scuffle between Hagan and the judge's son, Daniel W. Adams.[63] According to a report from a Jackson newspaper, *The Southron*,

> Mr. A. [Daniel Adams] met with Dr. H [Hagan] while the latter was returning from his boarding house to his office. When within a few yards of him, he called to Dr. H. and stated that a scurrilous article against his father had appeared in the Sentinel, which he then held in his hand, and he desired to know the author of it. Dr. H., without making any further reply, advanced upon Mr. A., who at the same time raised his walking cane and struck at Dr. H., who caught the blow on his arm, and immediately seized Mr. A. around the waist. They grappled with each other and after a short struggle both came to the ground, side by side, but Mr. A. being farther on the slope of the hill, Dr. H. succeeded in getting on top and fixing his hand upon the throat of Mr. A. While in this position, Mr. A. drew a pistol from his side pocket and shot Dr. H., the ball entering just below the left shoulder blade and ranging along the spine to the back part of the head. He died immediately.[64]

Even though there were several witnesses, this was a ritualistic display of manliness and honor and Adams was acquitted on the grounds of self-defense. Ironically, one of Adams' defense lawyers, Henry S. Foote, also was asked to give Hagan's eulogy, which he declined out of inappropriateness.[65] According to a July 4, 1843, article in the *Sentinel*, the community was so moved by Hagan's death that a monument was created to his name and memory. The large stone monument, which was erected in lot 17 of Cedar Hill Cemetery, has since fallen over and is on the ground.[66]

It might be easy to assume that Hagan's encounters with ritualized violence in lieu of defamation suits were an anomaly during this period. It also might be easy to assume that any violence faced by editors in the mid–nineteenth-century South was connected in some way to the growing controversy over slavery and nullification. However, a 1956 study of antebellum Mississippi newspapers located in the state archives, *Those Duelling Editors of Vicksburg, 1841–1860* by Monroe F. Cockrell, suggested differently. Cockrell read hundreds of pages of antebellum Vicksburg newspapers for evidence of dueling editors. In documenting his results, Cockrell wrote, "Notices about duels in other places appeared too frequently for me to keep track of them lest I lose sight of my own at Vicksburg."[67] Cockrell also wrote, "Incidentally I did not see a single line about slavery. The quarrels arose from political partisanship, differences about the banks and their paper money, skin plasters, repudiation of debts, the Choctaw Indian claims, etc.— all mixed up with hot-blooded personalities."[68] Cockrell's analysis was prompted by what he saw as a disproportionate number of Vicksburg editors involved in duels and near duels for a white population, which was approximately 1,968 in 1840. Counting all black males and females, free and slave, the population of Vicksburg in 1840 totaled approximately 3,104.

The legacy of the Vicksburg editors after Hagan further illustrates that his constant exposure to ritualized violence was not an anomaly. After about a month-long interim editorial stint by Hagan's executor, Dermot J. Brennan, John A. Ryan became editor of the *Sentinel*. It was clear that he did not get off on a good foot with his town rivals at the *Whig*. On August 22, 1843, *Whig* editor R.E. Hammet wrote, "Our new potato blossom over the way, whose sudden transition from the stool of the pedagogue to the chair editorial has given him imaginary importance."[69] The rivalry continued throughout the following months with such editorial exchanges as the *Whig* editor calling Ryan on September 21, 1843, "A compound of turf and potatoes" and the *Sentinel* editor promising to make the *Whig* editor fight or prove him a coward.[70]

The attacks between the two editors continued to escalate as the months wore on. There was some evidence that the Vicksburg authorities had tried to quell the impending ritual violence between them. The *Brooklyn Eagle* reported on November 18, 1843, that the editor of the Vicksburg *Whig* was jailed for being involved in an honor dispute. The report read, "To prevent a hostile meeting with another editor, the magistrate had required him [the *Whig* editor] to give bail in the sum of $2,000 to keep the peace. Declining to do so he was committed [on November 4]."[71] It was reported that the editor enjoyed the quiet hospitalities of the jail as much as working in his office.[72] On November 6, Hammet wrote that he was liberated on parole by the mayor until his trial and announced on November 8 that he was finally released from incarceration after five days.[73]

Apparently the jail term only temporarily quelled the antagonism between the two editors. Cockrell noted that they finally met on the field of honor on February 29, 1844. He wrote in his study:

> The Sentinel editorial said [quoting directly], "We are called upon to record the death of John A. Ryan, Esq., editor of this paper; being the second martyr who has fallen in the cause of Democracy within the last year. He fell on the fourth shot, at the distance of only ten paces, without the power of resisting. The bloody fight, (being according to the duello) beyond the limits of either suggestion or dictation. Which of his seconds can look towards Heaven and answer to their God, for the death this noble Son."[74]

The *Brooklyn Eagle* reported: "Fatal Duel.—A duel was fought at Vicksburg, Mississippi ... between Mr. Hammet, editor of the Vicksburg Whig, (and brother of the member of Congress from Mississippi,) and Mr. Ryan, editor of the Sentinel. They fought with pistols at the usual distance. At the fourth fire Mr. Ryan fell mortally wounded, being shot through the lungs. He died within ten minutes."[75] No record was found of whether Hammet was convicted on a charge of murder or dueling, but judging from the journalistic record in Vicksburg following Ryan's death, he most likely was acquitted.

Walter Hickey assumed the editorial role of the *Sentinel* after Ryan and was met with similar ritualized violence. He soon was involved in a public street fight with Dr. J.F. Macklin. The *Brooklyn Eagle*, via a news exchange, reported the outcome of the affair: "The Effects of Assaulting Editors.—Dr. C. F Marlin [*sic*], who was shot a few days since by the editor of the Vicksburg Sentinel, in a street recontre, has since died of his wounds. He declared, when about dying, that 'he would have acted as the editor did under the same circumstances.'—*Jersey Paper*."[76] This report was followed by a June 20, 1844, announcement that Hickey was unanimously acquitted on the charges of manslaughter.[77] The Mississippi Archives record that Hickey, "who had several difficulties and was wounded repeatedly," retired from the *Sentinel* and was subsequently killed in Texas through unrelated circumstances.[78]

The *Sentinel* editorship was assumed by John Lavins, who was publisher during Hickey's tenure.[79] There is evidence that both men during their stints had a tenuous relationship with the local government, as evidenced by a December 13, 1844, report in the *Brooklyn Eagle*:

> Conflict of Authorities.— Gov. Brown, of Mississippi, pardoned Mr. Hickey, the editor of the Vicksburg Sentinel, and Mr. Lavins, the proprietor, imprisoned on a charge of libel contained in a censure of Judge Coalter. The defendants were sentenced by Judge Coalter to six months' imprisonment and a fine of five hundred dollars each. On their being released by the Governor, Judge C. arrested both of the released persons again, and committed them on their former sentences. The Governor immediately procured a writ of habeas corpus and brought them from Vicksburg Jail before the High Court of Errors and Appeals (Judges Sharkey, Clayton and Thatcher,) now in session in the city of Jackson — since which, we have not heard how the affair has progressed. There is some talk of the Judge committing the Governor for contempt. Fortunately, the Governor has the pardoning power in his own hands, and can release himself.[80]

Whether both editors were eventually run out of town cannot be clearly ascertained, but it was recorded by Cockrell that these two editors were replaced by John Jenkins a short time after the controversy. According to Cockrell, who cited Jenkins' gravestone, the editor took over his duties on December 13, 1844.[81]

Jenkins, with F.C. Jones, was still editing the *Sentinel* in 1848 when he was killed by Henry A. Crabbe. During a heated political debate at a public meeting on September 12, Crabbe, a local lawyer, struck Jenkins with his hand and a scuffle ensued. The fight was broken up, but Crabbe became the subject of a Jenkins editorial two days later in the *Sentinel*. When the two next encountered each other in front of a local drugstore while Crabbe was carrying a cane,[82] the confrontation, as the *Whig* reported, turned violent:

> A difficulty occurred between Henry A. Crabb [*sic*], Esq., and John Jenkins, one of the editors of the Sentinel at the political meeting of Tuesday night, which was far from being allayed by an article referring to it in the Sentinel of Thursday. Yesterday the two gentlemen met on Washington Street — words ensued, Mr. Jenkins drew a knife and stabbed Mr. Crabb in several places, when the latter presented a pistol and shot the former in the heart, killing him almost instantly. It is thought Mr. Crabb is mortally wounded. Mr. Jenkins leaves an estimable lady and several children to lament his untimely death.[83]

Henry S. Foote recalled in his *Casket of Reminiscences* that Crabbe was a lawyer he knew for several years and was highly respected in the Vicksburg community.[84] According to the Mississippi Archives, Jenkins' partner, F.C. Jones, drowned himself not long after Jenkins died.[85] It is not known if there was foul play involved in Jones' death.

The Brooklyn *Eagle* did not miss the significance when it received a notice in 1860 from Vicksburg that the *Sentinel* was looking for someone to fill its editor position.

> The Vicksburgh [*sic*] *Sentinel* (Miss.) wants an Editor. The *Sentinel* frequently wants an editor, and probably the following brief history of men who have filled the position, will account for the constant recurring vacancies:
>
> "Dr. James Hagan took hold in 1837, had a number of street fights, fought a duel with his brother editor of the Whig, and was killed in 1842, in a street fight, by D.W. Adams. His assistant, Isaac C. Partridge, died of yellow fever in 1839. Dr. J.S. Fall, another assistant, had a number of fights, in one of which he was badly wounded, James Ryan, next editor, was killed by R. E. Hammet of the *Whig*. Next came Walter Hickey, who had several rows, and was repeatedly wounded; he killed Dr. Maclin, and was soon after himself killed in Texas. John Lavins, another editor, was imprisoned for the violence of his articles. Mr. Jenkins, his successor, was killed in the street by H.A. Crabbe.... F.C. Jones succeeded Jenkins, but soon afterwards drowned himself. It will be seen from this, that a considerable portion of the editorial matter of the Sentinel has been 'leaded.'"[86]

It is not known whether the *Sentinel* found an editor.

Olsen suggested in *Political Culture and Secession in Mississippi* that ritual responses of violence to the partisan language of newspapers during the nineteenth century signaled a weak political culture.[87] This was significant for incidents of libel or defamation because this anti-party tradition hinged on personal reputation and character, not necessarily political ideology. Thus, the traditional style of partisan journalism in the North, described by Dicken-Garcia as convincing readers of the correctness of one's position on an issue by destroying the opponent's credibility, proved disastrous to many editors in the South whose opponents' candidacy for office was based almost solely on their reputation in the community.[88] The fact that many Southern editors were actually born in the North and trained under Northern journalists could have only added to the confusion.[89] Add to the mix that by the last decade of the antebellum period the circulation of Southern newspapers almost doubled, and one can begin to understand why there was a surge of ritual violence against editors in the South.[90]

And so editorial dramas similar to that in Vicksburg played out in similar fashion in rural communities across the southern United States during the antebellum era. When Melzar Gardner, editor of Virginia's Portsmouth *Chronicle*, was killed trying to defend himself against a caning on March 30, 1843, his attacker, Mordecai Cooke, Jr., was acquitted by a jury. The Norfolk *Beacon* described the incident: "The parties, we learn, met accidentally at the Ferry Wharf when a conversation was held between them, upon which Mr. Cooke raised a stick which was dropped in the wrestle. Mr. Gardner drew one of Colt's revolving pistols from his pantaloon's pocket, and in the struggle, which lasted but a moment, one of the caps exploded, and one of the barrels was discharged. The ball penetrated Mr. G's heart and he expired in a few moments."[91] Although there was no proof to the contrary in this case, characteristically the types of meetings that preceded ritualistic beatings of editors, as in the case of the *Sentinel*, were seldom accidental.

In 1829, when the Lexington *Gazette* criticized one of Kentucky's most prominent politicians, Robert Wickliffe, it touched off a newspaper war with his son, Charles, who publicly rushed to his defense. Each side published anonymous articles under the names Coriolanus (Wickliffe) and Dentatus (Gazette) berating each other until it escalated to violence. The Lexington *Gazette* described the March 9, 1829, confrontation:

> Mr. [Charles] Wickliffe on Monday the ninth inst. after preparing himself with at least three pistols, invited a friend to go with him to the Gazette office, for the purpose of demanding the author of Dentatus. The friend required first to see the two essays, and having examined them declined going any further in the business, and advised him [Wickliffe] not to do it either. He however persisted and called at the Gazette office, where he saw Mr. [Thomas] Benning, and demanded the author of Dentatus. The editor requested him to call at five o'clock [*sic*], which he did. Mr. Benning at that interview told him that he must see the author, and that if he would call at eight o'clock the next morning he should have the name. This was strongly objected to by Wickliffe who insisted on instant information, but at length agreed to wait until the time specified, some conversation between them ensued in relation to a publication about Robert Wickliffe, which ended by Wickliffe calling Benning by some harsh epithet and advancing upon him in an attitude of attack. Benning, who had a small stick in his hand, attempted to raise it in his defence, but it was quickly taken from him, or thrown on the floor by Wickliffe, who at the same time was pulling out one of his pistols. Benning who was perfectly unarmed, attempted to make his escape through a back door of his office, and whilst going from his assailant, and endeavoring to avoid his attack, was mortally wounded by the discharge of the pistol.[92]

Charles Wickliffe was arrested for killing the Lexington *Gazette* editor, and a grand jury indicted him on a charge of manslaughter, not murder. Robert Wickliffe called on Secretary of State Henry Clay, among other top defense lawyers, to defend his son. Clay won an acquittal on the grounds that the defamatory publications in the *Gazette* caused the death of the editor. Many community leaders supported the defense, much to the chagrin of the *Gazette*, which wrote, "They [the community abroad] will perhaps doubt it, and consider us doing an injustice to our native Town. It is however strictly true. It is the monstrous fact, that there are many persons in this place, of reputable standing in society, who *justify* the murder of Benning, and some who *applaud* it."[93] Having Clay involved drew national attention to the case.

Wickliffe's acquittal did nothing to quell the controversy. The Jacksonian press, led by Benning's replacement, George J. Trotter, assailed Wickliffe in what was viewed by their adversaries as a partisan attack. Trotter himself saw Wickliffe's acquittal as jeopardizing freedom of speech:

> Now, in the first place we deny that "Charles Wickliffe has been ungener-
> ously assailed by the Jackson party." In commenting upon, as they
> believed, the unprovoked killing of Thomas R. Benning, the trial and
> acquittal of Charles Wickliffe, they exercised no more than their legitimate
> privilege. Would Mr. Smith deny them this? Could he expect them to
> stand tamely by — see the unwarrantable efforts made for the acquittal of
> Wickliffe, and fold their arms in silence?[94]

Trotter was responding to the editor of the *Kentucky Reporter*, who called upon the political enemies of Wickliffe "to consult their judgment rather than their party feelings."[95] Those who supported Wickliffe said there was nothing unfair about the acquittal, that "twelve honest men decided that he ought not be punished" and there was nothing further to debate.[96] Trotter retorted that Clay's interference led to Wickliffe's improper acquittal, and he was willing to let the issue rest. "But," Trotter wrote, "if the friends of Mr. Wickliffe are not satisfied, and intent to prolong the controversy, however much we may deplore it, we shall never shrink from the faithful performance of our duty, and when our humble opinions are called for, they will be pronounced in language neither to be *misapprehended* or *misapplied*."[97]

Trotter was probably able to enlist help nationally from his partisan allies by what Wilmer described as a technique of marking or circling specific paragraphs in a newspaper to attract the attention of editors who received the paper in the mail. According to Wilmer, "Each Journalist sends many copies of his paper, hundreds perhaps, to editors in different parts of the country, and receives their publications in return....

When a journalist receives a paper marked in the manner described, he considers himself requested either to copy the designated paragraph, or to embody the substance of it in an editorial article of its own."[98] An article such as Trotter's would be particularly significant since it involved Clay.

Ten days later on September 28, 1829, Trotter received a note from Wickliffe challenging him to a duel in response to what Wickliffe described as a "wanton and unprovoked attack" upon his feelings.[99] Trotter replied, "Your note was received on yesterday ... and whilst I cannot recognise your *right* to call on me in the manner that you have, still the satisfaction you ask for *shall not be denied.*"[100] The terms were set and the two met for a duel just outside the Fayette county line on October 9 at a distance of 8 feet. Wickliffe was killed on the second fire.[101]

Even though the affair was settled honorably, Trotter and his seconds still felt free speech and their lives were in danger. Of the duel, Trotter wrote:

> It now rests with the public to decide between me and my enemies. As it were I have stood alone. They have sought to overwhelm me by introducing witnesses, who, if they testified *truly*, had no right to be present. My Friend and Second is now a thousand miles away. Falsehood and slander have been tried in vain, and assassination doubtless is the "*future adjustment,*" of which Holeman [Wickliffe's ally] boasts. Fearless still I stand. I am pledged that *the press shall be free*— upon that pledge I will stake my life — FOR I WOULD RATHER DIE A FREEMAN THAN LIVE TO BE A SLAVE.[102]

At the time, editorial allies of Trotter did not view this as a personal confrontation but as an example of the struggles of a free press under the weight of the code of honor.[103] One of the newspapers that came to Trotter's defense was the New York *Evening Post*, which wrote:

> We are by no means the advocates of duelling; yet surely some extenuation may be found for the offence of which Mr. Trotter has been guilty, in the state of public sentiment where he resides, and in the fact of the obloquy which he would have incurred had he refused the challenge of Wickliffe. Besides, it is by no means certain, judging from previous occurrences, that it would have been safe for him to pursue a different course. The fate of his predecessor afforded him good reason to suppose that he would not be permitted to pursue an independent editorial career, without either exposing his life in private combat, or otherwise being liable to fall by the pistol of the assassin; and standing in such a calamitous dilemma, the alternative which he chose will meet with very modified censure from honorable men.[104]

Friends of Wickliffe in the community, Trotter maintained, were trying to misrepresent the facts of the duel in order to ruin his newspaper or justify an attempt on his life.[105]

The scenarios described thus far were not unlike the ritualistic confrontations that many antebellum editors, especially in the South and West, faced over incidences of defamation. It also was not uncommon for the sons of political figures to rush to their fathers' defense, as a knight might during medieval times, to protect the patriarch against defamation according to the rituals of honor. This might be seen as an American modification of dueling, and it had a direct impact on journalism and the local community. Because the nature of antebellum partisan relationships in the South required absolute loyalty and because it was a natural springboard to a political career, some Southern political figures installed their sons as editors of their state and local party organs as a first line of defense against defamation. For example, during O. Jennings Wise's tenure at the *Richmond Enquirer*, which began in 1857, he was involved in at least eight duels.[106] Many of his duels, suggested Holland, involved defending his father, Henry Wise, who was then the governor of Virginia, against defamatory remarks.[107] When Roger A. Pryor of the Richmond *Enquirer* criticized John M. Botts, a leading lawyer and political figure in Richmond, his son, B. B. Botts, challenged Pryor to a duel. The *New York Times* wrote of the event:

> ANOTHER VICABIOUS [*sic*] DUEL.— By the Telegraphic report it will be seen that young BOTTS and PRYOR, editor of the Richmond *Enquirer*, have gone to Washington to fight a duel. This is another of those family feuds which are becoming as common at the South as they used to be among the clans of the Scottish Highlands. YOUNG BOTTS has challenged PRYOR, not on his own personal account, but to sustain the honor of his father, just as the younger MAGRATH fought with the editor of the *Mercury* to defend the honor of his brother. It is a most unfavorable sign for the South, that not a solitary Southern journal, so far as we have seen, has had a word of disapprobation of these barbarous and irrational methods of settling a quarrel.[108]

The two met on the dueling field, but the police appeared before any shots took place and arrested everyone in attendance. It was suggested that the elder Botts tipped off the police.[109] That would not be the only time Pryor would participate in an affair of honor.[110]

The other duel mentioned in the *New York Times* passage referred to a Charleston, South Carolina, duel between W. R. Taber, editor of the *Charleston Mercury*, and Edward Magrath, brother of federal judge A.G. Magrath, which took place on September 30, 1856.[111] The *New York Times* reported:

McGrath [*sic*] challenged Messrs. HEART and TABER of the *Mercury* severally, to meet him on the charge of publishing and indorsing [*sic*] libelous attacks upon his brother. On the field efforts were made between each exchange of shots to effect a settlement without avail. After the fall of Mr. Taber, HEART appeared on the ground and notified MCGRATH of his readiness to meet him. MCGRATH replied that he had no further demand to make.[112]

Taber was killed on the third fire. As was often the case by the late-antebellum era, dueling laws prevented political and judicial figures such as A.G. McGrath from resorting to the code of honor in cases of defamation.[113]

In cases where journalism, family, honor and politics were not discrete, as in the case of the Wise family, the results were often ritualistic in the antebellum era when dealing with libel. Thomas Ritchie, editor of the *Richmond Enquirer*, and his sons William and Thomas, Jr., illustrated this idea. Throughout Ritchie's editorial reign of from 1804 until his retirement in 1851, his newspapers depended on political patronage in the form of the state's public printing.[114] Thus, his family became dependent on that money for survival; therefore a disparaging political attack on Ritchie, in concept, was akin to attacking the family farm or his primary source of income. As one of the leading journalistic voices in the antebellum era, he had everything to lose by dueling and so largely avoided honor disputes. However, in cases where honor disputes were unavoidable — as when William S. Archer, a U.S. senator from Virginia, attacked Ritchie on the street because of defamatory remarks — his sons would often step in on his behalf. In Archer's case, Ritchie's son William publicly slapped him in the face in retribution for his father and promptly received a challenge to a duel from the senator. The duel was never fought.[115]

This situation in Richmond was further exacerbated when Ritchie became editor of the *Washington Union*, the national organ of the Democratic Party in the Polk administration, and left his sons to edit the *Enquirer*. Thomas, Jr., and the editor of the *Richmond Whig*, John Hampden Pleasants, were involved in a heated rivalry before Ritchie's departure for Washington. His sons assumed the rivalry and both William and Thomas, Jr., were involved in honor disputes with Pleasants.[116] Pleasants was killed in a February 25, 1846, modified duel with Thomas, Jr. A February 28 report in the *Brooklyn Eagle* described the encounter:

BLOODY RECONTRE. — A most savage and brutal personal contest took place by appointment, on Wednesday morning, in Richmond, Va. The parties were Thomas Ritchie, Jr. and John H. Pleasants both editors of rival newspapers in Richmond. The combatants were placed 100 yards apart, armed with pistols, swords, and knives, and advanced towards each other, firing their pistols until they were sufficiently near to use their blades, with which they hacked and mangled each other until they were separated. Ritchie escaped with a few slight wounds upon the face and breast; but Pleasants was horribly mutilated, and received a terrible gash in the abdomen, which it is supposed will prove mortal. Ritchie fled to Washington the same day.[117]

Unknown to the elder Ritchie at the time, Pleasants had no intention of killing his son and had unloaded his pistol before the encounter. Thomas, Jr., was tried for murder but was acquitted without the jury even leaving the box.[118]

A further American modification of the duel, as was the case in the Cilley-Graves and Denver-Gilbert affairs, made it socially acceptable for a representative of a disparaged party to challenge an editor to a duel. This social norm was especially precarious for editors in a community that had state laws barring anyone from holding public office if they participated in a duel. It was precarious because it would often compel the defamed party, if he was in a position of power, to enlist a third party to challenge the editor on the defamed party's behalf. An example of this type of situation was the duel between William Walker, one of the editors of the San Francisco Herald, and Hicks Graham on January 15, 1851. According to San Francisco's Alta California, "The affair was caused ... by an article which appeared in the Herald ... relative to the Judge of the Probate Court and the Public Administrator, for which Mr. Graham challenged the Editor, on behalf of Judge Morrison."[119] The editor, among other criticisms, questioned in his columns the frequent absenteeism of the judge, suggesting corruption.[120]

After provoking a challenge from the editor, Graham met Walker on the dueling field. The terms of the duel were Colt revolvers at eight paces. Graham's actions led the Alta California to remark, "We thought the days of knight errantry had passed away."[121] The duelists were to get five shots each unless one of the parties was hit. Although accounts vary, the Alta California reported, "Two shots were exchanged. At the first fire Mr. Walker received his adversary's ball through the leg of his pantaloons, and at the second was shot through the fleshy part of the thigh."[122] Although Graham was arrested in connection with the duel, a January 16 report in the Alta California suggested that no one, including friends of Walker, would testify against him.[123] Walker, "the grey-eyed man of destiny," survived the event to eventually again acclaim — and the Latin American presidency — as a filibuster in Nicaragua.[124]

The *Alta California* saw the problems created by the Walker duel and the code of honor in California as indicative to those facing editors across the country. In a January 14, 1851, article, "Muzzling the Press," the editor of the *Alta California* wrote:

> Recent events would lead us to believe that the attempt which has been so often made in other portions of the Union to muzzle and silence the press is about to be renewed here. If we know ourselves and our cotemporaries, we can distinctly say that it will prove equally futile with all previous ones. We know our rights, our duty to the public, and no bullying, nor hints of street fights, and pistols and coffee, shall ever cause us to swerve one single hair's breadth from what we consider our proper and legitimate course.
>
> It was stated that half a dozen young gentlemen, including a relative of Judge Morrison, who had been employed by him in various capacities, had banded themselves together for the purpose of chastising any audacious editor who should dare question his official acts, and so publicly stated. This is monstrous: almost too preposterous for belief; but we can inform these young gentlemen that if we hear of any act of malfeasance on the part of that officer or any other, which we hope we shall not, that six men, nor ten times that number shall hinder us from exposing it. This is a poor place to attempt such gag law; and we look upon it as an outrage that a man should be driven to such a position as to fight another to redress the grievances a third part imagines he has received. It must not be tolerated.[125]

It is not known if the editor was criticized for this article.

As such, when the gold rush pushed settlers en masse to the West, the same patterns of ritual violence threatening editors in rural communities repeated itself. Another example besides Walker included the 1863 duel between Joseph T. Goodman, editor of Virginia City, Nevada's, *Territorial Enterprise*, and Thomas S. Fitch, editor of the *Virginia City Union*. Nevada's *Virginia City Evening Bulletin* described the event:

> A few days since, the editor of the Enterprise published an article severely reflecting on the private character of Thos. S. Fitch, the editor of the *Union*. The *Union* editor replied on the following morning in a comparatively mild manner, from which it was supposed that the difference would end there. But on the day before yesterday, a challenge was sent by Mr. Fitch to Mr. Goodman, demanding satisfaction. This challenge was accepted, and the terms of the fight arranged as follows: Navy revolvers, at fifteen paces for the first fire — then advance and fire as they chose.[126]

Before the duel could take place, however, the town marshal arrived, arrested them and took them before the local judge, who "ceased them to enter into bonds to keep the peace in the sum of $5,000 each."[127] It was reported that there were between 40 and 50 spectators at the dueling ground.[128]

By as early as 1855, there were editors who felt that dueling had reached epidemic proportions in California. *The Sacramento Union* wrote: "This savage and inhuman practice seems to be on the increase in our State. Latterly, it appears as if a dueling epidemic prevailed in California. When will the detestable practice be frowned down by public opinion and by the enforcement of the law against dueling? Of course, not while men in public station, and those occupying the higher walks of the professions, are guilty of violating the law, and of placing before the eyes of the public so pernicious."[129] Thus dueling was a widespread problem in the California community and not just a series of isolated incidents, and it would be safe to say that the code of honor had a tremendous influence in emerging journalism in the West in the same manner as the antebellum South.

The *Sacramento Union's* comments were in connection to a duel between Robert Tevis, a Downieville lawyer, and Charles Lippincott, a state senator from Yuba county, on July 14, 1855. The honor dispute arose from Lippincott's criticism in the columns of the *Sierra Citizen* of Tevis' July 4 speech.[130] Tevis responded by referring to him as a liar and slanderer in a newspaper called the *Old Oaken Bucket*.[131] According to the *Alta California* and various other reports, the two fought with double-barrel guns, at 40 paces, and Tevis died on the first fire with the ball striking him on the fourth rib of his left side, passing through his body and killing him almost instantly.[132] According to the *Sacramento Union*, Lippincott narrowly escaped death himself, as the ball from Tevis' gun passed so close to his head that he staggered and was thought by his second to be wounded.[133] Of the duel, an article signed "Pioneer" in the *Sacramento Union* declared, "It is not our purpose to comment upon this most unfortunate affair, but we cannot lose sight of the fact the life of one of our most promising young men has been taken, and that, too, by one of the members of the last Legislature, which passed "an act for the suppression of dueling." Shall this law, like many others, remain a dead letter upon our statute books, or shall it be enforced?"[134] Ironically, Tevis had been invited on July 4 to read the Declaration of Independence to a local audience.[135]

As long as the lifeblood of journalism was tied to politics through patronage and public approval, the lines between personal honor and civic duty were often blurred in the antebellum community. This blurring, coupled with weak laws and weak law enforcement, thrust many journalists into honor rituals, in defamation of defamation suits, as expected by social norms in the community.[136] Even when anti-dueling laws were eventually enacted regionally to protect journalists and others, many of those laws failed. Thus, it should not be surprising that many, if not all, antebellum editors faced the threat of ritualized violence at one point or another in their journalism careers.

CHAPTER FIVE

Influences of Honor Rituals in the Secession-Era Partisan Press

In some revisionist histories, the outbreak of the Civil War has been characterized as a large-scale duel.[1] If we continue under that assumption, then it follows that there must have been some ritual arbitration of insult and apology before any Confederate or Yankee soldier ever squared off on the field of honor for it to be truly considered a duel in the nineteenth-century sense. By using the evolution of the connection between honor rituals and journalism in antebellum America as a road map, one can begin to rearticulate the visceral reactions between North and South on the path to war from the Missouri Compromise in 1850 to South Carolina leading the South into secession on December 20, 1860. Instead of notes passed between two "seconds," a grammatical arbitration could be seen taking place in the press as political parties radically realigned into sectional alliances.

Thus, an understanding of the connection between honor rituals and the nineteenth-century press is critical in this scenario. In the North, it is true that the abolishment of slavery became a unifying cause that connected Union states in the Civil War.[2] However, during the years leading up to secession, the Republican Party endorsed only a slightly better version of white supremacy in the form of colonization, where slaves would be relocated into camps or deported.[3] Furthermore, it should be also noted that the Union states of Maryland, Delaware, Kentucky and Missouri all made allowances for slavery at the height of secession. There were mitigating political factors that compelled these "border states" to remain part of the Union, but the bottom line is slavery was still permitted in these

96

states as the war began.[4] On the other side of the coin, it could be argued that it was more than just pro-slavery sentiments that bound Southern states together in the Confederacy, it was a general compulsion for many Southerners to prove their worth of character in the wake of perceived Northern aggression with public displays of violence as demanded by the code of honor.

The point is not to prove or disprove the relevance of slavery, but to establish that the evils of racism and slavery were not unique factors to the Confederacy. The mere fact that slave states were permitted in the Union illustrated that the issue was more complicated than "North" and "South" sectional differences regarding the matter. Just as there was a strong movement in 1861 by the mayor of New York to secede the city from the rest of the state,[5] so were there strong anti-slavery sentiments within Southern states such as Missouri.[6] The issue in this chapter is not to rationalize or justify the idea of slavery or any government that condoned it. There can be no truly enlightened rationalization of history that condones American slavery.

When examining the motives for the initial conflicts of the Civil War, it is important to note that only a small percentage of Southern whites owned slaves. If that was the case, why were Southerners so committed to fighting? Even to this day, you might hear someone from the South refer to what is known popularly as the "Civil War" as the "War Between the States." Why is that? What's more, the honor codes, which had a history of drawing individuals into armed combat over defamation, were still an imposing force on American society during the years leading up to Civil War. What effect did they have in the march towards war?

What this chapter will do is examine some of the communication divides between Northern and Southern cultures to understand what roles the culture of honor and journalism may have played in motives to secede. Southern culture still had the remnants of English hierarchy, as illustrated in chapter one, which were honed and cultivated in an Americanized version of chivalry in the Jacksonian Era, as illustrated in chapter two. In chapter three, it was discussed how defamatory remarks could easily draw editors into ritualistic honor conflicts that may or may not have ended in violence. Chapter four discussed how politicians and editors began as the mid–nineteenth century approached to defend their group power base against perceived libel by utilizing the ritual of honor and acting as knight-errant figures. It would seem in hindsight that all of these elements would stew in a pressure cooker waiting to explode on July 21, 1861, in Manassas Junction, the site of the first battle of the Civil War.

A journalistic snapshot of the late antebellum period might offer a further glimpse of an American culture that seemed nearer to Europe with its social stratification, which may be difficult for a twenty-first century American reader to conceptualize. When Major Jefferson Davis, the future president of the Confederacy during the Civil War, delivered his "Eulogy on the Life and Character of Andrew Jackson" to a large audience in Vicksburg on June 28, 1845, America was mourning the loss of a national hero. Shortly after Jackson's death earlier that month in his Hermitage home in Tennessee, Vicksburg City Council adopted measures to show its respect for the memory of the former President.[7] The council chose Davis to deliver the keynote speech. Davis, who had wholly admired Jackson since his childhood encounter with the man, rose to the occasion.[8]

The Vicksburg newspapers described the pomp and ceremony of that Saturday morning. A parade of civil groups and military companies marched from the courthouse square to the Presbyterian church. Bearing the national flag was a former dragoon[9] under Jackson's command, and Davis, in a carriage with two friends, followed the procession. Reaching its destination, the parade halted in front of the church.[10] When Davis arrived, the companies and societies saluted as he passed through the ranks and into the building.[11]

In the crowded pews, a hymn and prayer preceded Davis' address. The audience was composed of both Whigs and Democrats, the two most powerful political parties in the South during that time.[12] The *Vicksburg Sentinel* reported that amid the silence of the crowd, tears filled more than one eye as Davis poured forth his eloquent portraiture of Jackson in the sweltering heat of that Mississippi morning.[13]

Two days later, the *Vicksburg Sentinel* printed in full Davis' address documenting the life and achievements of Jackson.[14] At the time of his death, Jackson, who was born on March 16, 1767, was older than the country itself.[15] As a child he grew up in the shadow of war against the British and was captured at the age of 14. Surviving imprisonment, he would rise in the army ranks to be the savior of the Union and gain worldwide fame in the Battle of New Orleans as the man who beat the army that defeated Napoleon.[16] In his oratory, Davis compared Jackson's heroics and military prowess to that of Napoleon, Frederick the Great and Henry V.[17] He said in his speech, "Not intending to say any thing which can wear a party aspect, allow me to observe, that high as I estimate his military prowess and his military genius, I esteem him as a Statesman more highly still."[18] Davis praised Jackson for putting honor above political partisanship.[19]

The Vicksburg newspaper accounts of Davis' eulogy give insight into communications patterns of the mid-century American partisan press. Newspaper accounts, such as the *Vicksburg Sentinel,* implied that men must be heroic to command respect and rise above their peers in both the local community and the national political arena. Military titles suggested class rank above the average citizen, and the appearance of Christian values was important. Davis' eulogy, referencing the military prowess of Napoleon, Frederick the Great and Henry V, demonstrates the influence of European society on an America still struggling for a cultural identity. Finally, the eulogy implied that a great military and political leader such as Jackson must live by the code of honor, which supported dueling and ritualized violence.

Examples that Davis and other politicians set forth in the partisan press during the mid–nineteenth century may seem inconsequential by twenty-first century standards, but to most Americans during this period simply reading descriptions of unfolding events was a new phenomenon.[20] The industrial revolution was changing the landscape of communications and politics. The technology of the penny press introduced in the 1830s through newspapers, such as the *Sun* and *Herald* in New York, enlarged newspaper readership nationwide and made newspapers affordable to almost anyone in major cities who could read.[21] These new readers were learning how to fit in and excel on every level of the political landscape, which made the examples set by established politicians increasingly influential.

This, in tandem with territorial expansion enabling a new segment of the public to participate in all levels of government, led to increased ethical paradoxes between the defamation laws and social norms in the post–Jacksonian political era. With a new audience, newspapers began to shift into a new concept of reporting that emphasized local news, more sensational news and the appearance of human interest stories. Also, with the Mexican War in 1844, newspapers began to utilize the railroad and telegraph as ways to transmit information quicker than had ever been previously possible. The New York Associated Press would form out of this greater demand for timeliness in reporting.[22]

The speed at which news was produced and the shift of the news concept also changed the nature of political responses to defamation in the partisan press with regard to the ritual of honor. So it would seem that in the absence of strong party leadership, weaker politicians rallied around stronger politicians in a patriarchal style of government characterized in the nineteenth century sometimes as political juntos. Acting as knight-errant figures, politicians defended their power base against perceived defamation by using the ritual of the duel, which again may or not have ended in violence. As such, a pattern developed where disparaging remarks made in a newspaper towards the keystone politician in a junto would solicit a ritualistic response from all members in the group, as justified by social norms. Partisan newspapers were a key component in organizing and rallying these political juntos. When juntoism developed on a sectional basis, this ritualistic response to partisan defamation could be seen as precipitating the initial conflicts leading to the Civil War.[23]

The rural nature of developing politics and the lack of strong leadership in the Democratic Party gave rise to more pronounced political juntoism. The juntoism that developed with the emergence of California statehood is a good example of this. With California growing by leaps and bounds in the decade before the Civil War, there was a strong movement to create a state government. Amid great fear that its induction into the Union would upset the balance of power between North and South, California became a state in part of the Great Compromise of 1850. Although Henry Clay was the impetus of the compromise, it was Stephen Douglas, a major power player in the national Democratic Party, who would push the bill through.[24] Arthur Quinn wrote in *The Rivals: William Gwin, David Broderick, and the Birth of California*, "The compromise had been passed, and so had the baton of leadership between the generations. Clay had proposed the compromise, but Douglas had gotten it through the Senate."[25] With the emergence of Douglas as a major power-broker, members of the Democratic Party would be caught between his junto, endorsing the idea of popular sovereignty as a blueprint for budding governments in the new territories, and the old ways of the chivalry adhered to by John C. Calhoun and eventually Davis, among other smaller factions.[26]

The admission of California and the rapid expansion into the new territories would re-ignite the national debate in newspapers over issues surrounding federal influence over popular sovereignty and state sovereignty. In the absence of strong national leadership, these factors helped to initiate a reorganization of political loyalties that seemed almost feudal in its characteristics. On May 25, 1850, the *Brooklyn Eagle* wrote: "Party discipline seems to have lost its potency, and individual representatives consult the sectional prejudices of their particular constituents rather than risk the sacrifice of personal popularity by taking the patriotic ground of broad National requirements. This is one of the evils of our Democratic system of government, and the remedy is far worse than the disease."[27] With these discussions also came fresh threats of disunion from Southern politicians who believed that the Missouri Compromise bill encouraged federal interference and usurped the ability for new territories and states to set to set their own domestic agendas, which sometimes included slavery.[28] In turn, as new territories in the West, such as Kansas, began to form their own political structures, rivaling political factions used the partisan press to start a newspaper war between juntos.[29]

It was the North, not South, who organized the first primarily sectional party in American politics.[30] One could consider that the New York Associated Press, which by 1860 had begun to overshadow nearly all chief news-gathering and news-transmitting agencies of the country, contributed greatly to the North speaking in a unified sectional voice.[31] With a history of not being able to separate personal from political attacks, many Southerners interpreted reactions to events in the 1850s, vocalized in the press, as evidence that the North no longer respected them as equal Americans and Christians.[32]

Citizens of the South, particularly the Deep South who were isolated economically and socially, thought they were under attack from an increasingly aggressive sectional Republican party.[33] A Republican party who many Southerners deemed, rightly or wrongly, was violating the Dred Scott decision handed down by the Supreme Court. By the time of the 1860 presidential race, what the Dred Scott decision seemed to do is help shift the political debate from point of law to point of morality and character.[34]

For those who followed the tenets of the Code of Honor, questions of morality and character were settled by providence on the field of honor. What follows is a snapshot of that debate as it appeared in the July 13, 1858, *Brooklyn Eagle* and many other newspapers across the country: "In the first place, he (Mr. Lincoln) sets out in his speech to say, quoting from Scripture that a house divided cannot stand; that the American Government, divided into an equal number of Free and Slave States, cannot stand. That they should all be the one or all be the other."[35] Lincoln's platform, similar in elements to Jackson's in the antebellum era, used qualities of honor and character to affirm and organize political fidelity by utilizing anti-slavery politics as the keystone. By framing the character debate in "either/or" terms, it initiated ritualistic language that, as illustrated in previous chapters, had a clear pattern of being settled with public demonstrations of violence in the name of honor.

Southern political leaders such as Stephen Douglas understood this at the time, which is why he and his followers may have chosen to argue the issue of slavery from legalistic terms instead of character: "It is no answer to this argument to say that slavery is an evil, and hence should not be tolerated. You must allow the people to decide for themselves whether it is a good or an evil."[36] This example is not to prove one political platform superior to the other, but to illustrate how honor rituals could have influenced the media debate during the years leading up to secession.

Adding to the confusion was the lack of uniformity in the states' treatment of blacks even in Free states. In Lincoln's home state of Illinois, blacks may have been technically "free," but could not vote, hold office, serve on juries or enjoy any political privileges. In Maine, however, blacks were permitted to vote equally to whites. In New York during this period, the state constitution provided that blacks could vote only if they owned $250 worth of property. With such diversity in opinion, how does one determine absolute moral correctness? This was a question that must have been pondered by many Southern leaders.[37]

To get at the heart of how honor ritual affected communication patterns in the secession era, it is imperative to understand what was being communicated and the context in which it was delivered through media outlets. Douglas' idea of popular sovereignty allowed for home rule to decide whether slavery would be allowed or not in the new territories. As proven by Kansas statehood, when given an equal chance, a majority of voters chose not to allow slavery in their state.[38] On the other hand, the insistence of the Republican platform of uniformity on the slavery issue was another step on the road to despotism in the eyes of many Southerners, a red-herring character argument distracting from the real issue of federal interference with home rule.[39] After all, even if Southern states had conceded to the unconditional emancipation of slaves before the 1860 election, antebellum Republican leaders still faced large divisions in their party if they advocated a policy of emancipation without deportation of all slaves.[40] These elements seemed to boil beneath the politic rhetoric exchanged in the partisan press.

Home rule was the backbone of Southern patron-client social hierarchies that depended on the communication and cultivation of an aristocratic-like set of "courtly" manners rooted in the history of honor rituals. The Civil War writings of the *Richmond Examiner* editor John Moncure Daniel, who was considered the pride and ornament of the Southern Press, give insight into how honor rituals still influenced communication patterns in the South even as late as the 1860s.

> Southern chivalry was always a favorite theme of ridicule with these people [Republicans]. While their heavy artillery of argument and slander was directed against our more serious and permanent objects of solicitude, the

missiles of ridicule were directed against our social peculiarities and domestic affections. The attempt to establish a more exalted code of manners and a more delicate morality was laughed to scorn as the insolent assumpt on of affected aristocrats. Strict equality was, in their opinion, to be secured by the libeling process.[41]

In our modern conception of the corporate journalism, it almost seems unfathomable that disparagement might lead to war. But in the era of the Party Press, unchecked defamation of character was an attack for which many Southern gentlemen of the ruling class were willing to engage in a life-and-death struggle to make right. As discussed in previous chapters, an impasse of opinion over defamation was often decided on the field of honor.

Daniel argued that political leaders of Northern states were using the guise of federal conformity to exploit the Southern states for their profit, similar to how Russia governed Poland or England governed Ireland during this period. Daniel wrote:

Slavery was the immediate occasion — carefully made so by them — it was not the cause. The tariff [of 1828], which almost brought about the disruption some years ago, would have much more accurately represented, though it did not cover, or exhaust, the real cause of the quarrel. Yet neither tariffs nor slavery, nor both together, could ever have been truly called anything lower, meaner, smaller, than that truly announced, namely the sovereign independence of our States. This, indeed, includes both those minor questions, as well as many others yet graver and higher. It includes full power to regulate our trade for our own profit, and also complete jurisdiction over our own social and domestic institutions; but it further involves all the nobler attributes of national, and even of individual life and character.[42]

To read "our own social and domestic institutions" and infer the passage as simply to mean the right to keep slaves would be true. But the Republican policies in a deeper sense, and therein may lie the true genius of Lincoln, appeared to strike at the very heart of the inherited European social hierarchies and honor codes that were still cultivated in many Southern states. This was a patron-client theory of democracy where social mobility was based on a mixture of birthright and reputations of honor, which in turn made it extremely sensitive to defamation. When Daniel and many other Southern editors used phrases such as "heavy artillery of argument and slander" and "missiles of ridicule," they were not necessarily being euphemistic or flowery in their language. They were deadly serious.

The infamous response by Congressman Preston Brooks of South

Carolina to the "Crime against Kansas" speech on May 18, 1856, by U.S. Senator Charles Sumner of Massachusetts is a significant example of how disparagement against the state could evoke a ritualistic response from its leading citizens. In his speech on the Senate floor, Sumner chastised Senator Andrew Butler, who was absent, and his home state of South Carolina over Butler's role in the Kansas-Nebraska Act of 1854. He said: "If the slave States cannot enjoy what, in mockery of the great fathers of the Republic, he misnames equality under the Constitution in other words, the full power in the National Territories to compel fellowmen to unpaid toil, to separate husband and wife, and to sell little children at the auction block then, sir, the chivalric Senator will conduct the State of South Carolina out of the Union! Heroic knight! Exalted Senator! A second Moses come for a second exodus!"[43] Upon reading a copy of the speech, Brooks sought out Sumner in the Senate chambers and violently beat him with his cane. Newspapers, such as the *Washington Star* and South Carolina's *Spartanburg Spartan*, confirmed that defamation was at the heart of Brooks' ritualistic response when they published his first-hand account of the incident: "I have read your speech carefully, and with as much disposition to do you justice as I could command; and I have deliberately come to the conclusion that you were guilty of a gross libel upon my State, and of a wanton insult to my absent and grey-haired relation, Judge Butler; and I feel myself under obligations to inflict on you a punishment for this libel and insult."[44] It was reported that Brooks said those words to Sumner right before he caned him.[45] Public canings were a ritualistic practice through which an insulted party communicated that the insulter was not honorable enough to challenge to a duel.

Southern editors, such as John Daniel, who was known for his unflinchingly pointed columns in the *Examiner*, were sensitive to the aristocratic etiquette that honor codes demanded. A veteran of many duels himself, perhaps one of Daniel's most famous affairs of honor was an aborted duel against Edgar Allan Poe. In the summer of 1848, Daniel was acquainted with the family of Sarah Helen Whitman, whom Poe was smitten with after receiving a valentine from her that year. Although accounts vary depending on the source, a letter from Whitman to Poe biographer John Henry Ingram broadly recounts the incident.[46] Poe, infuriated with Daniel, insisted that an acquaintance of his, J.R. Thompson, act as his second and deliver a hastily written challenge. Apparently the event which precipitated the encounter was associated with Daniel making public comment on Poe's budding relationship with Whitman. Thompson refused outright to deliver the challenge, and "Poe sought an interview with

Daniels [*sic*] and the offensive paragraph was withdrawn."[47] Although difficult to verify, George Woodberry delivers a popular account of the encounter in his book, *The Life of Edgar Allan Poe*. Based on recollections by Judge Robert W. Hughes, a writer for the *Richmond Examiner*, Woodberry wrote that when Poe entered the office of Daniel, he was extremely intoxicated.[48] According to the Hughes' account,

> When he [Poe] entered and saw Daniel he drew himself up to full height and demanded, in his haughty manner, why he had sent for him. Daniel was sitting near a table on which was displayed two very large, old-fashioned pistols, which the quick glance of Poe soon espied. Daniel in a cool and quiet manner asked Poe to be seated. Then he told him that he did not care to have the matter get to the police authorities, and suggested that instead of the usual formalities of the code they settle the dispute between them then and there.[49]

Woodberry wrote that Poe sobered up quickly and sought a peaceful resolution to the disagreement, which Daniel accommodated.[50]

As the Poe encounter helps illustrate, Southern secession-era editors, such as Daniel, were not simply political lapdog extremists with a printing press. They were often intellectuals who mingled with the political and literary elite of the day. The editorials of Daniel, who was a minister to Turin, Italy, in the 1850s during reunification, were undoubtedly influenced by that country's similar political struggle over whether it should be composed of a loose confederation of states or encompass a strong centralized government.[51] Daniel's editorial politics were probably influenced by European models of democracy that were inherently racist by their social stratification as demanded by the tradition of honor rituals, which many Southerners and Europeans justified biblically. This is an important distinction when unraveling nineteenth-communication patterns because there were two major political factions arguing about God and democracy, while expressing virtually two completely incongruent viewpoints.

That is not to say also, in theory, that slaves and other minorities could not have eventually been incorporated into this social hierarchy as freemen. Freed slaves, of course, in the eyes of this kind of society, would never have been seen as social equals to the gentlemen class in this scenario, but keep in mind most whites were not viewed as social equals to one another either. These were social hierarchies that early printers had to make inroads into during the early days of the country and that almost kept Andrew Jackson out of office. States of the North had their own version of this social stratification in the era of secession, which is likely why the Republican Party could not politically conceive of emancipation of the slaves without colonization.[52] These often unspoken forces were at work affecting and influencing sectional communications.

Adding to this communication confusion was the realignment of political parties in the North during the 1850s, which has been characterized by some historians as a mass revolt.[53] In the *Origins of the Republican Party*, William E. Gienapp described the antebellum realignment as "not simply a redistribution of voter loyalties but in the short period of three years nothing less than the death of one party (the Whigs), the rise and fall of another (the Know Nothings), and the emergence as a major party of yet a third (the Republicans)."[54] But as Gienapp also characterized, the rise of the Republican Party rested less on the conversion of Democrats and more on mobilizing the support of large numbers of previously indifferent voters.[55] Key to mobilizing this broad support was penny press editors such as Horace Greeley of the *New York Tribune*, whose support was instrumental to Lincoln's victory,[56] and *New York Times* founder Henry J. Raymond, who wrote the first platform for the Republican Party.[57]

The role of Francis P. Blair, Sr., in organizing the Republican Party is also worth noting. A *New York Times* account of the first national Republican convention said: "The appearance of the venerable gentleman on the train which arrived on Thursday, after a long delay upon the road, was the signal for a general outburst of enthusiasm. Mr. Blair was the bright particular star of the week, and his luster is by no means dimmed by his years."[58] This move by the Republican Party could have only fueled a political rivalry with Calhounites since Blair was a founding editor of the Jacksonian *Washington Globe*, the newspaper which ousted Green's *United States Telegraph* and Calhoun from the national spotlight in the 1830s.[59]

The second rise of Francis P. Blair, Sr., to power also helps support the idea that Lincoln was heavily influenced by a media strategy that tapped into ritualistic language, whether done so consciously or unconsciously. After his ousting by Polk as the Democratic Party editor, Blair set his sights on Northern politics by helping to organize the secession-era version of the Republican Party. His biographer, Elbert B. Smith, wrote in *Francis Preston Blair*, "In New York ... he had begun a useful relationship with John Bigelow, associate editor of the New York *Evening Post*. Until well after the Civil War, the *Post* was ready to print anything Blair wished to write. This gave the former editor a new opportunity for widespread influence and perhaps with greater illusion of power than he actually had."[60] Thus, as the elder Blair's journalism had played an integral part in organizing the Democratic Party during the Jacksonian era, so too was Blair an integral part in reorganizing the Republican Party.

Furthermore, the role of his son Francis "Frank" Blair, Jr., in the Republican Party could have only contributed to the perception of Southern leaders that the North was disingenuous over the slavery issue beyond breaking the political back of plantation owners with federalism. Although it made sense that Frank Blair, whose politics closely followed his father and Andrew Jackson's vision of a strong national government, would be an advocate of the burgeoning Republican Party, it was still inescapable that he himself owned slaves. In a speech that was reprinted in the October 3, 1860, edition of the Philadelphia *Press*, Frank Blair declared:

> The miscalled Democracy of to-day, following the example of all the defeated and discarded parties that have ever existed in this country, has taken refuge in that citadel of aristocracy, the Supreme Court, and maintains that slavery, which is a political institution, because it has some of the attributes of property, like those things which have no other attributes and are merely property and nothing else, must be the subject of judicial construction. Mr. Lincoln has confronted this pretention with the doctrine advanced by Jefferson and Jackson, and maintains that this is a political institution, of which the political power of the State has rightful cognizance, and that the Supreme Court cannot, under a pretence of deciding a right of property, establish or overthrow the political institutions of the people.[61]

Frank Blair, who was a strong advocate for deportation, was not arguing for treatment of slaves as equals to whites, he was arguing for a solution similar to Thomas Jefferson's idea of emancipation with colonization or the forced relocation of native-Americans initiated by Andrew Jackson.[62] Although there can be no argument that both alternatives were preferable to human beings treated as property, Lincoln and the Republican party still endorsed a policy of white supremacy in the years leading up to the war.

Also contributing to the secession-era breakdown in communication must have been the great upheaval in party politics in the North, which made political events in the middle to late 1850s seem almost out of control to many observers.[63] Propaganda in the partisan press only fueled the hysteria in both the North and South. On January 17, 1861, the *Daily Evening Express* in Lancaster, Pennsylvania, wrote that the sectional excitement unquestionably was owed in a great degree to the unscrupulous misrepresentations of the principles and purposes of political parties by the opposing party organs.[64] In comparison, Sandusky's *Daily Commercial Register* wrote, "And so it goes. The reading world gets shocked up, and the newspaper press forthwith makes it a principal business to shock them up more and more. All run in one channel and feed on one diet. No matter if it be bitter to the taste and unpalatable, it is the universal rage nevertheless."[65] Adding to the growing anxiety and hysteria was Republican sympathy for John Brown and the Harper's Ferry raid. Of the incident, the *New Orleans Bee* wrote on February 9, 1860:

> On the one hand the rank and file of the Black Republicans, in their dread of a reaction against them [John Brown was hanged], they are repudiating JOHN BROWN and his principles, and assuring the South that beyond a repugnance to the extension of slavery, they bear no animosity whatever to our section of the Union. On the other hand, the mass of the truly national and praiseworthy men who have steadfastly combated fanaticism, avail themselves of the opportunity to demonstrate the inevitable consequences of sectional feuds; to show that the attempt of BROWN and his associates at Harper's Ferry was the legitimate result of the tenets and teachings of Black Republicanism, and to warn the North against the fatal error it has so long cherished.[66]

So it would be that in a relatively short period of time, the Republicans would grow to be the most powerful political party in the nation,[67] pledging themselves in seemingly stark ritualistic terms in the partisan papers to an aggressive anti-slavery policy seemingly declared unconstitutional by interpretation of the Dred Scott case.[68] The issue at hand was not whether blacks were equal to whites; all sides argued from a position of white supremacy.

The Northern press, through newspapers such as the Chicago *Democrat*, helped to exacerbate the already intense political rivalry between the North and South.[69] On November 5, 1860, the *Democrat* wrote:

> Either the slave power will go on from conquering to conquer, driving every vestige of freedom before it, planting the institution of slavery on every foot of our land, degrading free labor, and erecting an oligarchy of capital and an aristocracy of wealth, the way for all which is already marked out by the decisions of the Supreme Court and the construction of existing laws; or else, driven to desperation, and deprived of the hope of obtaining redress through the ballot-box, the people of the North will rise against the oppressors and sweep them away forever.[70]

Many leading Southern papers, such as the *Richmond Enquirer*, warned that Lincoln's election would embody a terrible affront to Southern sensibilities and be perceived as a direct insult to Southern honor.[71] The *Enquirer* wrote on July 10, 1860:

> If the Southern States are to be ruined by "missiles" hurled by the hands of Lincoln and his followers, not from Illinois against Kentucky, but from

Washington City, with the power and patronage of the Federal Government, against the institutions and lives of the people of the Southern States, it will be a matter of small consequence whether that ruin follows the effort at independence or comes as the natural consequence of a servile submission to Black Republican rule.[72]

According to Olsen, it was a declaration of cultural superiority by the North that Southerners could not leave unchallenged.[73]

To combat the perceived character assassination of the Republicans, the South would turn to the ritual grammar of honor.[74] Encouraging this was the inflexible and unapologetic opposition of Republican congressman to Southern proposals designed to prevent civil war, wrote Dwight Lowell Dumond in *Southern Editorials on Secession*.[75] Before the 1860 election, many moderate Southern papers, such Lexington's *Kentucky Statesman*, were still advocates for union. The *Statesman* wrote on November 13, 1860: "We, therefore, counsel acquiescence in Lincoln's election, or rather in the recent verdict of the people, upon the distinct and unequivocal expression of strong hope, if not belief, that no real attempt will be made to carry out the measures avowed by his party. If we believed that the Federal administration would and could now be used to carry out the aggressions of fanaticism against slavery, our voice would now be for resistance. But we cling yet to a hope for the Union."[76] However, with Lincoln's victory becoming increasingly clear, some Northern papers, such as the Chicago *Democrat*, took a progressively hostile tone:

> The chivalry will eat dirt. They will back out. They never had any spunk anyhow. The best they could do was to bully, and brag, and bluster. John Brown and his seventeen men were enough to affright the whole mighty commonwealth of Virginia out of its propriety, and to hold it as a conquered province until recaptured by the federal troops, and to this day John Brown's ghost is more terrible than an army with banners, in the eyes of every southern cavalier. These knights of the sunny South are just heroes as Sancho Panza was. They are wonderful hands at bragging and telling fantastical lies; but when it comes to action, count them out.[77]

Editorials such as this were reprinted throughout the Southern press and helped rally a divided South into a uniform confederacy of secession.[78] Thus, moderate Southern newspapers, such as the *Kentucky Statesman*, used the grammar and rhetoric of the code of honor to unite Southerners against perceived Northern aggression. In a little over a month, the *Statesman* went from advocating the union to a call to arms against the North. On December 25, the *Statesman* wrote:

We can not mistake Kentucky's feeling on this subject when the Federal Government shall undertake to use bayonet and cannon to subjugate six or eight slave States to the Administration of Mr. Lincoln on the Chicago platform; we do not hesitate to believe that Kentucky, indignant and united, will take her position along with the section to which she belongs, and present her face to the enemy. In such a dread contingency we shall hear no more of party, but will only know each other as freemen and Kentuckians, impelled by a common sentiment and united by a common interest and one destiny. In such an emergency we should scorn to appeal to party feeling, and spurn the attempt to draw party lines. Old Kentucky! would be the cry, and in her defense of her honor and her cause, men would rally oblivious of old associations.[79]

Having both participated in honor disputes during their earlier political careers, Lincoln and Davis both intimately understood the culture of shame and honor.[80] Similar to political duels, newspapers had articulated the grammar of honor to a point where neither side could back down without losing esteem in the public forum. The construal of sectional newspaper insults within the context of honor made secession a reality and violence a self-affirming option.[81] Newark, New Jersey's *Daily Advertiser* wrote on January 12, 1861: "Why, are we not well aware, that it was the writers and not the actors of the day, who ushered in the horrid tragedies of the great French Revolution of '93?"[82]

When Jefferson Davis was inaugurated as President of the Southern Confederacy by the Provisional Congress set up by the seceded states of Mississippi, Alabama, Florida, Georgia, Louisiana and South Carolina, he believed that the South had done all it could to prevent the impending war.[83] Wrote the Philadelphia *Morning Pennsylvanian*:

> JEFFERSON DAVIS' election was not one whit more sectional in its character than ABRAHAM LINCOLN's. No Northern State helped to elect the former, neither did any Southern State help to elect the latter. If both the President and Vice President of the Southern Confederacy are Southern men and slaveholders, both the President and Vice President of this Confederacy are Northern men and free-soilers. Like begets like, and the sectional programme and anti-slavery policy of the Black Republicans drove the cotton States into the formation of a sectional Government and a slavery policy. But for the first, the last would not have existence.[84]

Lincoln's unyielding policy on slavery in the new territories was an important catalyst in mobilizing the North and South to war. However, his election was one objection in a line of sectional grievances that many Southerners believed had been growing since Jefferson, Madison, Monroe and others advocated secession from the Articles of Confederation in 1781.[85]

Thus, when the two sides mobilized for war, a divided South united on the battlefield to defend their culture of honor, which included slavery, from a perception of Northern hostility that was derived primarily from the hostile and condescending tone of the Republican partisan press. Wrote Wyatt-Brown, "The threat to slavery's legitimacy in the Union prompted the sectional crisis, but it was Southern honor that pulled the trigger."[86] And so, as ritual demanded, South would meet North at the field of honor in Manassas on July 21, 1861; both sides flying the Stars and Stripes with each claiming the right to its heritage and glory.[87]

CHAPTER SIX

The Culture of Honor on
Trial During the Civil War

The fighting of the Civil War, which by now was well into its fourth year of hostilities, had yet to reach Richmond, Virginia, when John M. Daniel, editor of the *Richmond Examiner,* and E. C. Elmore, treasurer of the Confederate States of America, met at dawn to duel on August 16, 1864. The site of the hostile encounter was a farm about two miles from the city, and the weapons used were, as the *Richmond Daily Dispatch* described, "ordinary smooth-bore duelling pistols" at ten paces.[1] The combat ended violently for the editor, according to the *Daily Dispatch*'s account of the affair:

> Mr. Elmore was the challenging party, and, in accordance with previous arrangements, each side was accompanied by one second, a surgeon, and other advisory friends. Mr. H. Rives Pollard, of the Examiner, acted as the immediate friend of Mr. Daniel, and Lieutenant Thomas Taylor, of South Carolina, held the same position towards Mr. Elmore. At the first fire neither of the combatants were hurt, whereupon Mr. Elmore demanded another shot, which put an end to the hostile meeting, Mr. Daniel being struck in the calf of the right leg, a few inches below the knee. In the opinion of his surgeon, the wound is not considered a dangerous one, though it is accompanied with great pain.[2]

Fortunately Daniel did not suffer a mortal wound, and it appeared that honor was satisfied between the two adversaries.

The dispute between the editor and the treasurer arose from an allegation printed in the *Richmond Examiner* that a high official in the Confederate Treasury Department was embezzling funds and trying to bribe a treasury department detective to keep quiet about the matter. Wrote the *Daily Dispatch,* "Subsequent to the publication of this piece, a correspondence ensued between the parties, the nature of which has not yet been made public."[3] Whether that high official was Elmore was never made clear in the report. It was apparent that Elmore had issued a challenge to Daniel, which drew this published response from the editor:

> I am ... to observe that you and your class labor under the hallucination because I was sincerely and openly desirous to avoid an engagement [duel], that my conduct was due to intimidation. Heaven permitting, I will teach you this lesson, that when gentlemen exhibit a disposition for peace it does not necessarily follow that you may safely bully them. For these and other reasons you shall have the duel which you and your class have so pertinaciously sought to fix on me; and the rest of the matter is now in the hands of [my second] Mr. H. Rives Pollard.[4]

There was obviously no love lost between the editor and the treasurer.

Later that afternoon on the same day as the duel, two police officers arrested Elmore and Daniel's second, fellow *Examiner* editor Rives Pollard, and brought them before the mayor of Richmond, Richard Mayo. Pollard was released on $3,000 bail, but the mayor refused to set bail for Elmore. Wrote the *Daily Dispatch*:

> The Mayor's refusal to bail Mr. Elmore was based upon the ground that there was strong reason on his part to believe that he (Mr. E.) had already shot Mr. Daniel. Mr. Pollard was arrested and bailed, not because of the part he had sustained in the affair which took place between the parties in the morning, but for the purpose of preventing a hostile meeting, which, it was believed, was in process of negotiation between that gentleman and some one whose name has not been made known.[5]

Even though the Daniel-Elmore duel was reported in the *Daily Dispatch*, all of the participants in the encounter were apparently conspiring to remain silent, as if the event never happened. This would set a chain of events in motion that would occupy the Richmond court system for several months.

During the Civil War era, 1861–1865, dueling was illegal in most states throughout the Union and Confederacy, including Virginia, but not generally considered murder or attempted murder if one of the combatants was hit. But the laws were only relevant if they were enforced. A March 2, 1861, article in the *Daily Dispatch* highlighted the problems with creating anti-dueling laws that seemed to be at odds with public sentiment: "Can the penalties of the anti-duelling law be enforced in Virginia? Is there not in the United States and in every State, 'Higher law' than that of any Government, the law of public opinion, the only supreme and recognized government acknowledged and obeyed in this country?"[6] Similarly, a May 11, 1861, column in Pennsylvania's *Columbia Spy* declared, "Whatever the moralists may say, or popular opinion may be, there is no class of 'sensation' reading more eagerly pursued than such as detail scenes of violence and bloodshed. The 'duello' has prevailed among all races, civilized and barbarian, from the remotest antiquity, and is not likely to be eradicated while men are urged by hot passion, or ideas of punctilious honor prevail in professions and communities."[7] So it would appear that throughout the Civil War era many local and state communities still struggled between public sentiment, which a majority often favored and encouraged dueling, versus laws that outlawed the practice.

This chapter will examine the tension between honor rituals and nineteenth-century mass communication on a micro and macro level. Common historical misperceptions are that anti-dueling laws and the wide-ranging sociopolitical effects of the Civil War caused the demise of dueling. This may be true to a point, but dueling in cases of defamation still persisted throughout the nineteenth century; therefore it certainly did not end during the Civil War. Furthermore, how did the communicative qualities of honor rituals, which were the precursor to any combat under the code of honor, impede or hasten dueling during the Civil War era? This chapter will explore these questions and illustrate that even though dueling as a popular practice may have begun its decline, it still had a profound impact on journalists throughout this time period.

By closely examining the arrests and court proceedings that followed the Daniel-Elmore encounter, an attempt will be made to draw a clearer picture of how duelists evaded prosecution for the crime in cases of defamation. On a micro level, the attitude of Richmond citizens, who resided in the primary capital of the Confederate government, was important because of these citizens' leadership role in the South. This begs the next question: as laws made dueling illegal during the Civil War era, were they primarily responsible for the end of dueling or did the laws simply drive the hostile encounters underground?

On a larger level, this chapter will also examine how the changing patterns of communication, such as the formation of the Government Printing Office in 1860, might have contributed to changes in ritualistic responses to defamation. It will also examine one of the period's most controversial documents, the Emancipation Proclamation, from a mass communication perspective. An attempt will be made to show that Lincoln's intimate knowledge of honor rituals may have influenced the decisions he made in constructing and articulating the proclamation.

Focusing back on the Daniel-Elmore duel, Pollard and Elmore were brought before the Richmond court, each with their attorneys, to answer for the charges that had been brought against them. The Richmond mayor, on calling the case, explained he had refused on the evening of the arrest to admit Elmore bail, because he learned that he had shot Daniel in a duel, which was considered a felony and necessitated committal. Pollard was given bail because he was about to participate in a duel with Elmore, not for role he played as second in the Daniel-Elmore exchange.[8]

The court of the Commonwealth then examined three witnesses: George W. Butler, J. Marshall Hanna and Dr. A. E. Peticolas. Wrote the *Daily Dispatch*:

> Mr. Butler, on being sworn, stated that he knew nothing of his own knowledge about the duel. — From a conversation with Mr. Elmore, he had learned that a fight had taken place between Mr. Daniel and himself with pistols, and that Mr. Daniel had been struck; but that he did not ascertain where or at what hour it came off.
>
> Mr. Hanna only knew of the duel from hearsay; learned about seven o'clock Tuesday morning that a fight had taken place, and that Mr. Daniel was wounded, but had not seen him since the duel.
>
> Dr. Peticolas concluded the examination. He stated, under a protest that he might implicate himself, that Mr. Daniel was wounded, and that he received his wound about two miles, or thereabouts, north of the city, west of the Central railroad, and about fifty yards north of a county road which runs west from the toll-gate on the Mechanicville road to the Brooke turnpike.[9]

So in essence, there were three witnesses who would not testify that they witnessed the duel or gunshots. Peticolas admitted that Daniel had been wounded but would not mention the specifics of the wound.

Perhaps the strategy of Peticolas admitting that he saw Daniel's wound, and not keeping silent altogether, was that the duel took place technically out of the jurisdiction of the Richmond court. This was undoubtedly a calculated move because this point was immediately brought up by the defense counsel, who pointed out that based on the testimony of the witnesses, the duel had taken place more than a mile beyond corporate limits in the county of Henrico. The strategy worked to some extent, as the Richmond mayor determined that the case was out of his jurisdiction. However, upon making this decision, he essentially took everyone in the courtroom in tow to seek out a county magistrate. They finally succeeded in finding Justice Riddick, who happened to be home as they drove up to his residence. By that time, however, it was too late to go into examination.[10]

Elmore was bailed and scheduled to appear at the county courthouse.

Pollard's lawyer, P.H. Aylett, requested that his client be released since his name had not been mentioned in connection with the duel. But the mayor objected to the editor's release, saying that even though he had an absence of witnesses to prove it as fact, he had good reason to believe that Elmore and Pollard were planning to duel. The case was continued, and Pollard was bailed.[11]

At the hearing the next day, the mayor stated that the correspondences which he had read in the *Examiner* that morning regarding the Elmore-Daniel duel were conclusive evidence that Pollard was involved in the affair. The mayor also declared that he should also be remanded to the county magistrate with Elmore and charged with being an accessory to a duel. According to the *Daily Dispatch*, Aylett strongly protested.

> Mr. P. H. Aylett, counsel for Mr. Pollard, desired to know whether the Mayor pretended to say that newspaper publications were sufficient evidence in point of law to base a charge of criminal prosecution upon against a party. If such was the rule in that court, it was different from any other in which he had practiced. On Wednesday, as he considered, there had been no charge made against his client of any connection with the duel which had already taken place, but he had only been required to enter into a recognizance to answer the offence of a meeting which it was apprehended was about to take place with Mr. Elmore. The Mayor had refused to disclose the name of his informant, and now, on the second day, he not only did not propose to enter into a hearing of the case, but desired to throw the onus of the charge upon his client. To hold a gentleman under bonds to answer a crime where there has been no accusation made against him, was unprecedented, and, while he (Mr. A.) did not desire to be discourteous, he still regarded it as an outrage. He therefore hoped that his Honor would see the propriety and the justice of discharging Mr. Pollard.[12]

In the end, the mayor disagreed with Pollard's lawyer, maintaining that he had the right to arrest him based on what was published in the *Examiner* and ordered him to appear before the county justice. In reference to the allegations against Elmore and Pollard of being about to break the peace by engaging in a duel, he would drop those charges based on their statements denying the incident.[13]

Pollard and Elmore finally appeared before Justices Riddick and Lee of Henrico County to answer to their charges. The *Daily Dispatch* reported that Dr. Peticolas, who had treated Daniel for his gunshot wound, refused to testify even when he was assured by the prosecuting attorney, John B. Young, that his testimony would not be used against him in the future.

Dr. Peticolas, indeed, was more reticent in his testimony than on the first examination, notwithstanding the fact that the prosecuting attorney for Henrico County, Mr. John B. Young, read from legal authority to show that fear of implicating himself by answering certain questions as a witness need not prevent him from disclosing all that he knew about the duel, as nothing which he might say as a witness could be brought to bear against him in any future criminal prosecution. On this subject some discussion ensued between the prosecutor and Hon. Humphrey Marshall, counsel for Mr. Elmore; but the question was not pressed by Mr. Young, and Dr. Peticolas was therefore permitted to remain silent.[14]

The prosecution's case was also hampered by the fact that key witnesses failed to appear on that day as scheduled.[15]

The case was continued until the next week. When resumed on August 29, the prosecuting attorney, John Young, called George W. Butler to the witness stand and asked him to confirm that a hostile meeting had taken place between Elmore and Daniel. Reported the *Daily Dispatch,* "To this question Mr. Butler replied that he did not say that Mr. Elmore told him anything about a 'hostile' meeting, but simply that there had been a meeting. If Mr. Young understood him to use the word 'hostile' at all, he was sure there was some mistake."[16] Butler left the stand, and Dr. Peticolas was called to replace him.

When asked about the time and place where the duel between Elmore and Daniel was fought, Peticolas refused to answer any questions. The prosecutor tried to reassure the doctor that he would not be prosecuted for his testimony. Wrote the *Daily Dispatch*:

> Mr. Young then read from the acts passed by the Legislature of Virginia in the month of January, 1859, the clause relative to dueling, which says that "every person who may have been the bearer of a challenge or acceptance, or otherwise engaged or concerned in any duel actually fought, may be required, in any prosecution against any person but himself, for having fought, or sided or abetted in such duel, to testify as a witness in such prosecution; but any statement made by such person, as such witness, shall not be used in any prosecution against himself," and again repeated the same questions, informing Dr Peticolas, at the same time, that if he persisted in his refusal to testify, painful as it was to him to have to do so, yet the oath which he had taken as the commonwealth's prosecutor required him to move for his (Dr. Peticolas's) commitment to prison for contempt of court, and he would not flinch from the impartial performance of his duty.[17]

The doctor replied to Young that he was not convinced that his testimony might indirectly lead to his prosecution and still refused to testify.

Young motioned for the doctor to be committed to jail for contempt of court.[18]

Naturally, the contempt motion was hotly contested by the defense counsel. The defense argued that even though Young's quoting of the statute's language was correct, in reality the courts did not often rule in this manner. The defense also cited the trial of *Richmond Enquirer* editor O. Jennings Wise, who was arrested for dueling when he shot Virginia Congressman Sherrard Clemens in a hostile encounter on September 24, 1858. Wise's second was a judge. However the defense counsel focused on Clemens' second, Roger Pryor, who refused to testify about the Wise-Clemens duel on the grounds that it might implicate him and was not further pressed on the subject. Continuing their argument, the defense insisted that if the current Virginia statutes were enforced as written, then they threatened to rob citizens of every right of independence and justice.[19]

The justices reserved their decision until the next day. When they reconvened, Young recalled Butler to the stand to challenge his previous testimony that he knew nothing of the Daniel-Elmore duel. According to the *Daily Dispatch*: "After the opening of the court, Mr. John B. Young, the prosecuting attorney, read from a city newspaper a certain local paragraph with reference to the testimony of Mr. George W. Butler, in which it alleged that [that] gentleman testified that, from a conversation which he had [had] with Mr. Elmore relative to a duel which had taken place between himself and John M. Daniel, he had heard Mr. Elmore say that he had [had] a hostile meeting with Mr. Daniel."[20] Although not specifically mentioned, one can most likely assume that they were referring to the *Daily Dispatch* article on August 18. But no matter how hard the prosecutor pressed, Butler denied any direct knowledge of the duel and blamed the reporter for misquoting him. The newspaper stated:

> His impression was that, on Saturday week, when before the County Justices, he testified that, in a conversation with Mr. Elmore, on the day on which it was said a duel had been fought between that gentleman and Mr. Daniel, he learnt from Mr. Elmore that a meeting had taken place; but he could not say that Mr. Elmore had used the words "hostile meeting." While on the street, he had heard from various parties that Mr. Daniel and Mr. Elmore had fought a duel, and soon after he met Mr. Elmore and approached him on the subject. In reply, Mr. Elmore informed him that he had met Mr. Daniel; but as to the manner and place, he (Butler) was unwilling to say that he received any information from him.[21]

Butler suggested that because it was impossible to separate the myriad of conversations he had on the street, with reference to the affair, that it was impossible to give an exact recollection of the conversation between himself and Elmore. The prosecutor declined to further press Butler and released him from the witness stand.[22]

Dr. Peticolas, who treated Daniel's gunshot, was recalled to the stand and again declined to answer any question about the Daniel-Elmore duel on the grounds that it would eventually lead to his own criminal prosecution. On this matter, Justice Lee responded that the doctor was legally bound to answer the prosecutor's questions. But Peticolas still refused. However, just as Peticolas was about to be condemned to prison for contempt of court, defense attorney Aylett drew a petition for a writ of habeas corpus in behalf of Peticolas. The county sheriff was ordered to bring Peticolas, who was admitted to bail, before Judge John Meredith at the state courthouse for a hearing.[23]

The case continued to take more twists and turns. On August 30, Dr. Peticolas appeared before Judge Meredith to address the contempt of court charge. After listening to both the defense and prosecution, Meredith concluded the hearing. After considering the arguments of the defense and prosecution for several days, the judge rendered his decision on whether Peticolas was bound to testify or not. According to the *Daily Dispatch*,

> Taking the ground that neither the statutes of the Legislature nor the Constitution and Bill of Rights of Virginia ever intended that a witness should testify against himself in a matter in which he was particept criminis [a partaker in the crime], the Judge decided that Dr. Peticolas could not be compelled to answer any questions which be thought might criminate himself; and therefore he reversed the decision of Justices Riddick and Lee committing the Doctor to jail for contempt of court in refusing to answer certain questions propounded to him by Mr. John B. Young, the county prosecutor.[24]

Young responded to Meredith's decision by announcing that he would file an appeal.

When the Elmore-Pollard hearing resumed the following Saturday, the prosecutor called a Confederate surgeon, Dr. M. Tally, to the witness stand. When asked if knew information about the time and place of the Elmore-Daniel duel, similarly to Dr. Peticolas, the surgeon declined to answer on the grounds that it might implicate him in a criminal prosecution. At this point, the *Daily Dispatch* announced, the prosecutor declared that he would not proceed any farther in the case until the Court of Appeals rendered their decision on Judge Meredith's opinion releasing Dr. Peticolas from testimony on the Elmore-Daniel duel.[25]

There is much to be learned about the relationship between honor rituals and journalism during the Civil War era from the Elmore-Daniel duel and subsequent hearings. For one, the language of honor was still very much part of the public discussion. Even under the weight of war violence, it seemed that many areas of the country still turned to the ritual of honor to settle disputes. For instance, in Mississippi it seemed that the culture of honor continued to thrive. An April 30, 1863, report in the *Philadelphia Press* noted that when a Vicksburg editor criticized the Confederate army for allowing Union ships to pass through a canal blockade, the artillerymen responded by referring to the *Code Duello*.

> The Confederates at Vicksburg are said to have been exceedingly chagrined and irate at the success of blockade-runners last Thursday night, and on the following morning declared they had sunk all the transports, three or four of the gunboats, and has destroyed at least 400 or 500 Yankees. One of the journals in the city made some such statements, but soon after partially corrected the error, and said the *Henry Clay* was the only vessel lost. After publishing the article, it reflected severely upon the artillerists, declaring that they were either asleep, intoxicated or absent from their posts, and demanded that they be dismissed in disgrace from service by allowing a dozen Yankee ships to run by the batteries and escape with the loss of only one.[26]

The *Press* wrote that the Vicksburg editor was sent challenges by half dozen of the men in the artillery unit.[27]

As in the case of Pollard, who served as Daniel's second, editors remained embroiled in the mechanics of the affair of honor as seconds, which signaled that the status and reputation of many Civil War editors remained connected to perceptions of honor. An example of this would be the duel on May 7, 1862, between Union Colonel Leonidas Metcalfe and William Casto in a field outside of Maysville, Kentucky, just over the county line. Casto, a former mayor of Maysville, was arrested for being a Southern sympathizer and sent to a federal prison in New York. Kentucky at this time was under federal control, and Casto blamed Metcalf for his imprisonment. When he was released, Casto returned to Maysville and soon sent a challenge to Metcalf through his second, Isaac Green. *Maysville Eagle* editor served as Metcalf's second and arranged the details of the hostile encounter with Green.[28] Wrote Ohio's *Norwalk Reflector* of the affair: "A duel was fought in Bracken County on the 8th inst., between Col. Metcalfe of the Federal army and W.T. Casto of Maysville. The duel was forced upon the former by the latter, who evidently thought Metcalf would not dare to fight. The weapons were rifles, and Casto was shot through the heart at the first fire, dying in fifteen minutes."[29] The two had never met each other before the encounter.

That Metcalf was part of the Union army also illustrates that honor rituals during this period were not a uniquely Southern phenomenon. It might be fair to say that dueling was more socially acceptable in the South and West than in the North. However, when one takes into consideration the secrecy involving the Daniel-Elmore affair, it raises the question of whether duels were happening in the North and just not publicized in the newspapers? If so, was this a concerted effort to not publicize, or reward, public figures for dueling? Or on the other hand, were newspaper editors acting as gatekeepers in some instances to protect public figures who dueled? We may never know the answers, but it is interesting to hypothesize.

It is clear, however, that affairs of honor continued to impact Northern culture and communication in the Civil War era. This is true, in part, because many of the politicians who had found acclaim through honor rituals earlier in the nineteenth century were still in power, Lincoln included. The disagreement between General James Watson Webb, an American minister to Brazil, and his British counterpart, W.D. Christie, underscores the lingering influence of honor codes in the North during this period. When a rivalry between the two became heated, Webb, the former editor whose hostile encounters have been documented in previous chapters, challenged the English minister to a duel. At first it seemed the minister accepted his challenge, but when the encounter became public Christie explained away the challenge in the doublespeak language of honor that was typical in the communication phase of honor rituals. In a written statement in the May 23, 1863, edition of the *New York Times*, Christie explained the confusion:

> Gen. Webb says ... that he was told that I had agreed to challenge him, and that a meeting must take place the next morning, unless the matter were immediately arranged, and that [he] replied that he was ready to give me a meeting at sunrise, &c. I not only did not agree to giving a challenge, but I stated to M. de Glinka at the outset, in M. D'Eichmann's presence, if not in his hearing, that I was not a duelist, and that with me there was no question of fighting. M. de Glinka misunderstood me at first, and thought I had or meant, "I am no duelist, but I will fight this time." However, I corrected M. de Glinka's mistake both to him and to M. D'Eichmann within a few minutes, and I am quite unable to explain, according to any ordinary mode of interpreting the conduct of the gentleman, how Gen. Webb should a week after have written this romance about a challenge and then published it.[30]

Whether or not Christie was telling the truth or exaggerating to save face was not clear. What was clear, and not to the surprise of a *Philadelphia Press* correspondent, was that the language of honor was being used to settle a dispute.

> To those familiar with the exceedingly-pompous bearing and testy disposition of General Webb, there is something very ludicrous in the idea of his being reprimanded over whist [silence], for "talking too much," by the equally testy British diplomatist. It must have been a scene worth seeing. We can readily believe, too, that Webb was quite ready to fight a duel about it; for it is one of his principles, that the duello is an inseparable adjunct of all gentlemanly civilization.[31]

As far as can be ascertained, the two never fired a shot at one another.

A *Philadelphia Press* correspondent was also not surprised when he reported earlier that March that Manton Marble, editor of the *New York World*, was trying to initiate an affair of honor with one of his rivals, Parke Godwin, editor of the *New York Evening Post.*

> And, while speaking of said facetious journal [the *World*], it may not be considered out of the line of newspaper gossip to note that its editor-in-chief, Mr. Manton Marble, is evidently anxious to provoke
>
> A DUEL
>
> with the eminent historian and essayist, Parke Godwin, Esq., editor of the *Evening Post*, the latter paper, which is unsparing in its criticism, has been rather personal in its recent references to the *World*, and Mr. Marble is out this morning with an article so directly abusive of the historian of France [Godwin] that pistols and coffee would seem to be a foregone conclusion.

It is not known whether the two actually met on the field of honor.

In terms of defamation, the vocabulary of honor was still influential enough during the Civil War years that calling someone a "liar" in a newspaper was equivalent to sending a challenge to a duel. When the Louisville *Journal* published a letter on November 6, 1863, signed by prominent Kentucky political figure General Leslie Combs, in which he harshly criticized Union Colonel Carl Schurz's action at the battle of Chancellorsville, the colonel responded with a vague death threat. Wrote Combs in the article, "Our children have fought in every battle-field, and never once fled, as Gen. Schurz and his gang of freedom-shriekers did at Chancellorville."[32] Schurz's reaction, which was first printed in the November 6 Louisville *Journal* and then around the country via news exchange, gives insight to the power that words and defamation still had during the Civil War era.

> I wish, therefore, to say, that in asserting that "Carl Schurz fled at Chancellorsville," Mr. Leslie *lies*. I choose the word "*lies*"—although with

extreme reluctance and regret — upon due consideration of its meaning; for, if Mr. Leslie Combs has inquired into the facts, he must know that he is saying what is false; and, if he had made no such inquiry, then he gives with unpardonable levity the sanction of his name to a statement which is most injurious to another man's reputation, and which he does not know to be true. I wish to add that, in saying "Mr. Leslie Combs lies," I hold myself responsible for what I say.

This may seem equivalent to a challenge — and so it is. But I do not, however, mean to fight a duel with Mr. Leslie Combs. Being a good pistol shot, I might perhaps easily kill him, which I should not like to do; or, if he is equally skillful, he might kill me — and I should be sorry to die on so trifling an occasion; or we might not hurt each other, and then it would be a farce. Besides, I am opposed to duelling on principle.[33]

Whether or not Schurz was actually opposed to dueling on principle, or was just being evasive in his language to avoid the legal fallout that nagged duelists such as Pollard and Elmore, was not evident. However, if Combs had pressed the issue of calling Schurz a coward, it would not be a stretch to say that Schurz might have dueled over it like many of his predecessors. In the end, the only challenge that was issued was one from Schurz, suggesting that Combs follow him into battle the next time and see if had the heart to repeat his statement or do the more honorable thing and retract it.[34]

Some scholars have suggested that the violence and bloodshed of the Civil War might have dulled the public sentiment toward dueling. However, the code of honor had its roots in the military, so it would be illogical to assume that in a highly militarized period in American society one would see a decline in honor rituals. This was true not only for soldiers from the South, but the North as well, as this August 18, 1863, column in the *Philadelphia Press* suggested.

A duel occurred in New Jersey, opposite the city of New York, on Friday last. The actors were a young officer of artillery — son of an eminent naval officer — and a lieutenant in the 8th Infantry, a detachment of which is at present quartered on Governor's Island. Pistols were the weapons. Three shots were exchanged without effect. The result of the fourth was more sanguinary. The challenger, struck in the neck by the bullet of his adversary, fell bleeding and senseless, but reviving within a few moments, inquired with undaunted pluck whether the time had arrived for "another round." His strength, however, failed to match his courage, and the duel was pronounced at an end.[35]

The duel, in this case, originated over an insult to a lady.[36]

Not surprising, newspaper editors reporting the war had to contend with a military that was extremely sensitive to defamation by tradition. The tension between these groups could have been only exacerbated by the sectional animosity bred during the war and the shame of defeat in the South. The Alabama duel between E. O. Hale of the *Mobile Times* and an ex–Confederate colonel, Chas. Forsyth, son of the *Mobile Register & Advertiser* editor, gives insight to this tension. *New York Times* correspondent Benjamin C. Truman wrote on November 2, 1865, that when Forsyth returned from war, there was a rumor that his wife had inappropriate relations with a man named La Vega. Subsequently, Forsyth attacked La Vega with a large knife at a local theater. [37]

According to Truman, the *Mobile Times* ran a column condemning Forsyth's actions as unbecoming of a gentleman. Forsyth responded by calling Hale a liar, thief and coward. Hale challenged him to a duel. Wrote Truman:

> Forsyth accepted, and named as weapons double-barreled shot-guns, with sixteen buck shot in each gun — this is the style of a high-toned gentlemen. Both circulated the facts that they were going to fight, and of course were arrested and put under bonds of five hundred dollars each to keep the peace. Both parties were accused by their friends of letting the cat out of the bag — they rallied their courage — this is the style of high-toned Southern gentlemen — and proceeded to the Magnolia Park, and *fired at each other from the hip at forty paces*. Of course, neither of them were hurt — neither of them could have hit a barn — their wounds were healed, they shook hands, resurrected their friendship, started for Mobile, arrived at Mobile, and drowned their sorrows in the flowing bowl — for *this* is the style of high-toned Southern gentlemen.[38]

The irony of Truman's condescending and mocking tone is that it would have probably elicited a dueling challenge from one of the parties involved if he had been writing for the *Mobile Times* and not the *New York Times*. But Truman also represented the changing face of journalism that was shifting from a personal journalism fueled by patronage to a more corporate structure: the reporter.

The reporter and the corporate structure of a newspaper involved more people in making the news, and therefore made it increasingly difficult to single out one individual for a duel. But even reporters weren't immune from honor rituals during the Civil War years. In Wisconsin, an honor dispute occurred when a correspondent of the *Kenosha Sentinel* mocked a poem written by J.H. Tracy of the *Kenosha Times* for the opening of the Academy of Music in Milwaukee. Reported the *Philadelphia Press*: "The name of G.W. Chapman was given by the *Sentinel* man, but

Chapman denied the authorship of the squib. Tracy then proceeded to challenge the *Sentinel* editor, one Wheeler, and got this reply: 'If a sanguinary meeting will put an end to your poetical efforts, I shall esteem myself a humble instrument in the hands of Providence, used for the benefit of society at large.'"[39] The duel was never fought, but when Wheeler's second, George E. Wright, responded to Tracy, he wrote that Tracy could choose from this list of weapons: broadswords, rolling-pins, shovels, fish-knives, ice-cream freezers, 18-pound carronades, injection pipes and sprinkling pots.[40]

The rise of the reporter and corporatism was likely significant to how defamation and libel were treated in communities. A correspondent such as Truman could report on the news in Mobile and then leave the community. He did not necessarily report on the people he saw every day in the general store, churches and other gathering places. In essence, the personal relationship between the editor and the community began to erode, which made it more difficult to justify or initiate an affair of honor. Also, one can probably safely assume that challenging a correspondent to a duel did not garner the same public esteem as an editor-in-chief. This was in stark contrast to the situations of editors such as Richmond's Daniel and Pollard, who were not only the public voices of their regional party politics, but likely depended on the patronage of political leaders in the community to keep their newspaper operations running.

Also feeding into this transition into corporatism on a macro level was Abraham Lincoln's refusal to give patronage to a partisan organ during his administration. In Hazel Dicken-Garcia's *Journalistic Standards in Nineteenth-Century America*, she wrote, "Lincoln rejected using a party newspaper to serve his administration, becoming the first president to do so; his action has often been pointed out as sounding the death knell of the party press, and surely it had some influence."[41] Up until that point, printing contracts were awarded to party editors as spoils for their loyalty and persuasiveness. This decision paved the way for the establishment of the Government Printing Office (GPO), which was created by Congress in 1860. Supporters of the GPO, such as the *Brooklyn Eagle*, wrote that its creation was necessary to remove party favoritism from public printing:

> It seems to be an inseperable [*sic*] condition of all government contracts that shall be more wasteful and less faithfully carried out than those entered into with private parties. Particularly is the case in elective governments like our own where a new administration goes into office every four years, with hosts of friends to reward and hordes of camp followers who clamor for patronage and spoil and for whom, it has come to be an admit-

ted political maxim, pap must be provided. Whether it is a printing job or
a job of any other sort, matters little. It is not the method of disposing of
the printing that causes the difficulty but the recognized propriety of sustaining official organs and a brood of hungry politicians.[42]

Thus, the GPO effectively removed major political parties from directly
sustaining popular journalism with patronage. Keeping in mind that
defamatory remarks borne from personal journalism often initiated ritualistic responses, the rise of newspaper as an industry in the latter half of
the nineteenth century must have made dueling seem as obsolete as the
party press model of journalism.

Was Lincoln's role in laying the foundation for the GPO a calculated
attempt to diffuse the power of honor rituals and its inherent social
stratification? A question such as this is difficult to determine. From his
aborted duel on September 23, 1842, with James Shields, who was the Illinois state auditor at the time, it can be ascertained that he was well-versed
in the power honor that rituals held over some men, but on an intellectual level considered them absurd. Wrote an October 6, 1842, *Brooklyn
Eagle* report of the encounter: "A Duel, Almost.—James Shields, Auditor
of the State of Missouri, and A. Lincoln, a lawyer of Illinois, attempted
to settle their differences near Alton, on the 23, ult. With broad swords,
but on the very verge of hostilities the 'sober second thought' prevailed,
and the parties separated with explanations and whole heads."[43]

The incident started when Lincoln criticized Shields in a satirical letter printed in the September 2, 1842, *Sangamo Journal*, of Springfield, Illinois, under the pseudonym of "Rebecca."[44] Since not only did he not sign
his name to the letter, but used a female pseudonym, Lincoln probably
thought he was safe from an honor dispute. However, Shields was known
as a notorious dueler and, upon discovering the origin of the letter, had
his second, General Samuel Whitesides, deliver a challenge.

In a letter of instruction to his second, Dr. Elias Merryman, Lincoln
took an almost satirical approach to the duel itself as well. If Shields would
not accept his apology, then Lincoln issued these instructions to Merryman:

> 1st Weapons — Cavalry broad swords of the largest size precisely equal in
> all respects — and such as now used by the cavalry company at Jack-
> sonville —
>
> 2nd Position — A plank ten feet long, & from nine to twelve inches broad
> to be firmly fixed on edge — on the ground, as the line between us which
> neither is to pass his foot over upon forfeit of his life — Next a line drawn
> on the ground on either side of said plank & paralel [*sic*] with it, each at

the distance of the whole length of the sword and three feet additional from the plank; and ... the passing of his own such line by either party during the fight shall be deemed a surrender of the contest....

3rd Time — On thursday evening at five o,clock [*sic*] if you can get it so; but in no case to be at a greater distance of time than friday evening at five o,clock —

4th Place — Within three miles of Alton on the opposite side of the river, the particular spot to be agreed on by you —

Any preliminary details coming within the above rules, you are at liberty to make at your discretion; but you are in no case to swerve from ... these rules, or to pass beyond their limits —[45]

Not only was Lincoln's choice of weapons, broad swords, in stark contrast to the pistol duels that were more common, his insistence on the plank was an obvious reference to the extreme height advantage he held over Shields.[46]

Several days after this encounter, Lincoln was involved in another honor dispute when he acted as a second for Merryman, who was challenged by Whitesides. In a letter to Joshua F. Speed, Lincoln wrote about this experience.

Dear Speed: You have heard of my duel with Shields, and I have now to inform you that the dueling business still rages in this city.... Yesterday Whitesides chose to consider himself insulted by Dr. Merryman, so he sent him a kind of quasi-challenge, inviting him to meet him at the Planter's House in St. Louis on the next Friday, to settle their difficulty. Merryman made me his friend [second], and sent Whitesides a note, inquiring to know if he meant his note as a challenge, and if so, that he would, according to the law in such case made and provided, prescribe the terms of the meeting.[47]

Whitesides appointed Shields as his second. It wasn't clear that the encounter took place; however, Lincoln wrote to Speed that a street fight was anticipated.[48]

What was unmistakable was that Lincoln had an intimate working knowledge of honor rituals and had a knack for diffusing the situation. This may seem an odd statement to make since he was President of an administration during one of the bloodiest wars in American history. However, separating Lincoln from the Republican agenda, one may be able to gain more insight to his deft handling of Southern patron-client power structures. One example was the formation of the GPO; another example to consider is the Emancipation Proclamation.

From a historical standpoint, revisionist scholars have seemed to downplay the importance of the Emancipation Proclamation. Some critics of Lincoln, such as *Forced Into Glory: Abraham Lincoln's White Dream* author Lerone Bennett, Jr., have declared the document to be a fraud, having no impact on the abolition movement at all.[49] He and Benjamin Quarles, author of *Lincoln and the Negro*, have gone so far as to suggest that the Emancipation Proclamation was strategically designed to sabotage the anti-slavery movement.[50] Even many of Lincoln's staunchest supporters, such as Edward Steers, Jr., editor of *The Trial: The Assassination of President Lincoln and the Trial of the Conspirators*, agreed that "Bennett is correct in concluding that the Emancipation Proclamation freed few if any slaves."[51] Most scholars for and against Lincoln cite this passage as one of the document's greatest weaknesses:

> Now, therefore I, Abraham Lincoln, President of the United States, by virtue of the power in me vested as Commander-in-Chief of the Army and Navy of the United States in time of actual armed rebellion against the authority and government of the United States, and as a fit and necessary war measure for suppressing said rebellion, do, on this first day of January, in the year of our Lord one thousand eight hundred and sixty-three, and in accordance with my purpose so to do publicly proclaimed for the full period of one hundred days, from the day first above mentioned, order and designate as the States and parts of States wherein the people thereof respectively, are this day in rebellion against the United States, the following, to wit:
>
> Arkansas, Texas, Louisiana, (except the Parishes of St. Bernard, Plaquemines, Jefferson, St. John, St. Charles, St. James, Ascension, Assumption, Terrebonne, Lafourche, St. Mary, St. Martin, and Orleans, including the city of New Orleans), Mississippi, Alabama, Florida, Georgia, South Carolina, North Carolina, and Virginia, (except the forty-eight counties designated as West Virginia, and also the counties of Berkley, Accomac, Northampton, Elizabeth City, York, Princess Ann, and Norfolk, including the cities of Norfolk and Portsmouth), and which excepted parts, are for the present, left precisely as if this proclamation were not issued.
>
> And by virtue of the power and for the purpose aforesaid, I do order and declare that all persons held as slaves within said designated States, and parts of States are, and henceforward shall be, free; and that the Executive government of the United States, including the military and naval authorities thereof, will recognize and maintain the freedom of said persons.[52]

Thus, most historians have conceded that Lincoln freed only the slaves in the Confederate areas of the country "in rebellion" where he had no control and that the system of slavery in territories under Union control remained status quo. Through modern cultural sensibilities, it is understandable how a literal interpretation of the Emancipation Proclamation might be perceived as ineffective at best or disingenuous at worst.

What has seemed to be missing so far in the twenty-first century debate over the relevance of the Emancipation Proclamation is a deep understanding of how honor rituals may have been a pivotal influencing factor on how it was conceived, delivered and perceived at the time. In the context of the code of honor, which we know from the Daniel-Elmore encounter, continued to be a powerful force in the Confederate capital of Richmond during this period, the real communicational power of the Emancipation Proclamation may have been lost in the passage of time. From this perspective, it seems likely that Lincoln's proclamation was less of a mandate for blacks, but rather more of a signal to the South in language they understood: honor. This is not meant to detract from its power in bringing the institution of slavery to end, but to reconsider the proclamation from a communication perspective.

In Michael Vorenberg's essay "After the Emancipation: Abraham Lincoln's Black Dream," included in the book *Lincoln Revisited*, he noted that even Lincoln himself admitted that the Emancipation Proclamation could have been outlawed by the Supreme Court or Congress, or be rescinded by his successor if he failed to be reelected.[53] This suggests that this document was frail from its incarnation.

However, similar to the grammar of a duel, the power of the Emancipation Proclamation was in its leverage of honor rhetoric. With one simple document, Lincoln reframed the war debate to focus squarely on slavery, not states' rights. By utilizing the rhetoric of honor, Lincoln was seemingly able to unite the conservative and radical elements in the Republican Party to politically endorse abolitionism while sending a clear signal to the South that it would not be allowed to re-enter the Union unless it submitted to federal control. This may have been done, in fact, to satisfy the conservative hawkish wing of his party. The same part of his power base, in contrast to the abolitionists, endorsed colonization and held fast to its customs of social stratification, which were inherently white supremacist through centuries of tradition. But the message of the Emancipation Proclamation was clear to the leaders of the South: there would be no reconciliation without submission as long as Lincoln was in power.

Modern Lincoln critics, such as Bennett, suggest that the Emancipation Proclamation had no "pizzazz" in its language and that historians have given meaning to the document that the author never intended.[54] What may be closer to the truth, for better or for worse, is the historical inability for many readers in the twenty-first century to conceptualize the complexity of nineteenth-century social and cultural forces that compelled Lincoln's strategy. This was still an overtly classicist, hierarchical society where social status was often determined by birthright. Social mobility was possible, but often it took demonstrations of violence and honor, either by affairs of honor or the military, to achieve "gentleman" status, a title reserved in America for only an elite segment of white males.

Thus Lincoln had to contend with a majority of the American public, living in both the North and South, who saw blacks inferior not only by their race, but by their class status and birthright as well. Andrew Jackson, as illustrated in previous chapters, was able to penetrate this Americanized aristocracy by overcoming the latter two obstacles as a politician and judge, a general in the military and through constant affirmations of honor. Lincoln, who was also somewhat of an outsider to this American aristocracy, must have been acutely aware of the social forces that black Americans had to face.

As far as pizzazz, Lincoln's proclamation had an instant, dramatic effect on the war and reshaping the political debate. Frederick Douglass, a former slave and pioneering intellectual within the abolitionist movement, used these words in his autobiography to describe the announcement of the proclamation: "The effect of this announcement was startling beyond description, and the scene was wild and grand. Joy and gladness exhausted all forms of expression from shouts of praise, to sobs and tears."[55] In all fairness, Douglass would later describe the proclamation in his autobiography as defective and not the document he had hoped it would be. But Douglass, who knew Lincoln, added:

> For my own part, I took the proclamation, first and last, for a little more than it purported; and saw I its spirit, a life and power far beyond its letter. Its meaning to me was the entire abolition of slavery, wherever the evil could be reached by the Federal arm, and I saw that its moral power would extend much further. It was in my estimation an immense gain to have the War for the Union committed to the extinction of Slavery, even from a military necessity. It is not a bad thing to have individuals or nations do right though they do so from selfish motives. I approved the one-spur-wisdom of "Paddy" who thought if he could get one side of his horse to go, he could trust the speed of the other side.[56]

Thus, even in the moment, abolitionist leaders were aware of document's impact.

Again in all fairness, one could argue that Douglass' view supports Bennett's claim that the document was given a meaning that the real author never intended.[57] However, Douglass and Southern leadership both understood, as did Northern leaders, that the conflict to this point had been one of mostly reconciliation and not conquest. Many Northern leaders, such as General George McClellan, who would be Lincoln's rival in the 1864 presidential race, thought the war should be fought as a well-mannered or "civil" duel between organized armies on the field of honor, sparing non-combatants.[58] This is similar to how the first battle of Manassas was undertaken in July 21, 1861.

From a nineteenth-century communications perspective, however, the language of the Emancipation Proclamation argued against the existence of slavery from a point of honor. Therefore, it made it virtually impossible politically for reconciliation between Northern Democrats and Southern plantation owners, who were the lynchpin of the Confederate power base. It also meant that there would be no restoration of the Union as it existed before the war, which had been discussed by both sides. Quite simply, anyone who owned slaves in the states outlined in the proclamation was a traitor. Therefore, those Northern political leaders who sought reconciliation with slave owners were siding with the traitors and therefore were traitors themselves against the Union. This gave Southern slave owners exactly two choices: submit or be conquered. Thus, arguably for the first time, slavery became a rallying point for Union armies.

Southern leaders understood the power of the Emancipation Proclamation in the moment. In a January 12, 1863, message to the Confederate Congress at Richmond, President Davis announced the irrevocable change:

> The proclamation will have a salutary effect in calming the fears of those who have constantly evinced the apprehension that this war might end by some reconstruction of the old Union, or some renewal of close political relations with the United States. These fears have never been shared by me, or have I been able to perceive on what basis they could rest. But the proclamation affords the fullest guaranty of the impossibility of such a result. It has established a state of things which can lead to but one of three consequences — the extermination of the slaves, the exile of the whole white population of the Confederacy, or absolute and total separation of these States from the United States.[59]

The entire Confederate press echoed his sentiment.[60]

It did not escape Douglass, however, that a glaring flaw in the proclamation was that it made a distinction between loyal slave owners in the border states and disloyal ones in the Confederacy. In his autobiography, Douglass wrote: "While he [Lincoln] hated slavery, and really desired its destruction, he always proceeded against it in a manner the least likely to

shock or drive from him any who were truly in sympathy with the preservation of the Union, but who were not friendly to emancipation. For
this he kept up the distinction between loyal and disloyal slave holders,
and discriminated in favour of the one, as against the other."[61] Once again,
this could be seen as supporting Bennett's claim that Lincoln tacitly supported slavery and thus was disingenuous to the abolition movement.
What seems more likely from a nineteenth-century communications perspective, however, is the idea that Lincoln was dismantling slavery in stages,
starting with the foundation.

In following this theory, Lincoln's strategy would have had a double-
edged effect. From one point of view, Lincoln did not undercut his anti-
emancipation, pro-colonization power base that he needed to have not only
for re-election in 1864, but to literally preserve the Union and ensure his
policy of abolition continued. If Lincoln was not elected to a second term,
the alternatives were that either the colonizationists or slave owners would
assume power if there was reconciliation. The political paths for both these
alternatives in North and South ended in white supremacy.

From the other side, it once again diffused the ability of the Confederate leadership, which included partisan newspaper organs, to utilize
honor rhetoric to rally counter-support. True, it emphasized Confederate
plantation owners as traitors first, slave owners second. But the use of
honor rhetoric by Lincoln in the proclamation made this a "for" or
"against" issue. When the war is brother against brother, how do you define
who a traitor is? Lincoln redefined Confederate slave owners and supporters of slavery as the enemy. This would have given Union forces a clear
target and shifted the battle from an honor dispute between armies over
states' rights to outright war against Southern slave owners.

Lincoln's proclamation also served up Southern slave owners as targets for the Northern press. Eradicating slavery in the South seemed to
take on a new urgency and focus in the debate. It appeared to be so effective that by August 2, 1864, leading Confederate editors, such as John
Daniel, were complaining in their columns that the North had lost sight
of the real cause of the sectional dispute.

> Mr. Davis, in a conversation with a Yankee spy, named Edward Kirk, is
> reported by said spy to have said, "We are not fighting for slavery; we are
> fighting for independence." This is true; and is a truth that has not
> sufficiently been dwelt upon. It would have been very much to be desired
> that this functionary had developed the idea in some message, or some
> other State paper, which would have carried it round the world, and
> repeated it in all languages of civilized nations, instead of leaving it to be

promulgated through the doubtful report of an impudent blockade-runner, who ought to have been put in Castle Thunder. The sentiment is true, and should be publicly uttered and kept conspicuously in view; because our enemies have diligently labored to make all mankind believe that the people of these States have set up a pretended State sovereignty, and based themselves upon that ostensibly, while their real object has been only to preserve to themselves the property in so many negroes, worth so many millions of dollars. The direct reverse is the truth. The question of slavery is only one of the minor issues; and the cause of the war, the whole cause, on our part, is the maintenance of the sovereign independence of these States.[62]

Even modern historians critical of Lincoln, such as Quarles, agreed that that the Emancipation Proclamation changed the character and tone of the war.[63]

The fact that Lincoln did not emancipate the slaves in Union territories, however, is still as controversial with scholars today as it was with Douglass in the moment. Lincoln advocates, such as Steers, are quick to point out that Lincoln did not have the Constitutional authority of the thirteenth amendment, which was enacted nearly two years later in 1865.[64] The harshest critics of Lincoln, such as Bennett, have suggested that he "betrayed the trust of the slaves so often and on so many levels, mocking their dreams with dialect stories and "darky" jokes and maneuvering behind the scenes to keep them in slavery and in need, never approached the Moses hope that covered Southern fields like dew."[65] More moderate critical historical views of Lincoln, such as that of Vorenberg, proposed that "enslaved blacks were ready for freedom, and they had been ready for freedom since the guns had fired in Charleston Harbor four years before. It was the whites who had yet to be educated for black freedom. And it was Lincoln's failure to see this basic truth that represents a genuine failing."[66] Taking into account Lincoln's practicable approach, all of these points bear some validity in varying degrees.

Yet, when coming to a consensus about Lincoln's proclamation strategy of freeing the slaves in the Confederacy and not the Union, many, if not all historians have failed to account for the levels of social stratification, communicated by honor rituals, which he had to contend with as president. It was not necessarily simply a case of blacks being equal to whites. That would assume in the nineteenth-century that all whites were considered equal to each other, which through the lens of honor rituals was clearly not the case.

With the rise of industry and corporatism, wealth became a pathway to social mobility in nineteenth-century America. Beyond birthright, however, navigating the culture of honor through verbal or physical assertions of violence, whether through dueling or in the military, seemed to be one of the few apparent opportunities for whites of lower economic standing to penetrate the antebellum gentleman class. In this way, Andrew Jackson's political triumph over the Whigs, outlined in chapter three, seems to epitomize this class struggle.

Thus, in theory, Lincoln's strategy of incorporating blacks into the military may have been a type of mass communication strategy to educate whites both in the North and South that the black race was one of honor and pride, not servitude. Studying it euphemistically, it may have been more about honor than guns in the field. Keep in mind that in the context of the times, abolitionism was still considered a radical movement, and the majority of whites in both the North and South, however unconscionable and appalling the idea may be, regarded blacks as inferior.

In essence, Lincoln was giving Northern blacks the opportunity for social mobility on the basis of a patriarchal system mediated by honor rituals. So to say that blacks earned their own social standing in post–Civil War America would not be completely incorrect and in truth may have been the way Lincoln wanted it to be perceived. Lincoln may have gambled that this was the best long-term solution for blacks, similar to poor, rural whites in the Jacksonian Era, to be assimilated into the social stratification of nineteenth-century America. The system was, of course, not perfect. In the beginning blacks in the military were often segregated, relegated to menial work and received less pay, but there was no reason to think that this situation might have been adjusted better if Lincoln had not been assassinated. Nevertheless, the potential positive social impact of Lincoln's incorporation of black regiments into the army in lieu of immediate emancipation cannot be ignored.

Comparing the similarities of the mass communication strategies of Lincoln with Jackson is not a far stretch considering both presidents shared close relationships with Francis P. Blair, Sr., arguably one of the most influential journalists of the antebellum era. As one of the major architects of the Democratic Party and the Southern rise to power, he knew the communicative power of honor rhetoric and used it to undercut the influence of the Whig party in his role as editor of the Washington *Globe*. With his first-hand knowledge of the Calhoun wing of the Democratic Party and experience during the nullification crisis of 1832, no one was in a better position to know the strength and weaknesses of the Southern political platform. *Richmond Examiner* Editor John Daniel was known as a devotee of Calhoun's vision of states rights.[67]

Blair had plenty of personal motivation in seeing the dismantling of the feudalistic Southern political structure in favor of a strong central government similar to that of the Jacksonian platform, which he helped create. He was also a master of manipulating honor rituals in the press. Regardless of what the motivating forces were for the Emancipation Proclamation, its powerful use of honor rhetoric in a mass communication setting may be the chief reason why we remember slavery as a central issue of the Civil War. This honor rhetorical could have only been augmented by its announcement following the successful military battle at Antietam.

How would historians articulate the Civil War if the issue of slavery had not been thrust into the spotlight by Lincoln's Emancipation Proclamation? To this we may look to Southern historians, who to this day still refer to the conflict sometimes as "The War Between the States" or "The War of Northern Aggression."[68] Conveniently lost in most histories of the Civil War was the Republican Party's white supremacist platform of colonization. It was not slavery, but it was far from black equality.

With Lincoln's assassination April 14, 1865, we may never fully understand the personal Lincoln apart from the political necessities forced upon him by war and the conservative wing of the Republican Party. Was Lincoln's mass communication strategy with the Emancipation Proclamation a token nod to the abolition movement or part of a greater design to viably incorporate black Americans into the social hierarchy of nineteenth-century America? The closest answer to that question may come from Frederick Douglass, the ex-slave and leading voice of the abolition movement. In his autobiography he wrote, "I have often said elsewhere what I wish to repeat here, that Mr. Lincoln was not only a great President, but a GREAT MAN — too great to be small in anything. In his company I was never in any way reminded of my humble origin, or of my unpopular colour."[74] Coming from a man who stood toe-to-toe with some of the greatest evils of American society, these comments should not be regarded lightly.

Confederate journalists knew by war's end that they had lost the propaganda war as well as the battle. The author of *The Lost Cause: A New Southern History of the War of the Confederates*, published in 1867, wrote:

> Outside the domain of party politics, the war has left another consideration for the people of the South. It is a remarkable fact that States reduced by war are apt to experience the extinction of their literature, the decay of the mind, and the loss of their distinctive forms of thought. Nor is such a condition inconsistent with a gross material prosperity that often grows upon the bloody crust of war. When Greece fell under the Roman yoke,

she experienced a prosperity she had never known before. It was an era rank with wealth and material improvement. But her literature became extinct or emasculated; the distinctive forms of her art disappeared; and her mind, once the peerless light of the world, waned into an obscurity from which it never emerged.[69]

That author was *Richmond Examiner* co-editor E. A. Pollard, brother of Rives Pollard.

For his part, Rives Pollard was never convicted for his role as second in the Elmore-Daniel duel or his subsequent affair as a primary with Elmore. On February 8, 1865, the *Richmond Daily Dispatch* announced that the Court of Appeals supported Dr. Peticolas' refusal to testify.

> Dr. A. E. Peticolas, the reputed physician for Mr. John M. Daniel in a duel recently fought between himself and Assistant Secretary of the Treasury Elmore, was discharged yesterday by the Court of Appeals from all obligation to give evidence relative to the matter. It will be recollected by our readers that soon after the difficulty occurred the Examining Court of Henrico County insisted upon Dr. Peticolas testifying in the matter, and, upon his refusal to do so, ordered his commitment to jail. Subsequently, the case was taken before Judge Meredith on a question of bail, when that functionary decided adversely to the opinion of the county justices, and admitted him to bail. The decision of the Court of Appeals, as we are informed, releases all persons from testifying in the matter of duels where it is alleged their evidence might implicate themselves and thereby subject them to criminal prosecution.[70]

That meant that neither Pollard, Elmore nor Daniel would ever be prosecuted for the duel.

The demise of the *Richmond Examiner*, the beacon of Southern rhetoric, seemed synonymous with the death of its brightest light, John Daniel, who died from complications of pneumonia on March 30, 1865. It was recorded that Dr. Peticolas was by his side. Of his death, the *New York Times* wrote under the headline, "The Last of the Leading Rebel Journal and its Editor:"

> Like perverts generally, when he had once cast his fortunes with the conspiracy against the nation's life, he outdid the most virulent of the traitorous crew in his abuse of the national Government and the political institutions under which he had risen to an honorable fame. His death, which is noted as an event synchronous with the overthrow of the Richmond *soi-disant* Government, points a lesson which will be long remembered by the political student, both North and South.

Less than a week later, Confederate President Davis would announce the inevitable fall of Richmond in his April 5 proclamation.[71] The *Examiner* would be revived again, but it would never again hold the same prominence in the national community as it did during the Civil War.

Following his tenure with the *Examiner*, Rives Pollard continued his journalism career as editor of the *Southern Question*. After disparaging the sister of a prominent Richmond tobacconist, James Grant, in a November 21, 1868, article, Pollard was shot and killed three days later in broad daylight outside his office. According to *Harper's Weekly*, "The shot was fired from a third-story window opposite [from the office], from a double-barreled gun loaded with buckshot."[72] Despite overwhelming evidence against him, Grant was acquitted by the jury. In a March 7, 1869, article, the *New York Times* reported some of the details of Grant's defense by his lawyer, John S. Wise, who suggested that the homicide was justified because it insulted a woman's virtue. The defense also claimed that Pollard engaged in a type of blackmail, by making money off the insult, and no other recourse except Pollard's death would have repaired Grant's family name.[73]

The crushing defeat of the Confederacy in the Civil War did not destroy the culture of honor or its role in mediating defamation in many cities across the country, especially in the South. Journalists, politicians and other public figures would continue to be acquitted of dueling on legal technicalities similar to the ones described in the trial of the Elmore-Daniel duel. Rives Pollard's death is a clear example of this. In post–Civil War America, however, the rise of Northern corporatism, in contrast to the Southern feudalistic patron-client hierarchy, seemed to mark a decline, as E. A. Pollard predicted, in the distinctive forms of thought of the South which centered on the culture of honor. In fact, the state of the South's political and journalistic structures might be best summed-up by E. A. Pollard in *The Lost Cause*.

> She [the South] must submit fairly and truthfully to *what the war has properly decided*. But the war properly decided only what was put in issue: the restoration of the Union and the excision of slavery; and to these two conditions the South submits. But the war did not decide negro equality; it did not decide negro suffrage; it did not decide States Rights, although it might have exploded their abuse; it did not decide the orthodoxy of the Democratic party; it did not decide the right of a people to show dignity in misfortune, and to maintain self-respect in the face of adversity. And these things which the war did not decide, the Southern people will still cling to, still claim, and still assert in them their rights and views.[75]

Thus many people were left to wonder, for better or for worse, would the South ever rise again?

CHAPTER SEVEN

The Decline of Dueling as a Resolution for Defamation

Dueling and other ritual violence as a resolution for libel did not immediately end with the Civil War, as some scholars would suggest. As this chapter will illustrate, editors in several parts of the country faced ritualized violence in lieu of libel suits from 1865 through 1900. This ritualistic violence was similar in its sensitivity to defamation and its need for public displays of manliness compared to that of the antebellum period. If the culture of honor did not disappear after the Civil War, how and why did it eventually cease being a factor for journalists?

This chapter posits that the rise of corporatism and the end of federal patronage gave major impetus to the ending of ritual violence as a resolution for defamation in many areas of the country. Also, in the post–Civil War era, authorities in the South and West now made concerted efforts to thwart violent ritual confrontations before they occurred. This would compel many duelists to go to extreme lengths in order to satisfy their honor. Also, some regions during this era, such as South Carolina, still refused as late as 1880 to convict those who responded to defamation with ritual violence, if it even was prosecuted in the first place.

Most states by the Civil War had anti-dueling laws on the books that outlawed not only the act of dueling, but in many cases the libelous or slanderous remarks that might instigate a violent ritual encounter. But it was only after the Civil War that many of these laws began to be enforced. This chapter suggests that when these laws were finally enforced, it led to the breakdown of the arbitration that prevented many violent encounters and gave rise to a phenomenon known as a rencounter, an unplanned hostile encounter. This was similar to the Wickliffe-Benning affair described in Chapter Four. Now instead of a formal challenge or public beating, many disparaged parties would seek out editors with guns drawn. In many cases post–Civil War newspapers began to use the term "duel" and "rencounter" interchangeably. Why was that the case? Clearly, seeking an editor out and shooting him on sight was the antithesis of the formality of dueling. Yet as the nineteenth century came to a close, there was much newspaper debate as to what actually constituted a duel, even though it had been a part of American culture for over a century. This chapter will examine those issues.

By the end of the Civil War, journalism came into its own as a business with news as its commodity. Dicken-Garcia wrote, "The Civil War signaled the end of the kind of journalism associated with the penny press era, in which an editor's personality dominated and people read the newspaper for his views."[1] This shift had a radical effect on the way journalism was interpreted in major metropolitan areas. In less than a decade, newspapers such as the *Louisville Journal* were declaring,

> The day when the editor of a newspaper itself was the embodiment of the peculiar views of its editor, has passed away, there will be no more Horace Greeleys perhaps. One man can no longer edit a daily journal. The entire business has been multiplied by ten; editors; printers; reporters; expenses. The best newspaper is that which gives the freshest news and more of it at the lowest market price. The rule that governs bacon governs the press. There is no spread-eagleism about it. There is no mystery. It is an open-and-shut affair, like a Barlow knife. The best paper gets the most readers; and of consequence advertising flows in upon it and so it prospers.[2]

So at least by the 1860s, newspapers were being seen as a business and not merely as a function of a well-structured political junto. Furthermore, with reporter by-lines now present, according to Dicken-Garcia, many more names appeared in a newspaper and readers started to identify them with their overriding interests.[3] These factors made it difficult to hold one individual accountable, as many editors had been in the past, for a dueling challenge or ritual violence when it came to defamation. This journalistic shift from partisan organ to a business model also may have caused less political strife between rivals, leading to fewer incidences of defamation, and therefore less dueling and ritual violence. The lack of a major two-party system in the early Reconstruction period could have only helped this condition.

The shift from the antebellum personal school of journalism rooted in politics to the marketing model which emerged after the Civil War, which Dicken-Garcia describes in her book, was not a smooth one, however.[4] Editors in many sections of the country, mainly in the South, were still struggling with ritual violence and dueling well into the late nineteenth century. A July 11, 1883, *Washington Post* article, quoting an editorial in the *National Republican* on July 10, illustrated the country's continuing struggle with the code of honor: "The larger volume of public opinion in the whole country is decidedly against dueling, but there are particular sections where the reverse is true. Yet there are in these latter sections a large number of the best and most highly respected citizens who deprecate and condemn the practice. Let these men make themselves heard and their influences felt."[5] In these sections of the country, editors still faced ritual violence and participated in duels in much the same way their predecessors had before the war.

The state of Virginia, particularly Richmond, was still a hotbed for ritual violence after the war and editors were still a prime target. On October 12, 1870, the *Atlanta Constitution* reported a challenge made by James Barbour, editor of the *Richmond Enquirer*, issued to Major James W. Walker, a member of the House of Delegates from Madison County. Walker had publicly assaulted Barbour near a train stop, and the editor's response was a peremptory challenge to a duel. Barbour declined the challenge on the grounds that the State Constitution disenfranchised participants in a duel.[6]

In places such as Richmond, dueling in cases of defamation often arose, as in the past, when personal honor was intertwined with politics and journalism. Even though Virginia had some of the earliest and most stringent anti-dueling laws in the country, it still did not prevent at least 10 challenges and six duels between political rivals from 1879 to 1883 in that state.[7] Some of the fighting editors during this period of conflict included Elam of the *Whig* and Beirne of the *State*, mentioned in the introduction. Not only did these editors duel each other, but they also dueled political rivals. State Senator J.W. Riddleberger was known for hostile encounters with political rivals, including editors. When Beirne denounced Riddleberger in the *State* during his senatorial campaign, the latter responded with a challenge.[8] The two met on the field but did not duel because there were no percussion caps for the pistols. On that same day Riddleberger also dueled with Congressman-elect George Wise. Shots were fired, but no one was injured.[9]

Editorials nationwide chastised the men who participated in duels. But, as often was the case, the criticism was because the duel was bloodless, not necessarily that the duel itself took place. An excerpt from an October 18, 1881, editorial in the *New York Times* illustrates that sentiment:

Time was when a duel was literally mortal combat; when the antagonists went to the field of honor with the intention and expectation that one or other of them would be left there dead or wholly disabled. Under these conditions dueling was unreasonable, but it compelled respect of a certain kind for those who practiced it…. But nowadays in Virginia there is ordinarily less danger in dueling than in railroad traveling. Men stand opposite each other and blaze away for a half-hour in entire security for both, and then they shake hands and go home. That there is much satisfaction in this way of doing things is clear, but it is not what was meant by the "satisfaction of a gentleman" in other days. A custom which is cruel, barbarous, and blood-thirsty in its apparent purpose cannot long survive after it has become harmless and ridiculous. All the homilies of all the moralists would never do so much to break down dueling as the spectacle of WISE and RIDDLEBERGER and a dozen other fierce devotees of the code walking about the streets, after numerous encounters, unharmed.[10]

Although unwavering in its condemnation of dueling, even the Northern *New York Times* could not disavow dueling altogether.

It did not go unnoticed that the outbreak of dueling violated Virginia state law. C.A. Harwell Wells wrote in *End of the Affair?*, "Law enforcement was no longer willing to turn a blind eye to duels. When several would-be duelists attempted to meet and duel in private, they found themselves forced to run from the Richmond and Washington police. Once caught, the duelists were required by local judges to post large bonds to guarantee their peaceful behavior."[11] Virginia's anti-dueling law prohibited duelists and their seconds from holding public office. Dueling was so widespread in Virginia during this period that many of its most prominent politicians and editors were disqualified. To circumvent this, a special bill was introduced to the state legislature that, according to the *New York Times*, provided "for the removal of the disabilities of all persons who engaged in duels [and participated as seconds] during the past two political campaigns."[12] Among those in the journalism profession affected by this bill were W.C. Elam, of the *Richmond Whig*; J.B. Walters, Elam's associate editor; Alexander Hunter, editor of the *Alexandria Capital*; J.B. Beirne and William Ryan, of the *Richmond State*; and W.B. Wilder, of the *Portsmouth Times*.[13]

It is difficult to say accurately how many editors in the post–Civil War era were faced with ritual violence and dueling. In many cases, as in the Coleman-Thompson affair mentioned in chapter four, duels may not have been publicized or reported out of fear of the players being arrested or disqualified for public office. In places in the Deep South where the culture of honor still flourished, anti-dueling laws were passed that targeted the language of the duel before it could escalate into violence. In "*End of the Affair?*" Wells wrote, "Mississippi and Virginia expanded their libel laws to make illegal any statement likely to lead to violence.... So stringent was Virginia's law that, unlike ordinary libel laws, it sometimes punished 'fighting words' even when they were true."[14] If they were enforced, laws like those would seemingly make it politically disadvantageous to seek public affirmation through dueling.

But even these strict laws did not prevent Virginia editors from seeking satisfaction through the ritual of honor. The *Washington Post* reported on February 22, 1884, that M. Glenman, editor of the *Norfolk Virginian*, and John W.H. Porter, editor of the *Portsmouth Enterprise*, were arrested on the eve of a duel between them. Both, according to the report, were leading politicians.[15]

Even as the nineteenth century came to a close, Virginia editors were still struggling with the code of honor. On October 8, 1893, the *Washington Post* reported that Jefferson Wallace, secretary of the city Democratic committee, was arrested for sending a challenge to Joseph Bryan, owner and editor of the Richmond *Times*.[16] The code of honor remained a threat to journalism as late as the twentieth century. The *Washington Post* reported that in 1903 E.M. Slack, editor of the *Abingdon Virginian*, received a challenge from a J.W. McBroom, a postal clerk and son of the local postmaster.[17] In both cases, it was not clear whether a duel was actually fought, but it illustrates that the language of honor was still in the public consciousness.

Louisiana, with its strong European ties, was also a region in post–Civil War America where the code of honor still held fast. The *Atlanta Constitution* reported that Col. R. Barnwell Rhett, Jr., editor of the New Orleans *Picayune*, fought and killed Judge William A. Cooley in a July 1, 1873, duel. About four years earlier, the *New Orleans Times* reported on June 3, 1869, that L. Placide Canonge, editor of the *Epogue*, received a challenge from Paul Alhaisa, one of the managers of an area opera house. The two fought with swords, and Canonge received a minor wound. The report said it was expected that he also would duel the other opera house manager in the following days.[18] In a pistol duel, Major H.J. Hearsey, editor of the *New Orleans Daily States*, and E.A. Burke, state treasurer and one of the proprietors of the *Democrat*, exchanged two shots before reaching an amicable agreement in a bloodless duel.[19]

As in Virginia, dueling continued for Louisiana editors well into the late nineteenth century. A.B. Roman, editor of the *New Orleans Louisianaise*, exchanged three shots in a bloodless duel with J.E. Poche.[20] After five shots, E.A. Burke was wounded in both thighs on June 8, 1882, in a duel with C.H. Parker, editor-in-chief of the New-Orleans *Picayune*.[21] As late as 1891, Louisiana editors were still resorting to ritual violence, according to a September 26 account in the Chicago *Daily Tribune* about New Orleans: "A Captain and twenty policeman patrolled Camp and Natchez streets this afternoon. They were there to prevent a hostile meeting between Col. John C. Wickliffe, editor of the *New Delta*, and Gen. George W. Dupre, editor of the *Evening States*. Shortly after, both parties were arrested on warrants for being about to commit a breach of the peace, and placed under bonds and the police were withdrawn."[22] Their argument was over the patronage Dupre was receiving as state printer.[23] He was not a stranger to dueling, having been wounded in the jaw in a June 6, 1891, duel with Dr. S. R. Oliphant of the Louisiana Board of Health.[24]

As was the case in the antebellum years, some communities after the Civil War still refused to convict duelists, which in turn left the community newspaper editor a target for ritual violence. Such was the case in Charleston, South Carolina, when Colonel E.B.C. Cash goaded W.M. Shannon into a duel on July 5, 1880. Shannon, a plaintiff attorney in a lawsuit which involved Cash's wife and her brother, was killed in the affair.[25] Only the second duelist in the history of the state to be put on trial for murder, Cash was acquitted after an initial mistrial.[26] Before and during the trial, the Colonel's son, W.B. Cash, went on what the *New York Times* described as a "crusade against newspaper editors."[27] The *New York Times* wrote: "The editors of the News and Courier treated Cash's demand that adverse criticisms 'must cease from date' with dignified contempt, but two of their correspondents, who live on the spot, seemed more seriously impressed with the situation. One publicly retracted all he ever said, and seems ready to affirm, under oath, that no duel occurred; the other took refuge behind the worn out excuse — 'typographical blunders.'"[28]

The threat of ritual violence was not a hollow threat, as the editor of the *Cheraw Sun*, a nearby newspaper, soon found out. According to the *Washington Post*, when the editor, Mr. Pegues (first name not given), denounced the duel in his newspaper, both the elder Cash and his son attacked him with drawn pistols. The report said, "Pegues was only saved by being thrust by his friends into an open doorway where he was locked up."[29] It was also evident by the report that Cash felt validated by the code of honor to suppress negative comments written about him in the press: "It is the avowed intention of this pair of brutal bullies to regulate the press of South Carolina. There must be no unpleasant allusions to the recent murder. Col. Cash must be treated as a man of unsullied honor, or he and his son, armed to the teeth, will fall on any editor who offends, and shoot him down like a dog.... The code has had its day, and even in its zenith it was never intended to shield such fellows as these Cashes from the blows of outraged law."[30] No arrests were made in this incident.[31] In addition, the *Washington Post* reported, under the headline "Political Ethics of Dueling," that by 1883, newspapers such as the *National Republican* were doing all that could be done to elect Cash to a seat in Congress.[32]

In areas in the South, it was not uncommon for journalists to cross over state lines, as they had before the Civil War, to avoid arrest in their own state for dueling. For instance, the *Atlanta Constitution* described a place called Sand Bar Ferry, located along the state line, as still a "favorite resort for belligerent parties from the States of Georgia and South Carolina."[33] Two South Carolina editors, J.T. Heyward, editor of the *Orangeburg Times*, and Malcom J. Browning, editor of the *Orangeburg News*, exchanged two shots there in a bloodless duel on December 8, 1873.[34] Georgia duelists would duel on the South Carolina side, and South Carolinians would duel on the Georgia side, thus avoiding the jurisdiction of their local authority.[35]

Journalists in the post Civil War era would go to great lengths to duel without interference by the authorities. When E. W. Carmack of the *Memphis Commercial* and W. A. Connolly, editor pro tem of the *Memphis Appeal-Avalanche*, feared arrest in Tennessee before they could duel, they decided to travel to Holly Springs, Mississippi, to evade the authorities. The *Washington Post* reported on May 7, 1893, that the authorities caught up with them before they reached their destination.[36] The *Washington Post* wrote:

> In arranging to have the meeting at a point seventy or eighty miles distant, the seconds invited the incredulity of every rational human being. By going to Holly Springs they simply quadrupled the difficulties of the case and in a corresponding ratio diminished the probability of a fight. They chose a point in reaching which they had to take the cars and incur the chance of arrest by telegraph at a dozen different points upon the route, even if they succeeded in eluding the authorities at the Memphis depot.[37]

The *Post* suggested the situation would have been better remedied if the editors had shot at each other six weeks ago.[38]

Other instances of editors traveling great distances to duel can be found in late nineteenth-century journalism. Two Virginia newspapermen, Captain W. E. Cameron, editor of the *Petersburg Index*, and Robert W. Hughes, a contributor to the *Richmond State*, traveled by train to North

Carolina and dueled 16 miles from the Norfolk and Petersburg railroad on July 12, 1869.[39] In Mississippi, the editor of the *Aberdeen Examiner*, J. Dalton, Jr., traveled near Memphis to duel W.B. Walker, a Democratic elector for the First Mississippi District.[40]

Although seemingly less frequently than in the South, editors in more western states also experienced threats of ritual violence. On October 29, 1895, the *Chicago Daily Tribune* reported from Wisconsin that George Koeppen, editor-in-chief of the *Germania*, and Edgar W. Coleman, editor of the *Milwaukee Herald*, were engaged in a newspaper war and close to dueling.[41]

> There has been considerable ill-feeling between the editors of the papers for some time. The "lie" has been passed back and forth between the editors several times during the last week.
>
> The friends of the editors are alarmed at the serious turn which the war of words has taken and are doing everything to smooth matters over and to prevent a personal encounter between them. Both men are greatly excited and thus far have refused to listen to any talk of peace.[42]

A truce was agreed to by the editors before any violence occurred. However, about three months later it was reported that the newspaper war between the two had resumed and a duel was probably imminent.[43]

Threats of ritual violence against editors in the West during the late nineteenth century seemed similar to that of other regions. The *Washington Post* reported on May 27, 1890, that Walter G. Smith, editor of the *San Diego Sun*, was challenged to a duel by a man identified only as Colonel Ferrer. The challenge, according to the report, was declined.[44] On July 12, 1886, the *Los Angeles Times* reported that H. Harris, editor of Washington's *Tacoma Sun*, was arrested for challenging W.A. Ryan, proprietor of the *News*, to a duel.[45] Similarly, the *Chicago Daily Tribune* reported on December 6, 1890, that Oklahoma editor Frank Greer of the *Capital* was preparing to meet a man identified only as Senator Brown for a duel.[46] The *New York Times* reported on September 15, 1882, that a duel was fought in tombstone, Arizona, between Samuel Purdy, editor of the *Epitaph*, and Patrick Hamilton, editor of the *Independent*.[47]

Although scant in comparison to other regions of the country such as the South, there is evidence that Northern editors did not completely avoid encounters with ritual violence after the Civil War. James Gordon Bennett of the *New York Tribune* was known as an expert duelist in the latter half of the nineteenth century.[48] One public account of his familiarity with ritual violence was in response to his public beating by Fredrick May, brother of Edith May, who was romantically linked to Bennett. On January 4, 1877, the *New York Times* reported details of the encounter:

> Mr. Bennett ... lit a cigar, and emerged from the entrance of the Union Club just as Mr. May reached the corner of Twenty-first street. The two gentlemen walked toward each other, and met midway between the corner of Fifth avenue and the club entrance. Without uttering a syllable, Mr. May raised a large rawhide [leather strap], which he had kept concealed on his person, and struck Mr. Bennett full in the face, blood following the stroke. A second and third blow followed, and before Mr. Bennett had time to recover his surprise at the suddenness of the attack, he had received two severe cuts on the face — one on the nose, and one over the left eye.[49]

May and the editor struggled until bystanders separated them.

After Bennett recovered, his response was a desire to challenge May to a duel. His friends advised against it, reported the *Times*.

> Those of his advisors ... who are thoroughly conversant with the "code of honor," say that this is impossible, as the person challenged cannot in honor, according to the code, fight a duel with an adversary who has been disgraced by the cowhide. The situation is looked upon by Mr. Bennett's most intimate friends as exceedingly embarrassing, but they hope that with sober reflection they may be able to find some way out of the difficulty which shall be consistent with the honor and outraged feelings of the unhappy young gentleman.[50]

As evidenced by the *Times* report, the stigma of shame in a culture of honor was still much a part of Northern society.

Bennett, whose credibility as an editor was derived from public opinion, decided that the best option to save his reputation was to demand satisfaction from May who, apparently against honor etiquette, accepted the challenge.[51] The two duelists and their parties met at a territorially ambiguous point along the Delaware and Maryland borders. According to the *New York Times*:

> A walk of 20 minutes across the fields brought them to the State line between Maryland and Delaware at a point on the farm of Mr. Nathaniel McGinnis. Here the ground was measured off, and, that neither might be hit by a wad, twenty paces — and long ones too — were measured off. The usual preliminaries were then gone through with, and the pistols were discharged almost simultaneously. As before stated, neither man received a scratch. Mr. Bennett said he was "satisfied," and proposed they leave the field.[52]

Bennett left very soon after the duel for Europe to avoid a possible arrest.[53]

Because no blood was drawn in the Bennett-May duel, the encounter was chastised for not being a demonstration ritual violence but being a false display of honor. The *New York Times* wrote:

> The so-called duel was a farce from the beginning, and it is idle for the friends of either party to attempt to put a different aspect upon it. Had either of the principals shot the other the fact would have been known in less than 24 hours after the occurrence, and no one would have been so quick to spread the news as the duelists themselves, who would have thus merited the belief, at all events, that they were really in earnest, and desired to hurt one another. But neither of them was touched by a bullet, and to create the impression that something serious was really intended, a profound and mysterious reticence has been kept up.[54]

In a separate editorial, the *Times* added, "Under such circumstances, it is not only fortunate that neither of the principals was injured, but that the fatal bullets — if bullets indeed there were — did not hit some of the spectators of the bloodless conflict. Any suggestion that a stray cow was wounded in the melee may be dismissed as frivolous."[55] That there was a cloud of mystery and disinformation was true, but that may have been more of an attempt to avoid prosecution by the parties involved.

The lengths that duelists, including journalists, would go to in order to fight were the target of scorn and chastisement from political and journalistic rivals. Newspapers such as the *New York Times* and the *Atlanta Constitution* suggested that a duel could "escape being ridiculous only by becoming tragical."[56] When the editor of the *Chicago Tribune* received a challenge from an infamous French duelist and former Dakota cattle rancher known as Marquis de Mores, the newspaper mocked the event:

> There is still great conflict of opinion as to the weapons which shall be used. Mr. Harrison [The *Tribune* editor's mock second], in his conference with the Marquis' seconds, will urge that the combatants be mounted on buffaloes and armed with Indian spears. A suggestion has been received from James W. Scott of the *Herald* that, instead of spears, loaves of French bread be the tilting weapons, the loser — who will of course be the Marquis — to eat all the broken loaves in full view of the spectators.[57]

The marquis was well known in America; he had recently been in a highly publicized French duel in which he killed a Jewish officer in the French army after he was challenged for his anti–Semitic remarks. The officer's death touched off a wave of Jewish protest across France.[58]

The fact that the marquis was in France when he challenged the *Tribune* editor was the impetus for the humorous response, but dueling and ritual violence were still a dangerous threat to journalists. Even though the custom was declining, reported a September 17, 1893, story in the

Washington Post, dueling was not a joking matter for those who participated in it. The *Post* wrote:

> One cannot but wonder if any of the editors who see so much to amuse them in duels and the telegraphic headliners who write the funny heads to the brief mention of these events that appear in the morning papers ever saw a duel. No man who has ever stood by and seen the life sent out of a living, breathing fellow human in a second by an ounce of lead, or witnessed the bright red stream as it poured from heart or jugular which a sharp three-cornered sword had pierced, would ever think of the affair with anything like a feeling that it was a matter of fun.[59]

The author went on to suggest that if any of the witty gentlemen who poked fun at dueling were to stand 10 or 12 paces in front of a gentleman holding a dueling pistol, the sensations would be directly the opposite of funny.[60]

The rise of stronger dueling laws led some newspapers to declare the demise of dueling as a general practice in America. An August 25, 1889, *Washington Post* article declared: "The practice of resorting to duels for the purpose of settling personal difficulties and of attesting one's courage and honor is rapidly dying out. There are occasional outcroppings, it is true, like the Calhoun-Williamson fiasco in Georgia, which furnish considerable amusement and do no harm, but the custom as a general practice is literally a dead-letter."[61] The article noted that the most stringent laws were in the Southern and Western states in order to prevent dueling.[62]

However, a brief survey of newspaper accounts of the period suggest that dueling and ritual violence still impacted journalism from the mid–1880s to the turn of the century. When a Georgia state legislator dueled an editor who criticized his bill to tax bachelors, the 1885 account of the affair suggested that dueling was still a common practice when dealing with incidences of defamation: "The usual Georgia duel followed. Both gentlemen chose friends, who opened negotiations which resulted in leaving the weighty issues to the arbitrament of three prominent gentlemen, who decided that both the editor and the member were wrong, and that both should apologize, which has probably been done by this time."[63] That names were not mentioned in this account may have been done to shield the participants from prosecution. Other Georgia editors involved in honor disputes included F.H. Morris, editor of the *Melledgeville Chronicle*, and Dr. F.H. Kenan, a member of the legislature. A December 30, 1886, *Washington Post* article reported that a duel between the two was imminent.[64] In 1884, the *New York Times* reported that J.F.

Meyers, editor of the *Itemizer*, fought and killed J.C. Coleman, a merchant, in a duel in Swainsboro. Thirteen shots were fired, and Coleman was shot in the abdomen.[65] The *Times* also reported in 1897 that H.C. Hanson, editor of the *Macon Morning Telegraph*, and Tom W. Loyless of the *Macon Evening News*, had been criticizing each other for several weeks and that a formal challenge was imminent.[66]

Throughout the South, editors had to defend themselves through ritual violence into the 1890s. In Florida, H.V. Sevier, editor of the *Evening Telegram*, and Benjamin Harrison, editor of the *Standard*, fought a duel at Moncrief Springs, near Jacksonville, on November 16, 1891.[67] It was reported from Birmingham, Alabama, on September 24, 1893, that Coleman, an editor of the *Huntsville Daily Argus*, challenged Lane, an editor of the *Huntsville Daily Mercury*, to a duel. The challenge was refused by Lane. However, the *Washington Post* reported, "A fight will follow when they meet."[68] A little more than three years later, it was noted that Coleman was involved in a bloodless duel with an editor O'Neil (no first name given) of the *Huntsville Daily Mercury* on October 21, 1895.[69] On December 17, 1894, it was reported that S.D. Perry, publisher of the *East St. Louis Herald*, was scheduled to duel with Lloyd R. D. Fayling, ex-editor of the same paper. According to the report, the duel was postponed from fear of police interference.[70]

In still other incidents of Southern editors dueling in the 1890s, a duel was fought between a Vicksburg editor C.E. Wright, and Charles Scott, president of a failed bank in Rosedale. It is uncertain to which publication Wright was connected, but the duel was not a farce according to an August 31, 1898, report in the *Washington Post*: "The fight took place with .38-caliber revolvers and smokeless powder was used. The first exchange was without result, but on the second Wright was slightly wounded. The field was the same upon which scores of famous Mississippi duels have been held in the past."[71] Also in 1898, the *Washington Post* reported on February 10, from Lexington, Kentucky, that Colonel Thomas E. Moore, an area politician, challenged Desha Breckinridge, editor of the *Herald*, to a duel. Although it was uncertain whether the duel was fought, it was clear by the report that defamation was at the root of the challenge: "The feeling between the men was engendered in the Breckinridge-Owens Congressional contest four years ago. Col. Moore was recently suggested as a penitentiary commissioner, and the Herald ridiculed him. This led to the challenge."[72] Since Colonel Moore, an ex–Confederate, was paralyzed in his right arm, he suggested that both men use left arms.[73]

In examining dueling as a resolution for defamation in America, there was unlikely one single overriding factor for its demise. As discussed earlier in the chapter, the end of federal patronage and the emergence of the reporter made it difficult for a disparaged person to hold one individual accountable for a challenge. The Civil War also led to the eventual decline of the patron-client social and political hierarchy, anchored by the Southern plantation owner, which promoted patronage, an aristocratic gentleman class and the code of honor. With the aristocracy of the South in decline, it was no longer necessary in many cases to prove loyalty and manliness as a means of social mobility and affirmation of social standing.[74]

Finally, dueling laws had an impact on ritual violence only in areas of the country where they were enforced. In many cases, laws were designed or modified to outlaw potentially libelous remarks or language in newspapers that encouraged dueling and ritual violence. Ironically, this may have led to increased violence in areas of the South that still held traditions of honor. When dueling laws in areas such as Mississippi were finally enforced, it may have led to a breakdown in the arbitration of insult and apology that was integral to the formality of the duel.

Without the arbitration, insulted parties would resort to ritual violence first, to avoid early prosecution by authorities, instead of as a last resort as was traditionally suggested by the code of honor. On May 2, 1888, the *New York Times* reported out of Jackson, Mississippi, that the local postmaster, General Wirt Adams, was involved in a duel with John H. Martin, editor of the *New Mississippian*. However, what the *Times* described was not a formal, arranged fight between two gentlemen:

> About 2:30 o'clock this afternoon Gen. Wirt Adams, in company with Mr. Ned Farish, were passing north on President-street. They had reached and crossed Amite street, when Mr. Martin was seen approaching from the north. The parties met very near the residence of Judge Brame, and there an encounter took place. Gen. Adams was going north and Mr. Martin south. Mr. Farish, who was walking with Gen. Adams, says that as they approached each other Gen. Adams accosted Martin, saying: "You d — n rascal, I have stood enough from you!" Martin replied: "If you don't like it," and simultaneously with the remark drawing a pistol, he fired and got behind a large china tree on the outer edge of the pavement, half a foot in diameter. Gen. Adams also fired about the same time: but Farish, though not certain, thinks that Martin shot first.[75]

Both men died in a conflict that resembled more of a rencounter, or what Wild West mythology might describe as a showdown, than actual formal combat under the *Code Duello*.[76]

Rencounters, such as the Adams-Martin affair, were often triggered by editorial remarks of the same sort that precipitated dueling. Because of its connection with honor, rencounters in cases of defamation became synonymous with dueling in some courts and newspapers. In events similar to the Adams-Martin affair, Jackson, Mississippi, editor Roderick Gambrell was fatally shot on May 6, 1887, by Colonel Jones Hamilton after repeatedly assailing the colonel's personal character in his publication, *Sword and Shield*.[77] Hamilton was arrested for Gambrell's death but was eventually acquitted.[78]

So, it would seem that in incidences of defamation, the formality of dueling became degraded in terminology and substance as the nineteenth century came to a close. A January 22, 1900, letter to the editor by Ezra Nat. Hill in the *Washington Post* illustrated the confusion between rencounters and duels that existed at the time:

> *Editor Post:* Permit me to criticize a head-line in The Post of the 17th. It is this: "Six Shot in Feud Duel." Webster [dictionary] defines a duel as "premeditated conflict between two persons, for the purpose of deciding some private difference or quarrel." The Encyclopedia [*sic*] Britannica says a duel is "A prearranged combat with deadly weapons between two private persons to settle some private quarrel." Webster, after giving the definition quoted above, says: "a sudden fight, not premeditated, is called a rencounter."[79]

Hill suggested that these definitions were not broad enough. He wrote that the "combat between David and Goliath, often spoken of by those who do not know what a duel is, as a duel, was in no sense a duel."[80] He wrote that even though Goliath had a standing challenge open to everyone in the Hebrew camp, the inequality of the weapons took this combat out of the class of duels.[81]

The inequality that existed in rencounters between combatants, which included journalists, in addition to the harm it posed to innocent bystanders, may have been the initial push that finally classified mortal combat in honor disputes as murder. The *Los Angeles Times* on September 15, 1894, reported that J.L. Goodman, editor of the *People's Voice*, and H.G. Armstrong, editor of the *Star*, were involved in a rencounter coined as a "street duel." Both men died, including an innocent bystander, in this honor dispute.[82] Similarly, under the headline, "Fatal Duel in Waco," the *Washington Post* reported on April 2, 1898, that W.C. Brann, editor of the *Inconoclast*, was involved in an honor dispute with Captain M.T. Davis. The *Post* reported the "combatants met just at 6 o'clock this afternoon on South Fourth street, in front of the Cotton Belt ticket office, and after exchanging a few words both began emptying their revolvers into each other's body."[83] Both men were likely to die, according to the same report. Although termed a duel, this could be more accurately described as a rencounter.

There are other examples in major American newspapers that confused the terminology of dueling with rencounter in the late nineteenth century. On October 10, 1899, the *Chicago Daily Tribune* reported that Dominick O'Malley, proprietor of the *Evening Item*, and C. Harrison Parker, editor of the *Delta*, fought a duel with each other in New Orleans. According to the *Tribune*:

> The trouble originated over a cartoon in the Item representing Colonel Parker as a little dog being led by a string by Governor Foster and labeled, "Me Too."
> About 3 o'clock this afternoon O'Malley came out of his office, accompanied by Parson Davies, and had walked only a few yards when Parker, who was across the street, started towards him. Both drew revolvers and firing, each continuing until his pistol was empty.[84]

Both men, it was reported, were seriously wounded in the encounter.

Post-Civil War dueling in cases of defamation differed from the antebellum years because it was no longer an unchecked part of Southern culture.[85] But long after dueling was in steady decline, the language of the code of honor persisted in newspapers and publications of the South well into the late nineteenth century. When newspapers, such as the *Washington Post* on August 24, 1897, tried to point out that the American press were mistaken when they classed together street fights, family feuds and vendettas under the term dueling, they were accused of trying to re-establish dueling as an institution.[86] But the *Post* pointed out that even though the *Code Duello* was probably dead in America forever, its deterioration and demise did nothing to curb the homicide rate in America. The paper also suggested that with the decline of the code, the carrying of concealed weapons became more prevalent, as did an increase in slanderous stories.[87] If this was true, then anti-dueling laws in the latter half of the nineteenth century may have hurt journalism more than it helped, at least in the interim. It may not have been detrimental to Northern newspaper editors and reporters, but in Southern cities such as Richmond and New Orleans, where honor rituals persisted, dueling laws took away a valuable part of the editor's defense: the arbitration before the hostile encounter. Sanders Garland, a *Washington Post* correspondent, wrote in 1897:

> Those who have practical knowledge and experience of the code are perfectly aware that its chief object is to prevent bloodshed. Those who are in

a position to tell the truth about it will indorse [*sic*] our statement that its operation has nearly always been to realize that object. The code of honor is, in effect, a system of arbitration, and should its history ever be written by a person at once competent and honest, the world will admit that it has forbidden a dozen encounters for every one it authorized.[88]

And so the nineteenth century came to a close, with American journalism still struggling to untangle itself from ritual violence and the code of honor.

CHAPTER EIGHT

Conclusions

What most journalism historians have failed to recognize is that a complete knowledge of honor rituals is essential for understanding the mindset of the nineteenth-century American journalist. Hazel Dicken-Garcia's *Journalistic Standards in Nineteenth-Century America*, referred to many times in this book, offers a valuable analysis of the dual role of editor and politician. But even she almost completely dismisses honor rituals as having any impact on that era.

As this study shows, that is an oversight. Ritual violence including dueling had a significant impact on journalism for nearly the entire nineteenth century. Was there a journalistic common denominator between the Alexander Hamilton–Aaron Burr duel in 1804 and the Richard F. Beirne–William C. Elam affair nearly eighty years later? The answer is yes. Instead of filing lawsuits, both Burr and Beirne took the field of honor with the expectation that their reputation would be restored by engaging in ritual violence over the public defamation they received in newspapers. This book has shown without doubt that a pattern existed where editors and politicians, whose professions were closely intertwined during much of the nineteenth century, consistently used the threat of ritual violence to attack and defend against criticism, defamation or libel in similar ways.

Few historians, save Bertram Wyatt-Brown, have been aware of the extent to which honor rituals have manipulated and influenced the communication patterns of nineteenth-century American culture. But as this book has shown, although honor rituals thrived in the South, they were not uniquely a Southern phenomenon. Thus, Wyatt-Brown's analysis can only take the journalism historian so far.

As many historians would agree, we have only recently begun to understand the sociopolitical forces that drove journalistic patterns during that era. Consequently, it is time to re-evaluate the impact of honor rituals on journalistic development in the nineteenth century. By having a clear understanding of the past, it may help journalism scholars recognize similar communication patterns as they re-emerge throughout time.

For instance, when conservative Democratic Georgia Senator Zell Miller gave the keynote speech at the 2004 Republican convention, he lauded President George W. Bush as a man with the willpower and backbone to protect his family. He announced to the thousands of audience members and millions of television viewers, "It is the soldier, not the poet, who has given us freedom of speech."[1] After listing all of the weapons systems he claimed that Senator John Kerry, the Democratic presidential nominee, had opposed over the course of his political career, Miller proclaimed, "This is a man who wants to be the Commander in Chief of our U.S. Armed Forces? U.S. forces armed with what? Spitballs?"[2] He finished his televised speech to a rousing ovation, declaring, "God bless this great country. And God bless George W. Bush."[3]

After the speech, Miller was interviewed by broadcast journalist Chris Matthews, host of MSNBC-TV's "Hardball with Chris Matthews." On his 6:00 P.M. show that preceded Miller's speech, Matthews asked a panel of political pundits, "Tonight, he's [Miller] going to endorse the Republican ticket for president and vice president. Do you think that's an honorable thing to do?"[4] After the speech, Matthews' television interview with Miller was full of aggressive candor and personal invectives from both men. Matthews questioned Miller's statement about freedom of the press, to which Miller antagonistically replied, "You didn't have anything to do with freedom of the press."[5] In a caustic tone, Matthews retorted, "Well, you could argue it was not nurses who defended the freedom of nursing. Why did you single out freedom of the press to say it was the soldiers that defended it and not the reporters? We all know that. Why did you say it?"[6] Both men continued to exchange verbal barbs with Matthews suggesting that Miller's comments about the press were designed as an applause line against the media at a conservative convention. The Georgia senator responded, "I wish we lived in the day where you could challenge a person to a duel."[7]

As the keynote speaker for the Republican political agenda, Miller's remarks pave the way for a discussion of the practical applications of nineteenth-century communication patterns to twenty-first century journalism study. As author and historian David McCullough once remarked, "How can we know who we are, and what we stand for, and where we are heading, if we don't know how we got to where we are and at what cost?"[8] That is not to say that the American political and journalistic arena is on course for a revival in the practice of dueling. But it does raise an important question: Is the study of honor rituals, which helped and hindered so many journalists in the nineteenth century, relevant to twenty-first-century journalism?

At the Workshop on Humiliation and Violent Conflict at Columbia University in 2004, Bertram Wyatt-Brown suggested that honor ethics still factor into decision making in many parts of the world, including the United States.

> The term [honor] is very much alive in two respects. First United States foreign policy functions under the rules of honor and dread of humiliation like those of other nations with ambitions for aggressive power.... Americans generally believe that a challenge to our power must be retaliated with greater might. Second, since Roman legions marched across Europe and Asia Minor, no armed services, ours included, has mustered without the discipline, sense of hierarchy for prompt obedience, and indoctrination of comradeship and unit loyalty — all things that the primarily male code cultivates.[9]

Thus, one might infer from this that honor rituals are more pronounced in times of war, which then may polarize the journalist into one of two categories: ally or adversary of the political party in control of administrative policy authorizing the war. This makes sense since the leader of the political party is also commander-in-chief of the armed forces.

To illustrate, after the attack on the World Trade Center on September 11, 2001, some journalists who criticized the administration's reaction were deemed unpatriotic or were censored. Dan Reeves wrote in a *New York Times* October 1, 2001, editorial, "Patriotism Calls Out the Censor,"

> You ... don't have to be that big man to lose your job — or be threatened by the White House if you don't shut up. Early casualties ... include Dan Guthrie, a columnist for the *Daily Courier* of Grants Pass, Ore., who accused President Bush and some of his advisers of "hiding in a Nebraska hole" immediately after the World Trade Center toppled and the Pentagon was bombed on Sept. 11. The Texas City *Sun*, in the president's home state, ran a front-page apology for an opinion by an employee. The offending opinion was that of the city editor, Tom Gutting, who wrote a column under the headline "Bush Has Failed to Lead U.S."
>
> Even comedians are not exempt from the patriotism monitors. Bill Maher, the host of "Politically Incorrect," lived up to his late-night talk show's title two days ago by saying, "We have been the cowards, lobbing cruise missiles from 2,000 miles away." Last Wednesday, Ari Fleischer, the White House spokesman, attacked Mr. Maher and warned others, saying, "Americans ... need to watch what they say, watch what they do, and ... this is not a time for remarks like that; there never is."[10]

Fleischer, in his book *Taking Heat,* defended himself by saying that his comments were not advocating censorship and that his position in situations such as the one described was that in all times, it is everybody's right to say things, no matter how wrong they may be.[11]

However, it still does not take away from the fact that Maher, whose show's premise was political criticism, was suddenly caught in a political controversy after he said the military was acting cowardly. Even though *Politically Incorrect* was not cancelled until May of the following year, the *New York Times* claimed it was that remark that led to the demise of the show.[12] That fact is interesting to note, considering the history of the word "coward" as a trigger for honor rituals.

Whether Fleischer's comments, as White House spokesman, were meant as an attack on free speech is a moot question in this debate. What was apparent at the time is that journalists critical of the administration, such as Maureen Dowd, felt that their free speech was being threatened because of their political views. "Even as the White House preaches tolerance toward Muslims and Sikhs, it is practicing intolerance, signaling that anyone who challenges leaders of an embattled America is cynical, political and — this the subtext? — unpatriotic," wrote Dowd in a September 30, 2001, editorial, "Liberties; We Love the Liberties They Hate" in the *New York Times.*[13] An item for future study might be whether this wartime honor ethic has been a driving force for increased partisanism in recent press trends. Another possible item for future study is whether this heightened wartime honor ethic could factor in Elisabeth Noelle-Nueumann's "spiral of silence" communication theory.

In this research, it was suggested that when personal honor intertwined with politics and journalism the result was antagonistic and often violent in the nineteenth century. The rise of Internet web logs, or blogging, as a journalistic trend, shares many characteristics to that of journalists in the early nineteenth-century party press era.[14] In a September 23, 2004, editorial in the *Fort Wayne News Sentinel,* Leo Morris wrote,

> What we're seeing today is the return of that penny press. Putting up a blog site is so cheap and easy that just about anyone can do it. And millions of people are doing it — lawyers and journalists and ordinary people of all kinds. Those who dismiss them as angry partisans in pajamas are forgetting — or don't even know — the origins of the press in this country. "The press" belongs to the masses now in a way it didn't even in the beginning.[15]

Although it was an apt assessment by Morris, it is probably more correct to say that we are seeing a return of the party press era values, which overlapped with the penny press era in the nineteenth-century. For example, as in the age of the party press, blogging promotes the kind of journalism, as Hazel Dicken-Garcia described in her book *Journalistic Standards in Nineteenth-Century America*, "in which an editor's personality dominated and people read the newspaper for his views."[16] Inevitably, the line between reporting the facts and partisan opinion is often blurred in blogging, as it was during the party press era. Similar to the nineteenth-century party press era, elements of personal honor and politics are seemingly mixed together in blog journalism with often antagonistic results that sometimes stop only short of outright violence.

Some media critics contend that blog journalism poses little threat to mainstream journalism because it lacks a business model. In a January 16, 2005, *New York Times* op-ed piece, "The Depressed Press," William Safire wrote:

> 1. *On the challenge from bloggers:* The "platform" — print, TV, Internet, telepathy, whatever — will change, but the public hunger for reliable information will grow. Blogs will compete with op-ed columns for "views you can use," and the best will morph out of the pajama game to deliver serious analysis and fresh information, someday prospering with ads and subscriptions. The prospect of profit will bring bloggers in from the mainstream to the mainstream center of comment and local news coverage.[17]

But what if bloggers are politically funded in ways analogous to antebellum patronage?

Similar to the party press era at the height of honor politics in America, the modern Republican Party appeared in 2004 to have resumed a pattern of awarding patronage to those journalists who best advanced its views. On February 18, 2005, Salon.com reported that journalist Jeff Gannon, aka James D. Guckert, and other seemingly independent bloggers were paid as part of a Republican strategy to discredit then Democratic Senate Minority Leader Tom Daschle during a hotly contested 2004 race for the senate against Republican John Thune. Salon.com reporter Joe Conason wrote:

> Gannon went much further, however, in accusing reporters at the state's most important newspaper, the Sioux Falls *Argus-Leader*, of shilling for Daschle and, worse still, of colluding with the senator in the intimidation of his political adversaries. Such wild attacks were then played back on the Thune-financed Web logs, which attracted substantial attention in the Senate race and influenced coverage in the South Dakota media. As the *National Journal* explained in a post-election analysis, the blog assault "opened a new and potentially powerful front in the war over public opin-

ion." The *National Journal* and local journalists agreed that the blog campaign against Daschle was "crucial." A top *Argus-Leader* editor conceded, "I don't think there's any way to say [the blogs] didn't" affect the paper's coverage.[18]

In addition, it was reported that seemingly independent blog journalists such as University of South Dakota law student Jason Van Beek and Jon Lauck, an associate professor of history at South Dakota State University, were paid thousands of dollars to advance Thune's candidacy. For his part, Gannon was a paid employee of Talon News, which was shown to be closely connected with GOPUSA, a Republican consulting group.[19] Gannon was then further legitimized by being regularly awarded White House press credentials until his connections were exposed.[20]

There is evidence that this pattern of political patronage is spilling over into the mainstream media. In a January 16, 2005, *New York Times* editorial, columnist Frank Rich wrote:

> By my count, "Jeff Gannon" is now at least the sixth "journalist" (four of whom have been unmasked so far this year) to have been a propagandist on the payroll of either the Bush administration or a barely arms-length ally like Talon News while simultaneously appearing in print or broadcast forums that purport to be real news. Of these six, two have been syndicated newspaper columnists paid by the Department of Health and Human Services to promote the administration's "marriage initiatives." The other four have played real newsmen on TV. Before Mr. Guckert and Armstrong Williams, the talking head paid $240,000 by the Department of Education, there were Karen Ryan and Alberto Garcia.[21]

Is this propaganda though? Or are we seeing a cultural shift in press values instigated by blog journalism that more closely mirrors the origins of American journalism? In response to criticism of journalistic bias, Gannon told Howard Kurtz of the *Washington Post*, "Call me partisan, fine, but don't let my colleagues [Washington Press corps] off the hook. They're partisan, too, but they don't admit it."[22]

Some supporters of blog journalism have suggested that the Internet has provided almost a spiritual rebirth of individualism in the American press. At a January 21, 2005, Harvard conference entitled, "Blogging, Journalism and Credibility: Battleground and Common Ground," a panelist and a Berkman fellow Chris Lydon suggested that websites such as Technorati.com, which track blog journalists, will metaphorically replace the *New York Times* as "God's memo on the day."[23] "It is very much to me like the Protestant Reformation, in which people's unmediated relationship to the truth, or Emerson would say, our individual participation in the mysteries of Nature and the divine spirit, have been democratized and opened up. And a lot of the phony claims, and artificial pyramids of authority, have been destroyed."[24] Similarly, a January 17, 2005, *Business Week* article, "The Future of the *New York Times*," suggested that profound changes in communications technology and political climate may have permanently eroded the mainstream media, including the "once–Olympian authority of the *Times*."[25] Quoted in the article was Orville Schell, dean of the University of California's journalism school, in support of this theory. "The Roman Empire that was mass media is breaking up, and we are entering an almost-feudal period where there will be many more centers of power and influence.... It's a kind of disaggregation of the molecular structure of the media," he said.[26]

But is the rise of blog journalism, as it currently exists, a revolution in free speech or reversal of fortune? Since it is not fed by a business model, blog journalists often depend on their reputation in the partisan group as a measure of success, which makes them susceptible to hierarchal social codes in ways similar to the code of honor in the party press era. At the luncheon address of the "Blogging, Journalism and Credibility" conference in 2005, Judith Donath, director of the sociable media group at the Massachusetts Institute of Technology media lab, told the Harvard audience that the assertion of reputation is a key component in the establishment of a blog journalist's credibility in the world of the Internet. According to Donath, blog journalists need to assert their credibility in innate ways similar to the animal kingdom.[27] To illustrate her point, she described an experiment done by an unnamed biologist testing the effect of reputation on the pecking order of sparrows, who garner respect and status by having black badges on their chest.

> He [the biologist] decided to see what would happen to a sparrow if he painted a badge of status on it and so it turned out if you do this for about an hour or so, this sparrow can hang out among all the other sparrows and he will get a lot of respect from them but then someone will probe this signal or peck at him and realize that he is not as strong as he seems and as soon as the sparrows realize that one of their own is wearing a fake badge of status, they will attack it mercilessly until they kill it.[28]

Donath contended that the sparrows responded with violence not because the bird was weak but because they thought it was lying.[29]

In comparison, Donath maintained that the communication structure of blog journalism as it currently exists behaves in a manner similar to the sparrows.[30] A real-world example of this idea might be when Eason Jordon, the chief news executive at CNN, was thought to have slandered

American troops at the 2005 World Economic Forum in Davos, Switzerland. The response by conservative bloggers was so overwhelming that he was forced to resign.[31] It was reported he had said that the U.S. military had purposely aimed at journalists and killed 12 of them. Even though he said that he never meant to imply that U.S. forces acted with ill intent, the suggestion that troops acted less than honorably evoked what the report described as a lynch-mob reaction from cyberspace.[32]

The sparrow analogy is important to keep in mind when factoring in the ramifications of free speech in a highly charged partisan atmosphere as it existed in the party press era and as it has re-emerged in the twenty-first century. After all, the sparrow with the black badge painted on did not create the falsehood but was a victim of someone with a larger organized agenda. There is evidence to suggest that blog journalism is currently struggling with similar issues. According to Joseph Lasica, senior editor of the *Online Journalism Review* at the University of Southern California in a November 1, 2004, article by Sacbee.com, an online division of the *Sacramento Bee*, the line between blog journalism and political rhetoric has become increasingly blurred: "Bloggers have become unofficial arms of the candidates' campaigns.... Just as the official spinmeisters work feverishly to put each candidate's performance in the best possible light, the partisan political bloggers are doing much the same, pointing out misleading statements uttered by the opposing candidate and arguing why their guy won."[33] What early American journalists knew, and what blog journalists are quickly discovering, is that the notion of impartiality in a partisan environment as blog journalism currently exists may be unattainable. According to the article "The Future of the *New York Times*,"

> What a growing, or at least increasingly strident, segment of the population seems to want is not journalism untainted by the personal views of journalists but coverage that affirms their partisan beliefs — in the way that many Fox News (FOX) shows cater to a conservative constituency. For years, major news organizations have been accused of falling short of the ideal of impartiality that they espouse. Now, the very notion of impartiality is under assault, blurring the line between journalism and propaganda.[34]

It would seem, then, that twenty-first-century journalism closely resembles Dicken-Garcia's description of the early nineteenth century press function where technological advances were overshadowed by an individual's "conceptual inability to separate a political from an information role."[35]

There are also signals that indicate that journalistic function, at least for the time being, may be influenced by a political junto mentality sim-

ilar to that of the party press era. In a March 2, 2005, Salon.com article
entitled "Tearing Down the Press," Eric Boehlert wrote:

> The White House and its media allies, echoing a deep-rooted conservative
> antagonism toward the so-called liberal media, say they are simply coun-
> tering its bias. But critics charge that the White House along with partners
> like Fox News and Sinclair Broadcasting, organizations whose allegiance to
> the Republican Party outweighs their commitment to journalism, is actu-
> ally trying to permanently weaken the press. Its motivation, they say, is
> twofold. Weakening the press weakens an institution that's structurally an
> adversary of the White House. And if the press loses its credibility, that
> eliminates agreed-upon facts — the commonly accepted information that is
> central to public debate.[36]

As with the Gannon incident, the conservative media junto is fueled by
blog journalists who are organized by a shared political platform and hyper-
links, which function strikingly similar in practice to nineteenth century
news exchanges, especially during the Jacksonian era. Bob Fertik said in
a 2005 *New York Times* article, "The way we perceive it ... is that that the
right-wing bloggers are able to invent stories, get them out on Drudge,
get them on Rush Limbaugh, get them on Fox, and pretty soon that spills
over into the mainstream media. We, the progressives, we don't have that
kind of network to work with."[37]

Seemingly, within this twenty-first century junto style of journalism
exists a patron-client style of honor and shame that is akin to the party
press era. In this system, as Bertram Wyatt-Brown described in the *Shaping of Southern Honor*, two parties of unequal power, but mutual interest,
agree to do favors for each other. In turn, clients look after their patron's
interests in exchange for things such as political appointments or access to
the patron's wealthy or influential inner circle.[38] This might be one way
to characterize Gannon's ascension into the White House press room. In
the case of the Republican Party, those media outlets that are sympathetic
to their political agenda, such as Fox News, are granted exclusive inter-
views with the president and vice president. In other cases previously mentioned, journalists are rewarded for their support of the administration.

Partisan journalists in this junto mentality must uphold the reputation of their chief patron as a measure of protecting their own status and
influence. Thus, when the patron's reputation is questioned or faces
defamation, it evokes a visceral reaction from its clients, or supporters. For
instance, when Dan Rather claimed he had discovered proof that President George W. Bush received special treatment in the Texas Air National
Guard, conservative bloggers responded with such fury to the defamation

that it was a major contributing factor to his early retirement.[39] Fortunately, reporters are beyond the days in American journalism when charges like that might lead to mortal combat. On the other hand, the new partisan journalism might benefit from a model based on the arbitration that the code of honor once provided in the absence of clear journalistic standards.

A potential subject for future study is whether a comparison between the party press era and blog journalism trends that includes honor ethics reveals certain qualities that are fundamental to a free press in a democracy. In a March 8, 2005, article in the San Francisco *Chronicle*, David Winer, who wrote some of the earliest blog software, commented that he saw no difference between bloggers and journalists. "We're more dependent on the independence of the bloggers than we have ever been, and we're going to be more dependent on the bloggers in the future," he said.[40] What may be emerging in blog journalism, however, is a pattern similar to what Dicken-Garcia described in her book, *Journalistic Standards in Nineteenth-Century America*, where Americans were praising a new individuality in the press while still conforming to a largely partisan model. At the heart of this struggle seems to be what journalists define as independent. "Through the 1830s and following decades, Americans decried the partisan press, enumerated its weaknesses, and increasingly lauded the independent newspaper. But what they called 'independent' papers generally supported particular parties and manifested other political propensities," wrote Dicken-Garcia.[41] So, too, it seems, that emerging blog journalism trends share this same identity crisis.

Journalism's modern role in feeding the culture of honor and shame may go well beyond politics. Pulitzer Prize winning journalist Fox Butterfield suggested in his 1995 book, *All God's Children: The Bosket Family and the American Tradition of Violence*, that modern minority gang violence in some instances may be a transmutation of Southern sensitivity to nineteenth-century honor codes.[42] In describing Willie Bosket, Jr., a violent African-American career criminal in the New York City area whose ancestry could be traced to nineteenth-century South Carolina, Butterfield wrote: "Willie started giggling. He felt like a big-time killer — something he had done had made the front page of the newspaper. He felt no remorse for the killings.... It was more as if he had scored a big victory in the most competitive game of all, violence. Living in a world where violence was essential for survival, Willie treated each encounter like a life-or-death duel, and he had proved to be the best by being the most violent."[43] In his book, Butterfield drew parallels between this type of modern violence and the incorporation of slaves into the social hierarchy of the nineteenth-century South after emancipation. In recounting the Bosket family tradition of violent reactions to insult, Butterfield wrote, "All this violence was not simple pathology. It grew out of the old white Southern code of honor, an extreme sensitivity to insult and the opinion of others. But where antebellum whites believed they were above the law, blacks at the turn of the century realized they were outside the law. The law was in the hands of the white man, the oppressor, and consequently, violence was the only alternative for resolving quarrels."[44]

Just as nineteenth-century males used media to amplify assertions of honor and reputation within their local community, so it would seem that some modern males, especially in gang-related or prison settings, have utilized the press and other modes of mass communication in a similar way within the hierarchy of their own social structures.

In drawing conclusions on the parallels between gang violence and honor rituals, Butterfield focused on the violent traditions of South Carolina. What might be a topic for future historical study is to compare and contrast the sectional perception of black Americans in the nineteenth-century media before and after the Emancipation Proclamation. The idea being that many slaves in the North were incorporated into the social hierarchy of honor rituals via the military. For instance, did slaves earning their citizenry through the military in the North after the Civil War need to affirm honor and reputation in similar ways as the Bosket family? Did they utilize the press or some other mass communication outlet to affirm this honor within the various black and white nineteenth century communities? These are some questions to ponder.

That is not to say, however, that the socio-political influence of South Carolina is not extremely relevant to discussions of modern parallels to nineteenth-century cultural attitudes in the media. As in the nineteenth century, the inherited traditions of the culture of honor in modern times are still fraught with symbolic imagery and ritualized grammatical cues. Take for instance, the flag known historically to Southerners as the canton of the Second National Confederate Flag, commonly referred to today as the "Confederate battle flag," which still flies over the South Carolina statehouse and is routinely spotlighted during presidential elections.[45]

During the 2008 South Carolina Republican presidential primary, the nuanced response of the candidates to the battle flag of the Confederacy illustrates that even nearly a century-and-a-half later, there is still confusion as to exactly what that symbol meant during the Civil War. In a January 18, 2008 *New York Times* article entitled "Confederate Flag Takes

Center Stage Once Again," Michael Cooper highlighted some of the candidates' responses to whether it was offensive to fly the flag over the South Carolina state capitol.[46] Fred Thompson remarked that, "for many Americans, it's a symbol of racism."[47] Arkansas governor and presidential candidate Mike Huckabee took a different angle, implying it was matter of states' rights: "You don't like people from outside the state coming in and telling you what to do with your flag."[48] He continued, "In fact, if somebody came to Arkansas and told us what to do with our flag, we'd tell them what to do with the pole; that's what we'd do."[49] That a symbol could be interpreted as both an emblem of independence and slavery seems almost paradoxical.

Along with Cooper's report, a January 18, 2008, article by Jim Kuhnhenn of the Associated Press, entitled "Confederate Flag Group Praises Huckabee," reported that a group called the American for the Preservation of American Culture (APAC), a federally registered political action committee, actually took out radio ads against campaign frontrunners Massachusetts Governor Mitt Romney and Arizona Senator John McCain for disparaging the symbolism of the Confederate battle flag.[50] The radio ad attacking McCain, which was also available for electronic download via APAC's Web site and Youtube.com, denounced the Republican frontrunners for calling the Confederate flag a symbol of racism:

> Mitt Romney's trying, but when it comes to bashing the Confederate flag he can't hold a candle to John McCain. McCain's been doing it, calling the flag a racist symbol, for years and he's still at it full steam ahead. After McCain, Arkansas Governor Mike Huckabee's stand is a breath of fresh air. Governor Huckabee understands that all the average guy with a Confederate flag on his pick-up truck is saying is: he's proud to be a Southerner. Mike Huckabee understands that we value our heritage and why. He says, "It's up to us to decide how."[51]

The irony with APAC's radio ad was that it could not define the group's position on the Confederate legacy of the Civil War discrete from racism any better than the efforts of the great Richmond editors of the period. For that, we may continue to thank Abraham Lincoln and the honor-laden language of the Emancipation Proclamation, which helped to forever link the evils of slavery to the rebellion of Southern state governments to federal control.

This, of course, becomes a mass communication issue because the general public depends on journalists and other members of the media to interpret and contextualize this symbolism and rhetoric. One could argue, as many Southerners still do, that the North also politically supported both colonization and slavery during the Civil War. Is this a simple case of "to the victor goes the spoils?" In a larger sense, has mainstream media on a visceral level tapped into the Judeo-Christian rhetorical power of honor rituals to categorize the symbolism of the Confederate flag? The idea is that the Union army was victorious in battle, so they were rewarded by providence. The Confederate army lost, so they along with every symbol that represented Southern philosophy, were wrong? This, in a fundamental way, illustrates how the media characterized duelists in the nineteenth century. What about the majority of Southerners who never owned slaves? Vice versa, what about the strong political elements in the North that either advocated slavery or colonization? Were they more correct historically because they happened to be on the side that won the war?

Confederate flag symbolism may seem like a non-issue in the twenty-first century, but keep in mind that symbols of the secession go beyond the South Carolina statehouse issue. States such as Mississippi, Georgia, Alabama, Florida, Texas and South Carolina still to this day include symbols of the secession-era in their state flag. Mississippi, the most obvious, incorporates the actual Confederate battle flag into its design. Georgia incorporated the Confederate battle flag into its state flag design also, but left it out when the flag was redesigned in 2003. Ironically, the current Georgia state flag appears to strongly resemble the original flag of the Confederacy, popularly known as the "stars and bars."[52] Texas incorporates the Bonnie Blue flag into its state banner, which was flown by Confederate soldiers in early Civil War battles.[53] South Carolina still flies the same flag it adopted in January 28, 1861, in response to their secession.[54]

Although the secessionist symbolism in the state flags of Alabama and Florida are vague compared to the flags of the previously named states, its kinship with the legacy of honor rituals may be more telling. Both carry a crimson saltire [cross] and are strongly suggestive of the Confederate battle flag design. In a deeper sense, however, the Alabama and Florida flags are emblematic of St. Patrick's Cross. The crimson saltire was adopted by the Order of St. Patrick, an Irish national order of chivalry, in 1783.[55] This is interesting to note since much of the American dueling protocol was based on the Irish *Code Duello* of 1777. The Confederate battle flag is said to have also been strongly influenced by the Saint Andrews cross, of Scottish origins. The common denominator to all of this symbolism, including the Confederate flag, is medieval Christianity.

Conversations about the Confederate flag seem to speak volumes towards how Americans communicate. One could argue that the stigma of the Confederate flag as racist has more to do with its adoption after the

Civil War by segregationists and extremist Southern hate groups such as the Ku Klux Klan. This, ironically, highlights a communication problem shared by those of both Confederate Southern heritage and Islam. What happens when your symbols get hijacked by extremism? For example, on May 19, 2003, a truck driver of Indian descent named Avtar Singh was shot multiple times in Phoenix because he was wearing a turban, a tradition in his Sikh religion, and mistaken for an Arab. According to the *New York Times* report, the two young white assailants yelled, "Go back to where you belong!" just before they attacked him. [56] Often mistaken for Hinduism or Islam, Sikhism is, of course, its own distinct religion.

The swastika is another modern example of extremists hijacking symbolism. Since World War II, the swastika is probably forever linked in Western culture with the atrocities perpetrated by Adolf Hitler and Nazism. Similar to the Confederate flag, the swastika has been adopted by hate groups as a symbol of hate, racism, anti–Semitism and white supremacy because of its Aryan links. However, the history of swastika is significantly rooted in the mythology of Buddhism, Hinduism and some Native American tribes. According to Indian mythologist Dr. Devdutt Pattanaik, the swastika communicates many different meanings to a variety of cultures: "To the Western eye the swastika is the symbol of Hitler and the Holocaust. To Hindus it is associated with auspiciousness and fertility. No one knows the swastika's origins, but because of the highly influential Nazi discourse on the Aryan race we tend to associate it with ancient Indo-European solar traditions. Hindus believe the word swastika comes from su-asti, which means, 'let good things happen.'"[57] As advances in communications and transportation bring once divided cultures closer together, it seems reasonable that symbolism would become an ever-important communication device when attempting to bridge language barriers.

With the advent of the Internet and its instant communication of words and images to millions of people in hundreds of cultures in a matter of seconds, the implications for twenty-first century journalism seem obvious. From a historical perspective, if we consider that the chief precipitator of the Civil War was an honor dispute between sectional cultures, then maybe we can learn from the communication successes and failures of that event and apply that knowledge to present-day decision making. This not only applies to the Civil War, but the connection between honor rituals and journalism during and before the nineteenth century. For example, when the Danish newspaper *Jyllands-Posten* published a cartoon depicting the Prophet Muhammad wearing a bomb as a turban on September 30, 2005, many Muslims viewed this as defamatory.[58] This in turn provoked assertions of violence from Muslim extremists in which several people died in attacks on Danish embassies across the world.[59]

Kurt Westergaard, the Danish artist who created the inflammatory image, said the origin of the drawing came from his desire to show how fanatical Islamists or terrorists use religion as a kind of spiritual weapon.[60] The problem with this logic is that in his communication process, he did not disassociate extremism discretely from Islam. With the warrior logic of honor rituals, this in turn had a polarizing effect and created exactly the opposite results intended. Wrote Harvard law school fellow Emran Qureshi in a February 12, 2006, *New York Times* op-ed:

> In a world of wrenching change, the Danish cartoon affair has widened a growing fissure between Islam and the West. The controversy comes at a time when many in the Islamic world view the war on terrorism as a war on Islam. They draw on memories of colonization and of the Crusades, when Western invaders ridiculed the Prophet Muhammad as an imposter.
>
> Sadly, the recent polarization obscures a rich humanistic tradition within Islam — one in which cosmopolitanism, pluralism and a spirit of open-minded inquiry once constituted a dominant ethos.[61]

This becomes a mass communication issue because there seemed to be confusion over what exactly the dispute was over. Those supporting the Danish cartoon did so decrying freedom of speech against extremism. By contrast, those who denounced the cartoon felt insulted because it denigrated Islam. Thus, how can there be a resolution without common ground?

As the Muslim culture, deeply rooted in honor rituals, is increasingly introduced to a Western-style concept of free press through the Internet and other communication advances, courts of law have tried to provide this common ground. Some of the main concerns at the 2007 Organization of Islamic Conference were non-violent resolutions to what Muslim leaders perceived as a rise in the defamation of Islam in a free press.[62] They described this phenomenon as Islamophobia. About this conference, *San Jose Mercury News* reporter Rukmini Callimachi wrote in a March 14, 2008, article, *Muslim Nations: Defame Islam, Get Sued?*: "The [Organization of the Islamic conference] report urges the creation of a 'legal instrument to crack down on defamation of Islam. Some delegates point to laws in Europe criminalizing the denial of the Holocaust and other anti–Semitic rhetoric. They also point to articles with various U.N. charters that condemn discrimination based on religion and argue that this should be ramped up."[63] It would seem, then, that a key issue for traditional Muslim communities is how to handle a free press within their highly ritualized social structures. With this being the case, a look into America's dueling past will likely provide some useful insight in drawing parallels. Studies of honor rituals and how they impact a free press system may become increasingly important as democracy is introduced into Islamic countries such as Iraq. Per se, the introduction of a free press system may have dramatic implications as much for editors in Muslim communities, such as Baghdad, as it did in 1840s Vicksburg or when a free press was introduced to some Italian communities in the late nineteenth century during the Risorgimento period.

Theoretically speaking, honor rituals may represent a type of fundamental communication building-block that pre-dates Islam and Christianity itself. Like the nineteenth-century American South, as Wyatt-Brown has pointed out many times, honor rituals permeate the fundamental core of Islamic culture.[64]

> The honor code encompasses a set of sanctions and prescriptions that function most especially in tribal communities but also in many parts of the world, including the U.S. Psychohistorians should consider the violent tendencies inherent in the honor code, which is a set of warrior principles predating Islam and Christianity. When combined with a powerful ideology like Islamic faith, the honor code (which Mohammed like Christ protested) may be explosive. In all international relations, we must keep a skeptical eye on the traditions — ours as well as others' — that honor constructs.[65]

This generally leaves one to wonder to what extent extremism leverages honor rituals as a communication device to manipulate fear and promote negative cultural stereotypes. This again harkens back to Noelle-Neumann's "spiral of silence" theory. Perhaps then we can isolate and diffuse the polarizing "for or against" extremist rhetoric that has led to American human rights atrocities, such as the relocation of Native Americans in the 1830s and more recently the forcible internment of Asian Americans during World War II, not to mention the reoccurrences of genocidal behavior throughout history in places such as Germany, Russia, Armenia, Bosnia and Darfur.

Another possible subject for future historical study is how the introduction of a free press system to Islamic communities compares and contrasts to similar points in time in the past of Western civilization. Although it is highly unlikely that journalists will be compelled to duel in cases of libel, it is not beyond the vocabulary of Iraqis. For instance, in October 2, 2004, Taha Yassin Ramadan, an Iraqi vice president, announced to the world media that Bush and Saddam Hussein should fight a duel as an alternative to war. According to a *New York Times* report, Ramadan suggested that the two meet on neutral territory and the mortal combat could be officiated by United Nations Secretary General Kofi Annan.[66] Just as a duel never materialized between the two men, it would be highly unlikely that the code of honor would rematerialize in the Middle East. What might be more realistic is that many Islamic journalists in a free press system would face situations similar to rencounters in late nineteenth-century America.

There is still much to be learned about how honor rituals have affected, and continue to affect, a free press system in a democracy. "History is both now and then, today and yesterday," said McCullough.[67] As certain patterns in the press re-emerge through time, journalists can use the successes and failures of predecessors as a roadmap for discussions of contemporary issues. One clear example of this is Fischer's astonishing claim in *Albion's Seed* that during the first two centuries of American history, every president except two was descended from one or more of the four original English cultural streams that formed our country.[68] Analyzing how these remnants of English culture affect contemporary American society becomes increasingly significant as today's plethora of media outlets take on characteristics similar to the party press era. Understanding how the cultural forces of honor ethics manifest themselves throughout history will lead journalism researchers to better understand the unquantifiable and often paradoxical forces that drive journalism press values in the present.

Appendix: Accepted Practices Under the Code of Honor

As Faced by Nineteenth Century Journalists

1. **An editor writes his column.**
2. **A person is publicly insulted by the editor's column and seeks satisfaction.**
3. **The person appoints a "friend" or "second" to have custody of his honor and facilitate the affair on his behalf.**
   - The libeled individual should never send a challenge in the first instance, for that precludes all negotiation. The libeled individual should send a note in the language of a gentleman, and let the subject matter be truly and fairly set forth, cautiously avoiding attributing to the adverse party any improper motive.
   - Written communications are entitled to a written reply, and it is the business of the second to require it.
4. **The second calls on the editor with a note from the principal.**
   - If the editor called on by the second, refuses to receive the note he bears, then the second is entitled to demand a reason for such refusal. If he refuses to give any reason, and persists in such refusal without explanation, the second has the right to challenge or post him.
   - If the editor refuses the note based on inequality, then the second is bound by the Code to tender himself in his stead. If

Source: *Code of Honor; or, Rules for the Government of Principals and Seconds* by South Carolina Governor John Lyde Wilson, published in 1858; slightly edited.

the editor also refuses to meet the second, then the second is entitled to post the editor as dishonorable.

5. **When the editor receives the note, etiquette requires that the second try to heal the breach of honor.**
   - The editor must be given an opportunity to explain his conduct and the second must do in all his power to diffuse the situation.

6. **The editor then appoints a second of his own to handle his affairs and deliver his response.**
   - Both seconds should search diligently into the origin of the misunderstanding. When they have discovered the original ground of error, each exchange of notes should work towards restoring harmony.

7. **If reconciliation cannot be agreed upon, the party aggrieved sends a challenge to the editor, which is delivered by the second.**
   - At this point, the editor has no choice but to accept the challenge.

8. **Upon the acceptance of the challenge, the seconds make the necessary arrangements for the duel, in which each party is entitled to a perfect equality.**
   - Traditionally, the editor being the challenged party would be required by protocol to name the time, place, distance and weapon.
   - The usual distance for a pistol duel is from ten to twenty paces, whatever is agreed on. The seconds in measuring the ground usually step three feet to mark off a pace.

9. **After all the arrangements are made, the editor and the aggrieved party will meet on the field of honor.**
   - The parties meeting at the grounds should consist of at least the principals, seconds and one surgeon to each principal.
   - Any number of friends can also be admitted to the grounds if agreed to in advance by the seconds. These friends are expected to abstain from any objectionable words or behavior not befitting a gentleman. Also, they should not stand near the principals or seconds, or hold conversations with them.
   - The seconds will load the agreed-upon weapons in plain view of each other, which traditionally were smooth-bore pistols not exceeding nine inches in length.

10. **The seconds must determine the giving of the word and position.**
    - The decision is made by a coin toss and whoever wins gets their first pick of either position or word, he cannot have both.
    - At all times the principals are to be respectful in the encounter and devoid of any outward emotion.

11. **The duelists take their position and the seconds hand them the loaded pistols.**
    - Once at their position, they are not allowed to leave under any circumstances.
    - The second, in presenting the pistol to his friend, should never put it in his pistol hand, but should place it in the other, which is grasped midway [up] the barrel, with muzzle pointing in the contrary way to that which he is to fire, informing him that his pistol is loaded and ready to use.
    - The second giving the word will demonstrate the manner in which it will be delivered when the parties are at liberty to fire.
    - Before the word is given, the principal grasps the butt firmly in his pistol hand, and brings it round, with the muzzle downward, to the fighting position.
    - The fighting position, is with the muzzle down and the barrel from you; for although it may be agreed that you may hold your pistol with the muzzle up, it may be objected to, as you can fire sooner from that position, and consequently have a decided advantage, which ought not to be claimed, and should not be granted.
    - If one of the principals fires before the word or time agreed on, the adversary's second is at liberty to fire at him.

12. **Shots are exchanged.**
    - If one of the principals [is] hit, then the duel should end as a matter of etiquette.
    - If no one is hit, it is the duty of the second of the challenged to approach the second of the challenger and say: "Our friends have exchanged shots, are you satisfied, or is there any cause why the contest should be continued?" The second of the party challenging should reply: "The point of honor being settled, there can, I conceive, be no objection to a reconciliation, and I propose that our principals meet on middle ground, shake hands and be friends."

- If the insult is considered serious, the aggrieved party can demand another shot from the editor until one or the other principals [is] hit.

13. **Honor is satisfied.**

- Either the editor is vindicated, or the insulted party's reputation is restored. Either way, both men gain esteem in the community for holding their honor and reputation above their lives.

Chapter Notes

Introduction

1. Don C. Seitz, *Famous American Duels* (New York: Thomas Y. Crowell, 1929), 32.

2. "News of the Morning." *New York Daily Tribune*, July 1, 1883, 4.

3. "The Duel Fought at Last." *New York Times*, July 1, 1883, 1.

4. "Appealing to the Code." *New York Times*, June 22, 1883, 1.

5. Ibid.

6. Ibid

7. "An Averted Duel." *New York Herald*, June 23, 1883, 1.

8. "Appealing to the Code." *New York Times*, June 22, 1883, 1.

9. "An Averted Duel." *New York Herald*, June 23, 1883, 1.

10. "Latest Southern Duel." *New York Daily Tribune*, June 26, 1883, 1.

11. "The Duel Fought at Last." *New York Times*, July 1, 1883, 1. The senator was Riddleberger.

12. "Appealing to the Code." *New York Times*, June 22, 1883, 1.

13. "An Averted Duel." *New York Herald*, June 23, 1883, 1.

14. "Latest Southern Duel." *New York Daily Tribune*, June 26, 1883, 1.

15. "An Averted Duel." *New York Herald*, June 23, 1883, 1.

16. "Latest Southern Duel." *New York Daily Tribune*, June 26, 1883, 1.

17. "An Averted Duel." *New York Herald*, June 23,1883, 1.

18. "Searching for Beirne and Elam" *New York Daily Tribune*, June 24, 1883, 1.

19. "Latest Southern Duel." *New York Daily Tribune*, June 26, 1883, 1.

20. "That Duel." *New York Daily Tribune*, June 27, 1883, 4.

21. "Duellists Still Apart." *New York Times*, June 26, 1883, 1.

22. "Bloodthirsty Babies." *New York Times*, June 24, 1883, 4.

23. "Duellists Still Apart." *New York Times*, June 26, 1883, 1; and "No Duel Fought Yet." *New York Times*, June 25, 1883, 1.

24. "The Richmond Duelists." *New York Times*, June 28, 1883, 4.

25. Ibid.

26. "The Impending Fight." *New York Herald*, June 26, 1883, 1.

27. "The Duel Fought at Last." *New York Times*, July 1, 1883, 1.

28. "The Impending Fight" *New York Herald*, June 26, 1883, 1.

29. "The Beirne-Elam Affair." *New York Daily Tribune*, June 25, 1883, 1.

30. "That Duel." *New York Daily Tribune*, June 27, 1883, 4.

31. "The Richmond Duelists." *New York Times*, June 28, 1883, 1.

32. "Beirne Wounds Elam." *New York Daily Tribune*, July 1, 1883, 1.

33. "The Duel Fought at Last." *New York Times*, July 1, 1883, 1.

34. "The Field of Honor." *New York Herald*, July 1, 1883, 1.

35. "The Duel Fought at Last." *New York Times*, July 1, 1883, 1.

36. "The Field of Honor." *New York Herald*, July 1, 1883, 1.

37. "The Duel Fought at Last." *New York Times*, July 1, 1883, 1.

38. "Beirne Wounds Elam." *New York Daily Tribune*, July 1, 1883, 1.

39. "The Duel Fought at Last." *New York Times*, July 1, 1883, 1.

40. In the account given in "The Duel Fought at Last," *New York Times*, July 1, 1883, 1, the command was cited as "One, two, three,

fire." However, the *Tribune's* account seems more logical and is explained in greater detail.

41. "The Duel Fought at Last." *New York Times,* July 1, 1883, 1.

42. "Beirne Wounds Elam." *New York Daily Tribune,* July 1, 1883, 1.

43. Ibid.

44. "The Duel Fought at Last." *New York Times,* July 1, 1883, 1.

45. "Beirne Wounds Elam." *New York Daily Tribune,* July 1, 1883, 1.

46. "The Duel Fought at Last." *New York Times,* July 1, 1883, 1.

47. "Beirne Wounds Elam." *New York Daily Tribune,* July 1, 1883, 1.

48. "The Duel Fought at Last." *New York Times,* July 1, 1883, 1.

49. "Beirne Wounds Elam." *New York Daily Tribune,* July 1, 1883, 1.

50. Ibid.

51. "Beirne's Driver Arrested as Witness." *New York Daily Tribune,* July 1, 1883, 1.

52. "News this Morning." *New York Daily Tribune,* July 1, 1883, 1.

53. "Mr. Elam's Condition Critical." *New York Times,* July 3, 1883, 1.

54. "Elam's Wound Very Serious." *New York Daily Tribune,* July 3, 1883, 1.

55. "A Possible Consequence of the Duel." *New York Daily Tribune,* July 2, 1883, 1.

56. "The Fighting Editors." *New York Times,* July 2, 1883, 1.

57. Ibid.

58. Hazel Dicken-Garcia, *Journalistic Standards in the Nineteenth-Century America* (Madison: University of Wisconsin Press, 1989).

59. Frank L. Mott, *American Journalism: A History 1690–1960* (New York: Macmillan, 1962).

60. Lambert A. Wilmer, *Our Press Gang; or, A Complete Exposition of the Corruptions and Crimes of the American Newspapers* (Philadelphia: J.T. Lloyd; London, S. Low, Son and Co., 1859).

61. Joanne B. Freeman, *Affairs of Honor: National Politics in the New Republic* (New Haven: Yale University Press, 2001).

62. Bertram Wyatt-Brown, *The Shaping of Southern Culture: Honor, Grace, and War, 1760s–1880s* (Chapel Hill: University of North Carolina Press, 2001).

63. Bertram Wyatt-Brown, *Southern Honor: Ethics and Behavior in the Old South* (New York: Oxford University Press, 1982).

64. C.A. Harwell Wells, "The End of the Affair? Anti-Dueling Laws and Social Norms in Antebellum America," *Vanderbilt Law Review* 54 (2001): 1813–1846.

65. Patricia L. Dooley, *Taking Their Political Place: Journalists and the Making of an Occupation* (Westport, Conn.: Greenwood Press, 1997).

66. Allan Nevins, *The Evening Post* (New York: Boni and Liveright, 1922), 51.

Chapter 1

1. Benjamin Franklin, "The Autobiography," in *The Norton Anthology of American Literature,* 4th ed. Vol. 1, ed. Nina Baym et al. (New York and London: W.W. Norton, 1994), 550. Capitalizations are original text.

2. Jeffrey L. Pasley, *"The Tyranny of Printers": Newspaper Politics in the Early American Republic* (Charlottesville and London: University Press of Virginia, 2001), 152. Basche was grandson of Benjamin Franklin.

3. Ibid., 190–191.

4. David Hackett Fischer, *Albion's Seed: Four British Folkways in America* (New York: Oxford University Press, 1989), 412.

5. Ibid., 396–397.

6. Ibid., 785–788.

7. Ibid., 383. In this specific instance, Fischer is referring to America in the seventeenth century. However, he does suggest that these examples of social orders were carried into the late eighteenth century.

8. Bertram Wyatt-Brown, *Southern Honor: Ethics and Behavior in the Old South* (New York: Oxford University Press, 1982), 19.

9. Pasley, *"The Tyranny of Printers": Newspaper Politics in the Early American Republic,* 285.

10. Ibid., 106.

11. Ibid., 296.

12. Ibid., 137.

13. Ibid., 156.

14. Ibid., 104.

15. *Merriam-Webster's Collegiate Dictionary,* 11th rev. ed., 2003, s.v. "duel."

16. Bertram Wyatt-Brown, *The Shaping of Southern Culture: Honor, Grace, and War, 1760s–1880s* (Chapel Hill and London: University of North Carolina Press, 2001), 61–65.

17. Hazel Dicken-Garcia, *Journalistic Standards in the Nineteenth-Century America* (Madison: University of Wisconsin Press, 1989), 71.

18. Bertram Wyatt-Brown, *The Shaping of Southern Culture: Honor Grace, and War, 1760s–1880s,* 62.

19. Bertram Wyatt-Brown, *Southern Honor: Ethics and Behavior in the Old South* (New York: Oxford University Press, 1982), 351.

20. Robert Baldick, *The Duel: A History of Dueling* (London, New York: Spring, 1965), 11–12.

21. Ibid., 22.

22. Barbara Holland, "Bang! Bang! You're Dead," *Smithsonian Magazine,* October 1997, 3.

23. Ibid.

24. Hamilton Cochran, *Noted American Duels and Hostile Encounters* (Philadelphia and New York: Chilton Books, 1963), 5.

25. Baldick, *The Duel: A History of Dueling,* 33.

26. Cochran, *Noted American Duels and Hostile Encounters,* 16.

27. Holland, "Bang! Bang! You're Dead," 4.

28. Baldick, *The Duel: A History of Dueling,* 33.

29. Ibid.

30. According to Baldick's *The Duel: A History of Dueling,* in European countries the choice of weapons was determined by the challenger, which differed from American tradition, 39.

31. Ibid., 38–40.

32. Cochran, *Noted American Duels and Hostile Encounters,* 17.

33. According to Baldick in *The Duel: A History of Dueling,* stance was important at this point. The principal would often stand sideways with feet close together, with his right hand aiming the pistol over his left arm shielding his body or vice versa, 47.

34. Cochran, *Noted American Duels and Hostile Encounters,* 17–18.

35. Joanne B. Freeman, *Affairs of Honor: National Politics in the New Republic* (New Haven: Yale University Press, 2001), 167.

36. Cochran, *Noted American Duels and Hostile Encounters,* 37–40.

37. Virginius Dabney, *Pistols and Pointed Pens* (Chapel Hill, N.C.: Algonquin, 1987), xvi.

38. Dicken-Garcia, *Journalistic Standards in the Nineteenth-Century America,* 36.

39. Frank L. Mott, *American Journalism: A History 1690–1960* (New York: Macmillan, 1962), 113–115.

40. Wm. David Sloan, James G. Stovall, editors; James D. Startt, associate ed., *The Media in America: A History* (Worthington, Ohio: Publishing Horizons, 1989), 69.

41. Dicken-Garcia, *Journalistic Standards in the Nineteenth-Century America,* 36.

42. Mott, *American Journalism: A History 1690–1960,* 113–115.

43. Dicken-Garcia, *Journalistic Standards in the Nineteenth-Century America,* 33.

44. According to Sloane et al., in *The Media in America: A History,* 67, newspapers rarely sold individual copies and instead charged yearly subscription rates, making it very pricey for the average American.

45. Mott, *American Journalism: A History 1690–1960,* 115.

46. Ibid., 153.

47. Dicken-Garcia, *Journalistic Standards in the Nineteenth-Century America,* 80.

48. "Williamsburg (Virginia)," *Pennsylvania Packet,* July 1, 1777.

49. Cochran, *Noted American Duels and Hostile Encounters,* 102–103.

50. Dicken-Garcia, *Journalistic Standards in the Nineteenth-Century America,* 36.

51. Sloane, *The Media in America: A History,* 64.

52. Dicken-Garcia, *Journalistic Standards in the Nineteenth-Century America,* 21–25.

53. Ibid., 58.

54. Ibid., 39.

55. Ibid., 34.

56. Ibid.

57. Ibid.

58. Michael Emery and Edwin Emery, *The Press and America: An Interpretive History of the Mass Media* (Englewood Cliffs, N.J.: Prentice Hall, 1992), 61. According to Emery and Emery, there were two groups struggling for power in the early development of American politics: those who believed in a strong central government, the Federalists, and Anti-Federalists, who favored more of a confederacy. The Republican party identity did not solidify until the rise of Jefferson's presidency.

59. Mott, *American Journalism: A History 1690–1960,* 147.

60. Dicken-Garcia, *Journalistic Standards in the Nineteenth-Century America,* 34.

61. Virginius Dabney, *Pistols and Pointed Pens* (Chapel Hill, N.C.: Algonquin, 1987), xvi.

62. Pasley, *"The Tyranny of Printers": Newspaper Politics in the Early American Republic,* 275.

63. Ibid., 276.

64. Ibid., 283.

65. Ibid., 284.

66. William Peter Van Ness, *The Speeches at full length of Mr. Van Ness, Mr. Caines, the Attorney-General [Ambrose Spencer], Mr. Harrison, and General Hamilton, in the great cause of the people, against Harry Croswell, on an indictment for a libel on Thomas Jefferson, President of the United States* (New York: G. & R. Waite, 1804), 47.

67. Ibid., 77.

68. Ibid., 73.

69. Freeman, *Affairs of Honor: National Politics in the New Republic,* the chapter "Art of Paper War," 105–158.

70. the Twelfth Amendment fixed this problem.

71. John Tebbel, *Compact History of the American Newspaper* (New York: Hawthorn Books, 1963), 71–72. Fleming, *Duel: Alexander Hamilton, Aaron Burr and the Future of America,* 367.

72. Mott, *American Journalism: A History 1690–1960,* 114.

73. Sloane, 71. There were, however, minor partisan papers in existence before the arrival of the *GUS.*

74. Jean Folkerts and Dwight L. Teeter, Jr., *Voices of A Nation: A History of Media in the United States* (New York: Macmillan, 1989), 81.

75. Sloane, *The Media in America: A History,* 72.

76. Folkerts, 101. The weekly edition was known as the *Herald.*

77. Sloane, *The Media in America: A History,* 74.

78. Mott, *American Journalism: A History 1690–1960,* 185.

79. "By Yesterday's Mails." *Columbian Centinel,* September 24, 1800.

80. Dicken-Garcia, *Journalistic Standards in the Nineteenth-Century America,* 109.

81. Meaning the protocol leading up to the duel.

82. "Extract of a letter...," *New York Evening Post,* September 21, 1802. Italicized in the original.

83. "Washington City," *National Intelligencer,* September 22, 1802.

84. "From the *Raleigh Register,*" *National Intelligencer,* September 24, 1804.

85. See "Monday, September 27," *New York Evening Post,* September 27, 1804; "From the Newbern Gazette of Sept. 10," *American Citizen,* September 27, 1804; and "By the Last Mails," *Columbian Centinel,* October 2, 1804.

86. "From the Newbern Gazette of Sept. 10," *American Citizen,* September 27, 1804.

87. Dicken-Garcia, *Journalistic Standards in the Nineteenth-Century America,* 81.

88. Ibid., 37.

89. Bertram Wyatt-Brown, *The Shaping of Southern Culture: Honor Grace, and War, 1760s–1880s,* 62.

90. Freeman, *Affairs of Honor: National Politics in the New Republic,* 167.

91. Ibid., 189.

92. Thomas Fleming, *Duel: Alexander Hamilton, Aaron Burr and the Future of America* (New York: Basic Books, 1999), 14–15.

However, Freeman, in *Affairs of Honor: National Politics in the New Republic,* suggests that the Reynolds' love letters were coded messages discussing the insider speculation and suggests that many political insiders, including Thomas Jefferson, suspected that at the time but could not prove it. See pages 70–71.

93. Fleming, *Duel: Alexander Hamilton, Aaron Burr and the Future of America,* 21.

94. Ibid., 231–232.

95. Freeman, *Affairs of Honor: National Politics in the New Republic,* 187–188.

96. Ron Chernow, *Alexander Hamilton* (New York: Penguin Press, 2004), 684.

97. Ibid., 668.

98. Ibid.

99. Ibid., 669.

100. Ibid.

101. Dicken-Garcia, *Journalistic Standards in the Nineteenth-Century America,* 115.

102. "New-York Evening Post," *New York Evening Post,* July 12, 1804.

103. Dicken-Garcia, *Journalistic Standards in the Nineteenth-Century America,* 226.

104. "New-York Evening Post," *New York Evening Post,* August 20, 1804.

105. "New-York Evening Post," *New York Evening Post,* July 24, 1804.

106. Freeman, *Affairs of Honor: National Politics in the New Republic,* 123. Newspapers were the most effective and far-reaching propaganda tools for American political parties. This fact, coupled with news exchanges and the *Evening Post*'s influence, made Coleman's month-long campaign against Burr politically devastating.

107. Dicken-Garcia, *Journalistic Standards in the Nineteenth-Century America,* 117.

108. Chernow, *Alexander Hamilton,* 684.

109. Dicken-Garcia, *Journalistic Standards in the Nineteenth-Century America,* 80–82.

110. Freeman, *Affairs of Honor: National Politics in the New Republic,* 184.

111. Ibid., 184.

112. Mott, *American Journalism: A History 1690–1960,* 186.

113. Freeman, *Affairs of Honor: National Politics in the New Republic,* 183.

114. Chernow, *Alexander Hamilton,* 673.

115. Ibid., 677.

116. Fleming, *Duel: Alexander Hamilton, Aaron Burr and the Future of America,* 189–190.

117. Ibid., 209–210.

118. "General Hamilton's Death," *American Citizen,* July 23, 1804. Italicized in the original.

119. Freeman, *Affairs of Honor: National Politics in the New Republic,* 248–249.

120. Ibid., 185.
121. Ibid., 177–178.
122. Ibid.
123. "Washington City," *National Intelligencer*, March 14, 1808.
124. "By the Mails," *Columbian Centinel*, March 2, 1808.
125. "Extract of a Letter From Our Correspondent," *New York Evening Post*, March 7, 1808; and "The Duel," *Columbian Centinel*, March 12, 1808.
126. "The Duel," *Columbian Centinel*, March 12, 1808.
127. "Washington City," *National Intelligencer*, March 14, 1808.
128. "New York City," *American Citizen*, March 8, 1808.
129. "Communication," *Richmond Enquirer*, March 8.
130. Freeman, *Affairs of Honor: National Politics in the New Republic*, 184.
131. Ibid., 192–193.
132. Ibid., 193.
133. Fleming, *Duel: Alexander Hamilton, Aaron Burr and the Future of America*, 367.
134. For instance, a dramatic image of Hamilton's coffin was also printed in *Columbian Centinel*, July 18, 1804.
135. Mott, *American Journalism: A History 1690–1960*, 160.
136. Ibid., 159.
137. Ibid., 196–197.
138. "New Orleans, March 4," *New York Evening Post*, March 29, 1808.
139. "It is with deep regret...," *Richmond Enquirer*, April 15, 1808.
140. The duel was not significantly reported upon in the *National Intelligencer*, *American Citizen*, or *Columbian Centinel* in the months of March, April or May of 1808.
141. Freeman, *Affairs of Honor: National Politics in the New Republic*, 145.
142. Mott, *American Journalism: A History 1690–1960*, 161.
143. Dicken-Garcia, *Journalistic Standards in the Nineteenth-Century America*, 117.
144. "A Letter from Washington says...," *New York Evening Post*, February 12, 1819.
145. "The Late Savage Duel," *Columbian Centinel*, February 24, 1819. The italics are in the original.
146. Ibid.
147. "Melancholy Event," *Richmond Enquirer*, February 11, 1819.
148. "The Late Savage Duel," *Columbian Centinel*, February 24, 1819.
149. "Melancholy Event," *Richmond Enquirer*, February 11, 1819.

150. "The Late Savage Duel," *Columbian Centinel*, February 24, 1819.
151. By the 1850s, Americans would become so desensitized to ritualized violence that dueling only became a useful political tool if the opposition died. For an example, see "The Affairs of Edward Gilbert.— Correspondence," *Weekly Alta California*, August 21, 1852.
152. Mott, *American Journalism: A History 1690–1960*, 256–257.
153. Dicken-Garcia, *Journalistic Standards in the Nineteenth-Century America*, 35.
154. Ibid., 31.
155. Ibid., 30.
156. Ibid.
157. Fleming, *Duel: Alexander Hamilton, Aaron Burr and the Future of America*, 19.
158. Freeman, *Affairs of Honor: National Politics in the New Republic*, 184.

Chapter 2

1. William Oliver Stevens, *Pistol at Ten Paces* (Boston: Houghton Mifflin, 1940), 73.
2. Frank L. Mott, *American Journalism: A History 1690–1960* (New York: Macmillan, 1962), 255–257.
3. Ibid., 215–216.
4. Hazel Dicken-Garcia, *Journalistic Standards in the Nineteenth-Century America* (Madison: University of Wisconsin Press, 1989), 44–45.
5. Ibid., 41.
6. Bertram Wyatt-Brown, *The Shaping of Southern Culture: Honor, Grace, and War, 1760s–1880s* (Chapel Hill and London: University of North Carolina Press, 2001), 58.
7. William David Sloan, James G. Stovall, eds.; James D. Startt, associate ed., *The Media in America: A History* (Worthington, Ohio: Publishing Horizons, 1989), 81.
8. Mott, *American Journalism: A History 1690–1960*, 256.
9. "Tennessee," *Richmond Enquirer*, July 1, 1806.
10. "Nashville, June 7," *New York Evening Post*, July 7, 1806.
11. "Nashville, May 24, 1806," *American Citizen*, July 14, 1806.
12. James Webb, "Pistols for Two: Coffee for One," *American Heritage*, February 1975, 71.
13. Ibid., 78.
14. Robert V. Remini, *Andrew Jackson and the Course of American Freedom: 1822–1832* (Baltimore and London: Johns Hopkins University Press, 1981), 1–2. Remini wrote: "The second bullet lodged against his bone in

the heavy muscle of the left arm just below the shoulder. During a gunfight on September 4, 1813, with Thomas Hart Benton [who would later reconcile his differences with Jackson] and his brother Jesse, Jackson was shot twice by Jesse: once in the left shoulder and once in the left arm. Over the next six months bits of bone were expelled from the arm, and Jackson sent them to his wife as 'souvenirs.' It was a long time before he could even slip his arm into the sleeve of his jacket, but the inflammation never totally subsided, and osteomyelitis set in."

15. Wyatt-Brown, *The Shaping of Southern Culture: Honor, Grace, and War, 1760s–1880s*, 75.

16. Ibid.

17. Sloan, Stovall and Startt, *The Media in America: A History*, 79–81.

18. Remini, *Andrew Jackson and the Course of American Freedom: 1822–1832*, 51–53.

19. Burstein, *The Passions of Andrew Jackson*, 131–133.

20. Ibid., 145.

21. Ibid., 127.

22. Mott, *American Journalism: A History 1690–1960*, 253–254. See also Sloan, Stovall and Startt, *The Media in America: A History*, 79.

23. Dicken-Garcia, *Journalistic Standards in the Nineteenth-Century America*, 36.

24. Remini, *Andrew Jackson and the Course of American Freedom: 1822–1832*, 79–81.

25. Wyatt-Brown, *The Shaping of Southern Culture: Honor, Grace, and War, 1760s–1880s*, 69–70.

26. "Denouement," *Richmond Enquirer*, February 12, 1825.

27. "Washington, Jan. 25, 1825," *Vermont Gazette*, February 15, 1825.

28. Ibid.

29. Ibid.

30. Joanne B. Freeman, *Affairs of Honor: National Politics in the New Republic* (New Haven, Conn.: Yale University Press, 2001), 122–126.

31. "Connecticut Courant," *Connecticut Courant*, February 15, 1825.

32. "Washington, Jan. 25, 1825," *Vermont Gazette*, February 15, 1825.

33. Ibid.

34. "Scenes of the Senate," *Vermont Gazette*, May 9, 1825.

35. Wyatt-Brown, *The Shaping of Southern Culture: Honor, Grace, and War, 1760s–1880s*, 69.

36. "Scenes of the Senate," *Vermont Gazette*, May 9, 1825.

37. Mott, *American Journalism: A History 1690–1960*, 179–180.

38. "Extract of a letter from Washington, April 11," *Richmond Enquirer*, April 18, 1826.

39. Ibid.

40. Hair triggers wreaked havoc on inexperienced duelists. According to William Oliver Stevens in the book *Pistol at Ten Paces*, "With the flintlock type and its priming pan, the pistol was usually carried at half-cock to prevent accidental blows causing a spark." Even though they were sometimes precarious, the hair trigger might give a slight advantage to the person with the quicker reflexes. Also because the hair trigger went off so easily, the gun was likely to fire even if the duelist was himself shot. See Stevens, *Pistols at Ten Paces*, 136–137.

41. "The Duel," *Richmond Enquirer*, April 14, 1826.

42. Ibid.

43. Ibid.

44. Ibid.

45. Ibid.

46. Ibid.

47. Wyatt-Brown, *The Shaping of Southern Culture: Honor, Grace, and War*, 1760s–1880s, 69.

48. Dicken-Garcia, *Journalistic Standards in the Nineteenth-Century America*, 223.

49. Bertram Wyatt-Brown, *Southern Honor: Ethics and Behavior in the Old South* (New York: Oxford University Press, 1982), 19.

50. Ibid.

51. Ibid.

52. C.A. Harwell Wells, "The End of the Affair? Anti-Dueling Laws and Social Norms in Antebellum America," *Vanderbilt Law Review* 54 (2001): 1823.

53. Bertram Wyatt-Brown, *Southern Honor: Ethics and Behavior in the Old South* (New York: Oxford University Press, 1982), 20.

54. Wyatt-Brown, *The Shaping of Southern Culture: Honor, Grace, and War, 1760s–1880s*, 63.

55. Mott, *American Journalism: A History 1690–1960*, 179.

56. Ibid.

57. Dicken-Garcia, *Journalistic Standards in the Nineteenth-Century America*, 36.

58. Mott, *American Journalism: A History 1690–1960*, 70.

59. Ibid.

60. Wyatt-Brown, *Southern Honor: Ethics and Behavior in the Old South*, 350.

61. Ibid., 14.

62. Ibid, 15

63. Dicken-Garcia, *Journalistic Standards in the Nineteenth-Century America*, 109.

64. Wyatt-Brown, *Southern Honor: Ethics and Behavior in the Old South*, 64.

65. Mott, *American Journalism: A History 1690–1960*, 255.

66. Ibid., 179.

67. Sloan, Stovall and Startt, *The Media in America: A History*, 84.

68. Mott, *American Journalism: A History 1690–1960*, 254.

69. Ibid., 20.

70. Wells, "The End of the Affair? Anti-Dueling Laws and Social Norms in Antebellum America," 1807.

71. Mott, *American Journalism: A History 1690–1960*, 354.

72. "A Duel," *Richmond Enquirer*, November 23, 1827.

73. Ibid.

74. "We grieve to learn that Henry W. Conway...," *Richmond Enquirer*, December 6, 1827.

75. Dicken-Garcia, *Journalistic Standards in the Nineteenth-Century America*, 107.

76. Ibid., 40.

77. Ibid., 103.

78. Ibid., 106.

79. Remini, *Andrew Jackson and the Course of American Freedom: 1822–1832*, 292.

80. Ibid.

81. Ibid., 299.

82. Harry L. Sloan, *Liberty of Power: The Politics of Jacksonian American* (New York: Hill and Wang, 2001), 174.

83. Sloan, Stovall and Startt, *The Media in America: A History*, 82.

84. Ibid.

85. Remini, *Andrew Jackson and the Course of American Freedom: 1822–1832*, 303–304.

86. Dicken-Garcia, *Journalistic Standards in the Nineteenth-Century America*, 167.

87. Lambert A. Wilmer, *Our Press Gang* (Philadelphia: J.T. Lloyd; London: S. Low, Son and Co., 1859), 297.

88. "From the St. Louis Beacon," *Richmond Enquirer*, September 23, 1831.

89. "From the St. Louis Beacon of August 27," *Richmond Enquirer*, September 13, 1831. Italicized in the original.

90. Dick Steward, *Duels and the Roots of Violence in Missouri* (Columbia and London: University of Missouri Press, 2000), 4.

91. See "From the St. Louis Beacon," *Washington Globe*, September 16, 1831, and "From the St. Louis Beacon," *Richmond Enquirer*, September 23, 1831.

92. Ibid.

93. "Monument to Mr. Pettis," *United States Telegraph*, September 10, 1831.

94. Wyatt-Brown, *The Shaping of Southern Culture: Honor, Grace, and War, 1760s–1880s*, 67.

95. Steward, *Duels and the Roots of Violence in Missouri*, 9.

96. Cochran, *Noted American Duels and Hostile Encounters*, 19.

97. Wells, "The End of the Affair? Anti-Dueling Laws and Social Norms in Antebellum America," 1827–1828.

98. Cochran, *Noted American Duels and Hostile Encounters*, 11.

99. Wyatt-Brown, *The Shaping of Southern Culture: Honor, Grace, and War, 1760s–1880s*, 65.

100. Ibid., 64.

101. Freeman, *Affairs of Honor: National Politics in the New Republic*, 187.

102. "House of Representatives: Monday, Feb. 12, 1838," *Congressional Globe*, February 19, 1838.

103. Ibid.

104. Ibid.

105. Ibid.

106. "From the New York American: The Late Duel at Washington," *Springfield* (Mass.) *Republican*, March 24, 1838.

107. Ibid.

108. "House of Representatives," *Washington Globe*, February 26, 1838. Italics are in the original.

109. Ibid.

110. Ibid.

111. Ibid.

112. Ibid.

113. "From the New York American: The Late Duel at Washington," *Springfield* (Mass.) *Republican*, March 24, 1838.

114. Ibid.

115. "House of Representatives," *Washington Globe*, February 26, 1838.

116. "From the New York American: The Late Duel at Washington," *Springfield* (Mass.) *Republican*, March 24, 1838.

117. Ibid.

118. "House of Representatives," *Washington Globe*, February 26, 1838.

119. Ibid.

120. Ibid.

121. Ibid.

122. Ibid.

123. Ibid.

124. "The Late Fashionable Murder —," *Springfield* (Mass.) *Republican*, March 3, 1838.

125. C.A. Harwell Wells, "The End of the Affair? Anti-Dueling Laws and Social Norms in Antebellum America," 1806.

126. "Congress," *Springfield* (Mass.) *Republican*, March 10, 1838.

127. Ibid.

128. "The Disastrous Duel," *Richmond Enquirer*, March 3, 1838. Italicized in the original.

129. "The Late Duel," *Congressional Globe*, July 9, 1838.
130. "Congress," *Springfield* (Mass.) *Republican*, March 10, 1838.
131. C.A. Harwell Wells, "The End of the Affair? Anti-Dueling Laws and Social Norms in Antebellum America," 1830.
132. Ibid., 1829.
133. Dicken-Garcia, *Journalistic Standards in the Nineteenth-Century America*, 134.
134. Ibid.
135. "The Cilley Duel," *Brooklyn Eagle*, April 27, 1843.
136. "Tract No. 1." *Brooklyn Eagle*, March 15, 1844.
137. "Mr. Clay on Duelling," *Brooklyn Eagle*, August 26, 1844. Italicized in the original.
138. Ibid.
139. Ibid.
140. Ibid.
141. C.A. Harwell Wells, "The End of the Affair? Anti-Dueling Laws and Social Norms in Antebellum America," 1824.
142. Elbert B. Smith, *Francis Preston Blair* (New York: The Free Press, 1980), 167.
143. Steward, *Duels and the Roots of Violence in Missouri*, 79.
144. Dicken-Garcia, *Journalistic Standards in the Nineteenth-Century America*, 46.
145. Ibid.

Chapter 3

1. "The Affairs of Edward Gilbert.— Correspondence," *Weekly Alta California*, August 21, 1852.
2. Ibid.
3. Ibid.
4. Ibid.
5. Ibid.
6. Ibid.
7. Ibid.
8. This theory is justified in the fact that Denver wasted his first shot to keep from killing Gilbert. See George C. Barnes, *Denver, the Man: The Life, Letters and Public Papers of the Lawyer, Soldier and Statesman* (Strasburg, Va.: Shenandoah Publishing House, 1949), 58.
9. Ibid., 58.
10. Ibid., 46–5
11. Ibid.
12. Barnes writes, "Thus, on entering state politics, General Denver found himself lined up with the faction know as the Bigler Democrats, and opposed, for the most part by Broderick and his friends. This alignment continued for some years, the General entering the Senate as a Bigler Democrat and continuing as such until he was appointed Secretary of State, Bigler, and thereafter until the election in November, 1854, when he ran for Congress, and was opposed by his former friend, the Governor." See Barnes, *Denver, the Man*, 63.
13. Dick Steward, *Duels and the Roots of Violence in Missouri* (Colombia and London: University of Missouri Press, 2000), 145.
14. Affairs of Edward Gilbert.— Correspondence," *Weekly Alta California*, August 21, 1852.
15. Barnes, *Denver, the Man*, 58.
16. Ibid., 57–59.
17. Ibid., 44.
18. Ibid.
19. Ibid., 58.
20. Wyatt-Brown, *The Shaping of Southern Culture: Honor, Grace, and War, 1760s–1880s*, 62–71.
21. Barnes, *Denver, the Man*, 61.
22. Wells, "The End of the Affair? Anti-Dueling Laws and Social Norms in Antebellum America," 1807.
23. Barnes, *Denver, the Man*, 61.
24. "Duelling in California," *Brooklyn Eagle*, July 12, 1853.
25. According to Quinn, Gwin was the personal secretary of Andrew Jackson in 1831 and received generous patronage from him in subsequent years. See Quinn, *The Rivals: William Gwin, David Broderick, and the Birth of California*, 13.
26. Ibid.
27. Quinn, *The Rivals: William Gwin, David Broderick, and the Birth of California*, 148.
28. "Duelling in California," *Brooklyn Eagle*, July 12, 1853.
29. Ibid.
30. Ibid.
31. Ibid.
32. "The News by the Illinois," *New York Times*, July 12, 1853.
33. Ibid.
34. "Important News from California," *New York Times*, October 10, 1859.
35. Ibid.
36. Ibid.
37. Ibid.
38. Quinn, *The Rivals: William Gwin, David Broderick, and the Birth of California*, 256.
39. "Important News from California," *New York Times*, October 10, 1859.
40. "The California Duel." *New York Times*, October 13, 1859.
41. Ibid.
42. Ibid.

43. Ibid.

44. Ibid.

45. David A. Williams, *David C. Broderick: A Political Portrait* (San Marino, Calif.: Huntington Library, 1969), 240.

46. An October 17 account of the duel in the *New York Evening Post* was reprinted eight days later in the *Richmond Enquirer*. See "From the N.Y. Evening Post, Oct. 17," *Richmond Enquirer*, October 25, 1859. To further illustrate, an October 10 editorial regarding the duel in the *New York Herald* was reprinted ten days later in the *Augusta* (Ga.) *Chronicle*. See "American Politics — A Sad Picture," *Augusta Chronicle*, October 20, 1859.

47. "The Political Aspects of Killing Broderick," *New York Times*, October 13, 1859.

48. Quinn, *The Rivals: William Gwin, David Broderick, and the Birth of California*, 237–238.

49. "Political Murder." *New York Times*, October 10, 1859.

50. Ibid.

51. Williams, *David C. Broderick: A Political Portrait*, 249.

52. "Mr. Buchanan and Fortnet," excerpt from *Philadelphia Press* reprinted in *Augusta* (Ga.) *Chronicle & Sentinel*, October 16, 1859.

53. Ibid.

54. Ibid.

55. Wells, "The End of the Affair? Anti-Dueling Laws and Social Norms in Antebellum America," 183.

56. "American Politics — A Sad Picture." *Augusta* (Ga.) *Chronicle*, October 20, 1859.

Chapter 4

1. Patricia L. Dooley, *Taking Their Political Place: Journalists and the Making of an Occupation* (Westport, Conn.: Greenwood Press, 1997), 93.

2. Ibid.

3. Ibid., 93–108.

4. Allan Nevins, *The Evening Post: A Century of Journalism* (New York: Boni and Liveright, 1922), 51.

5. Ibid., 51.

6. Lambert A. Wilmer, *Our Press Gang* (Philadelphia: J.T. Lloyd; London: S. Low, Son and Co., 1859), 295.

7. Nevins, *The Evening Post*, 47.

8. Ibid., 48.

9. Ibid.

10. Ibid.

11. Ibid.

12. Wilmer, *Our Press Gang*, 294.

13. Ibid.

14. Nevins, *The Evening Post*, 49.

15. Christopher Olsen, *Political Culture and Secession in Mississippi: Masculinity, Honor, and the Antiparty Tradition, 1830–1860* (New York: Oxford University Press, 2000), 172.

16. Barbara Holland, *Gentlemen's Blood: A History of Dueling from Swords at Dawn to Pistols at Dusk* (New York and London: Bloomsbury, 2003), 175.

17. Nevins, *The Evening Post*, 49.

18. "The Duel," *Brooklyn Eagle*, June 27, 1843.

19. Wilmer, *Our Press Gang*, 304. Parentheses are Wilmer's own.

20. Henry Graham Ashmead, *History of Delaware County, Pennsylvania* (Philadelphia: L.H. Everts, 1884), 481.

21. Wilmer, *Our Press Gang*, 304.

22. Clement Eaton, *The Growth of Southern Civilization, 1790–1860* (New York: Harper, 1961), 2.

23. Ibid., 268.

24. Nevins, *The Evening Post*, 49.

25. Christopher Olsen, *Political Culture and Secession in Mississippi: Masculinity, Honor, and the Antiparty Tradition, 1830–1860*, 175.

26. C.A. Harwell Wells, "The End of the Affair? Anti-Dueling Laws and Social Norms in Antebellum America," *Vanderbilt Law Review* 54 (2001): 1823.

27. Hazel Dicken-Garcia, *Journalistic Standards in the Nineteenth-Century America* (Madison: University of Wisconsin Press, 1989), 98.

28. Olsen, *Political Culture and Secession in Mississippi: Masculinity, Honor, and the Antiparty Tradition, 1830–1860*, 57.

29. Ibid., 56.

30. Dicken-Garcia, *Journalistic Standards in the Nineteenth-Century America*, 109.

31. "The Vicksburg Sentinel," in the Mississippi Department of Archives and History, S/F "Dueling."

32. "Some Notes on James Franklin Hagan," in the Mississippi Department of Archives and History, S/F "James Hagan."

33. Henry S. Foote, *Casket of Reminiscences* (Washington, D.C.: Chronicle Publishing Company, 1874), 378. "Sentinel" is not italicized in the original.

34. "A Difficulty Between Hugh C. Stewart and Dr. James Hagan," in the Mississippi Department of Archives and History, S/F "James Hagan."

35. Ibid.

36. Ibid.

37. Ibid.

38. Dicken-Garcia, *Journalistic Standards in the Nineteenth-Century America*, 39.

39. Foote, *Casket of Reminiscences*, 380.

40. "The Duel," *The Mississippian*, April 26, 1839, transcript found in the Mississippi Department of Archives and History, S/F "William H. McCardle."

41. "A Difficulty Between W.G. Kendall and Dr. James Hagan," in the Mississippi Department of Archives and History, S/F "James Hagan."

42. Ibid.

43. Ibid.

44. Ibid.

45. Ibid.

46. Ibid.

47. Ibid.

48. Ibid.

49. Ibid.

50. Wilmer, *Our Press Gang*, 283.

51. *Vicksburg* (Miss.) *Whig*, February 28, 1842, quoted in Cockrell, "Those Duelling Editors of Vicksburg, 1841–1860," 3, in the Mississippi Department of Archives and History, S/F "Dueling."

52. Ibid.

53. Ibid.

54. *Vicksburg* (Miss.) *Sentinel*, December 3–7, 1838, quoted in Cockrell, "Those Duelling Editors of Vicksburg, 1841–1860," 2, in the Mississippi Department of Archives and History, S/F "Dueling."

55. "The following letter...," *The Mississippian*, April 22, 1842, transcript found in the Mississippi Department of Archives and History, S/F "James S. Fall."

56. Ibid.

57. Ibid.

58. Ibid.

59. *Vicksburg Whig*, March 4, 1841, quoted in Cockrell, "Those Duelling Editors of Vicksburg, 1841–1860," 3, in the Mississippi Department of Archives and History, S/F "Dueling." Incidentally, this was the same Flagg who was a lawyer, well-traveled writer, poet, and playwright as well as a journalist. See *Early Western Travels Vol. 26, Part I of Flagg's the Far West, 1836–1837*. Edited by Reuben Gold Thwaites (Cleveland, Ohio: A.H. Clark, 1906.

60. *Vicksburg Whig*, May 14, 1841, quoted in Cockrell, "Those Duelling Editors of Vicksburg, 1841–1860," 3, in the Mississippi Department of Archives and History, S/F "Dueling."

61. *Vicksburg Whig*, May 18, 1841, quoted in Cockrell, "Those Duelling Editors of Vicksburg, 1841–1860," 3, in the Mississippi Department of Archives and History, S/F "Dueling."

62. Foote, *Casket of Reminiscences*, 381.

63. Cockrell, "Those Duelling Editors of Vicksburg, 1841–1860," 3, in the Mississippi Department of Archives and History, S/F "Dueling."

64. *The Southron*, June 14, 1843, transcript in the Mississippi Department of Archives and History, S/F "James Hagan." There are no italics in the transcript.

65. Foote, *Casket of Reminiscences*, 384–385.

66. "Some Notes on James Franklin Hagan," transcript in the Mississippi Department of Archives and History, S/F "James Hagan."

67. Monroe F. Cockrell, "Those Duelling Editors of Vicksburg, 1841–60," 2. This is not to be confused with Monroe F. Cockrell, *After Sundown: Those Duelling Editors of Vicksburg, 1841–1860*; and "Casket of Reminiscences," by Henry S. Foote, 1874 (Evanston, Ill.: M. Cockrell, 1961), call number CR4595.U6 C63 1961 (McCain) found at the University of Southern Mississippi, which may or may not be the same thing.

68. Ibid.

69. *Vicksburg Whig*, August 22, 1843, quoted in Cockrell, "Those Duelling Editors of Vicksburg, 1841–1860," Appendix 1, in the Mississippi Department of Archives and History, S/F "Dueling."

70. *Vicksburg Whig*, September 21, 1843, quoted in Cockrell, "Those Duelling Editors of Vicksburg, 1841–1860," Appendix 1, in the Mississippi Department of Archives and History, S/F "Dueling."

71. "Comfortable," *Brooklyn Eagle*, November 18, 1843, and *Vicksburg Whig*, November 4, 1843, recorded in Cockrell, "Those Duelling Editors of Vicksburg, 1841–1860," Appendix 2, in the Mississippi Department of Archives and History, S/F "Dueling."

72. "Comfortable," *Brooklyn Eagle*, November 18, 1843.

73. *Vicksburg Whig*, November 6, 1843, and November 6, 1843, recorded in Cockrell: "Those Duelling Editors of Vicksburg, 1841–1860," Appendix 2, in the Mississippi Department of Archives and History, S/F "Dueling."

74. *Vicksburg Whig*, March 1, 1843, quoted in Cockrell, "Those Duelling Editors of Vicksburg, 1841–1860," Appendix 1, in the Mississippi Department of Archives and History, S/F "Dueling." There are no italics in the transcript.

75. "Fatal Duel," *Brooklyn Eagle*, March 14, 1844. There are no italics in the account.

76. "The Effects of Assaulting Editors," *Brooklyn Eagle*, May 25, 1844. "Vicksburg Sentinel" is not italicized in the original account.

77. "A True Bill for Murder," *Brooklyn Eagle*, June 20, 1844.

78. "The Vicksburg Sentinel," in the Mississippi Department of Archives and History, S/F "Dueling."

79. Ibid.

80. "Conflict of Authorities," *Brooklyn Eagle*, December 13, 1844. "Vicksburg Sentinel" is not italicized in the original account.

81. Cockrell, "Those Duelling Editors of Vicksburg, 1841–1860," 5, in the Mississippi Department of Archives and History, S/F "Dueling."

82. The September 19 account of this encounter cites an eyewitness account that Crabbe was carrying a cane. See "Various painful...," *Vicksburg Tri-Weekly Whig*, September 19, 1848.

83. "Fatal Affray," *Vicksburg Tri-Weekly Whig*, September 16, 1848. "Vicksburg Sentinel" is not italicized in the original account.

84. Foote, *Casket of Reminiscences*, 385.

85. "The Vicksburg Sentinel," in the Mississippi Department of Archives and History, S/F "Dueling."

86. "The Vicksburg Sentinel (Miss.)," *Brooklyn Eagle*, November 21, 1860.

87. Olsen, *Political Culture and Secession in Mississippi: Masculinity, Honor, and the Antiparty Tradition, 1830–1860*, 175.

88. Dicken-Garcia, *Journalistic Standards in the Nineteenth-Century America*, 109.

89. Eaton, *The Growth of Southern Civilization, 1790–1860*, 266–267.

90. Ibid., 269.

91. "Unfortunate Recontre and Loss of Life," *Norfolk* (Va.) *Beacon*, March 31, 1843.

92. "A Statement of Facts," *Lexington* (Ky.) *Gazette*, March 20, 1829.

93. Ibid. Italicized in the original.

94. "From the Kentucky Gazette of Sept. 18, 1829," *Argus of Western America* (Ky.), October 28, 1829.

95. Ibid.

96. Ibid.

97. Ibid. Italicized in the original.

98. Wilmer, *Our Press Gang*, 282.

99. "To The Editor of the Argus," *Argus of Western America* (Ky.), October 28, 1829.

100. Ibid. Italicized in the original.

101. Ibid.

102. "Geo. J. Trotter, Esq.," *Argus of Western America*, November 18, 1829. Italicized in the original.

103. "The Argus," *Argus of Western America*, October 28, 1829.

104. "Society of Lexington, Ky.," *Argus of Western America*, October 28, 1829.

105. "Geo. J. Trotter, Esq.," *Argus of Western America*, November 18, 1829.

106. Holland, *Gentlemen's Blood: A History of Dueling from Swords at Dawn to Pistols at Dusk*, 178.

107. Ibid.

108. "Another Vicarious Duel," *New York Times*, October 7, 1856.

109. "Mr. Pryor, of the Richmond Enquirer...," *Brooklyn Eagle*, October 8, 1856.

110. Pryor shot Dr. O.B. Finney, Virginia state senator, in a duel not more than a month later. See "The Duel Near Richmond," *Brooklyn Eagle*, November 7, 1856.

111. "The Fatal Duel at Charleston," *New York Times*, October 8, 1856.

112. "The Charleston Duel," *New York Times*, October 9, 1856.

113. "The Bloody Code," *New York Times*, October 3, 1856.

114. Virginius Dabney, *Pistols and Pointed Pens* (Chapel Hill, N.C.: Algonquin Books, 1987), 4.

115. Ibid., 32–33.

116. Ibid., 33.

117. "Bloody Recontre," *Brooklyn Eagle*, February 28, 1846.

118. Dabney, *Pistols and Pointed Pens*, 35.

119. "Duel," *Alta California*, January 13, 1851.

120. Albert H.Z. Carr, *The World and William Walker* (New York: Harper and Row, 1963), 64.

121. "Duel," *Alta California*, January 13, 1851.

122. Ibid.

123. "The Duellists," *Alta California*, January 16, 1851.

124. Carr, *The World and William Walker*, 64.

125. "Muzzling the Press," *Alta California*, January 14, 1851.

126. "An Affair of Honor," *Virginia* (Nev.) *Evening Bulletin*, August 1, 1863.

127. Ibid.

128. Ibid.

129. "Dueling," *Sacramento Union*, July 18, 1855.

130. "Death of Robert Tevis, Esq.," *Sacramento Union*, July 17, 1855.

131. "The Fatal Duel," *Alta California*, July 19, 1855.

132. Ibid.

133. "The Late Robert Tevis," *Sacramento Union*, July 21, 1855.

134. "Death of Robert Tevis, Esq.," *Sacramento Union*, July 17, 1855.

135. Ibid.

136. Wells, "The End of the Affair? Anti-Dueling Laws and Social Norms in Antebellum America," 1832.

Chapter 5

1. Bertram Wyatt-Brown, *The Shaping of Southern Culture: Honor, Grace, and War, 1760s–1880s* (Chapel Hill and London: University of North Carolina Press, 2001), 178.

2. Simeon D. Fess, *The History of Political Theory and Party Organization in the United States* (Boston: Ginn and Company, 1910), 297.

3. Abraham Lincoln, "Speech in Springfield, Illinois, June 26, 1857," in *The Complete Works of Abraham Lincoln* , Vol. 2, ed. James G. Nicolay and John Hay (New York: Francis D. Tandy, 1905), 337.

4. William Robertson Garrett and Robert Ambrose Halley, *The History of North America, Vol. 14: The Civil War from a Southern Standpoint* (Philadelphia: George and Sons, 1905), 71.

5. "Mayor Wood...," *Brooklyn Eagle*, January 8, 1861.

6. "Republicanism in Missouri," *New York Times*, May 26, 1860.

7. "Testimonials of Respect for the Memory of General Jackson." *Vicksburg Sentinel*, June 23, 1845.

8. Felicity Allen, *Jefferson Davis, Unconquerable Heart* (Columbia and London: University of Missouri Press, 1999), 42–44.

9. Considered at the time some of the bravest and most honorable soldiers in the U.S. armed forces. The Mississippi Dragoons, which were represented at Jackson's eulogy in Vicksburg, won commendation from Jackson for their willingness to ride full speed up to enemy lines during a battle and fire upon the soldiers. See Allen, *Jefferson Davis, Unconquerable Heart*, 41.

10. "Funeral Ceremonies of Saturday," *Sentinel and Expositor*, July 8, 1845.

11. *Vicksburg Tri-Weekly Whig*, June 26, July 1, 1845, in *The Papers of Jefferson Davis*, Vol. 2, ed. James T. McIntosh (Baton Rouge: Louisiana University Press, 1974), 264n.

12. "Funeral Ceremonies of Saturday," *Sentinel and Expositor*, July 8, 1845.

13. Ibid.

14. "Eulogy on the Life and Character of Andrew Jackson," *Vicksburg Sentinel and Expositor*, July 15, 1845, in *The Papers of Jefferson Davis*, Vol. 2, ed. James T. McIntosh (Baton Rouge: Louisiana University Press, 1974), 266.

15. Andrew Burstein, *The Passions of Andrew Jackson* (New York: Alfred A. Knopf, 2003), 3.

16. Ibid., 266–275.

17. Ibid., 273, 276.

18. Ibid., 278.

19. Ibid., 279.

20. Garcia, 82.

21. Frank L. Mott, *American Journalism: A History 1690–1960* (New York: Macmillan, 1962), 241–243.

22. Walter R. Mears, "A Brief History of AP," in Reporters of the Associated Press, *Breaking News: How the Associated Press Has Covered War, Peace, and Everything Else* (New York: Princeton Architectural Press, 2007), 403.

23. See chapter three for a more detailed description of the juntoism phenomenon.

24. Arthur Quinn, *The Rivals: William Gwin, David Broderick, and the Birth of California* (New York: Crown Publishers, Inc., 1994), 86–91.

25. Ibid., 91.

26. James L. Huston, *Stephen A. Douglas and the Dilemmas of Democratic Equality* (Lanham, Md.: Rowman and Littlefield, 2006), 161.

27. "Congress." *Brooklyn Eagle*, May 25, 1850.

28. Ibid.

29. Mott, *American Journalism: A History 1690–1960*, 286.

30. Gienapp writes, "Whatever the pattern, by the end of the decade the basic outline of a new party system had taken shape throughout the North. Following Lincoln's election in 1860, the Republican Party came to national power, and the Civil War quickly ensued. Such a cataclysmic event had been difficult to imagine as long as the Whig and Democratic parties remained dominant, for both were national organizations committed to sectional harmony, and each enjoyed widespread popular support in the North and South. The collapse of the Whig party heralded the onslaught of a realignment era in American politics from which the Republican Party ultimately emerged." See William E. Gienapp, *The Origins of the Republican Party, 1852–1856* (New York and Oxford: Oxford University Press, 1987), 11.

31. Mott writes, "The early history of the New York Associated Press is filled with its effort to control the news-gathering field, if not to monopolize it; this effort was fairly successful by 1853. When the Western Union Telegraph Company was organized in 1855, agreements were made which gave the A.P. low rates and the Western Union a monopoly of newspaper business." See Mott, *American Journalism: A History 1690–1960*, 251–252.

32. Christopher J. Olsen, *Political Culture and Secession in Mississippi: Masculinity,*

Honor, and the Antiparty Tradition, 1830–1860 (New York Oxford: Oxford University Press, 2000), 183.

33. Ibid., xi.

34. "The Speech of Senator Douglas." *Brooklyn Eagle,* July 13, 1858.

35. Ibid.

36. Ibid.

37. Ibid.

38. Dr. Hermann Von Holst, *The Constitutional and Political History of the United States: 1859–1861; Harper's Ferry to Lincoln's Inauguration* (Chicago: Callaghan, 1892), 222.

39. "The Speech of Senator Douglas." *Brooklyn Eagle,* July 13, 1858.

40. "Lincoln and Politics of Black Colonization," Michael Vorenberg in *For a Vast Future Also: Essays from the Journal of the Abraham Lincoln Association,* Thomas F. Schwarz, ed. (New York: Fordham University Press, 1999), 44.

41. John Moncure Daniel, *The Richmond Examiner During the War or, The Writings of John M. Daniel* (New York: Printed for the Author, 1868), 120.

42. Ibid., 210.

43. "The Crime Against Kansas," Charles Sumner in D.A. Harsha, *The Life of Charles Sumner: With Choice Specimens of His Eloquence, A Delineation of his Oratorical Character, and His Great Speech on Kansas* (New York: Dayton and Burdick, 1856), 171.

44. "Brooks and Sumner," *Spartanburg* (S.C.) *Spartan,* May 29, 1856.

45. Ibid.

46. "Letter from Sarah Helen Whitman, Providence, ALS, to James Ingram," February 27, 1874, in John Henry Ingram's Edgar Allan Poe Collection in the University of Virginia Special Collections.

47. Ibid.

48. George Woodberry, *The Life of Edgar Allan Poe* (Boston and New York: Houghton Mifflin, 1909), 2:2, 444.

49. *Richmond Examiner* writer Judge Robert W. Hughes quoted in George Woodberry, *The Life of Edgar Allan Poe* (Boston and New York: Houghton Mifflin, 1909), 2:2, 444.

50. George Woodberry, *The Life of Edgar Allan Poe* (Boston and New York: Houghton Mifflin, 1909), 2:2, 444.

51. D.R. Anderson, ed., *Richmond Historical Papers* (Richmond, Va.: Richmond College, 1915), 1:1, 79–80.

52. Vorenberg, "Lincoln and Politics of Black Colonization," 44.

53. Gienapp, *The Origins of the Republican Party, 1852–1856,* 446.

54. Ibid.

55. Ibid.

56. Mott, *American Journalism: A History 1690–1960,* 340.

57. Ibid., 281.

58. "Republican Convention," *New York Times,* February 26, 1856.

59. Mott, *American Journalism: A History 1690–1960,* 179.

60. Elbert B. Smith, *Francis Preston Blair* (New York: The Free Press, 1980), 216.

61. "Frank P. Blair." *Philadelphia Press,* October 3, 1860.

62. John Hopkins University, *The Johns Hopkins University Studies in Historical and Political Science* (Baltimore: John Hopkins University Press, 1914), Vol. 32, 230–231.

63. Gienapp, *The Origins of the Republican Party, 1852–1856,* 447.

64. "The Licentiousness of Party," *Lancaster* (Pa.) *Daily Evening Express,* January 17, 1861, in *Northern Editorials on Secession,* Vol. 2, Howard Cecil Perkins, ed. (Gloucester, Mass.: Peter Smith, 1964), 1045.

65. "Southern Outrages," reprinted in *Daily Chicago Times,* December 14, 1860. In *Northern Editorials on Secession,* Vol. 2, Howard Cecil Perkins, ed. (Gloucester, Mass.: Peter Smith, 1964), 1041.

66. "Cause and Effect." *The New Orleans Bee,* February 9, 1860, in *Southern Editorials on Secession,* ed. Dwight Lowell Dumond (Gloucester, Mass.: Peter Smith, 1964), 236.

67. Gienapp, *The Origins of the Republican Party, 1852–1856,* 448.

68. Perkins, ed., *Northern Editorials on Secession,* Vol. 1, 6–7.

69. Gienapp, *The Origins of the Republican Party, 1852–1856,* 448.

70. "The Great Battle," *Chicago Daily Democrat,* November 5, 1860, in *Northern Editorials on Secession,* Vol. 1, Howard Cecil Perkins, ed. (Gloucester, Mass.: Peter Smith, 1964), 76.

71. Olsen, *Political Culture and Secession in Mississippi: Masculinity, Honor, and the Antiparty Tradition, 1830–1860,* 180.

72. "The Cry of Disunion," *Richmond Enquirer,* July 10, 1860, in *Northern Editorials on Secession,* Vol. 1, Howard Cecil Perkins, ed. (Gloucester, Mass.: Peter Smith, 1964), 140–141.

73. Olsen, *Political Culture and Secession in Mississippi: Masculinity, Honor, and the Antiparty Tradition, 1830–1860,* 181.

74. Wyatt-Brown writes, "To be sure, white supremacy ... was the 'central theme' of Southern culture. Yet the language for expressing it was largely framed in terms of honor and shame." See Wyatt-Brown, *The Shaping*

of Southern Culture: Honor, Grace, and War, 1760s–1880s, 199.

75. Dumond, ed., *Southern Editorials on Secession*, xx.

76. "Submit to the Constitution, But Resist the First Attempt to Enforce the Principles of the Republican Party," *The* (Lexington) *Kentucky Statesman*, November 13, 1860, in *Southern Editorials on Secession*, ed. Dwight Lowell Dumond (Gloucester, Mass.: Peter Smith, 1964), 233.

77. "Newspaper Provocations," reprinted in the *New York World*, November 28, 1860. In *Northern Editorials on Secession*, Vol. 2, Howard Cecil Perkins, ed. (Gloucester, Mass.: Peter Smith, 1964), 1037–1038.

78. Ibid., 1037–1039.

79. "The Force Policy," *The* (Lexington) *Kentucky Statesman*, December 25, 1860, in *Southern Editorials on Secession*, ed. Dwight Lowell Dumond (Gloucester, Mass.: Peter Smith, 1964), 370.

80. For an account of Lincoln's honor dispute with Illinois state auditor General James Shields, refer to the following chapter. For an account of Davis's honor dispute with William Bissell, in which Shields acted as second for Bissell, see "From William H. Bissell," February 27, 1850, in *The Papers of Jefferson Davis*, Vol. 4, ed. Lynda L. Crist (Baton Rouge: Louisiana University Press, 1983), 86.

81. Olsen, *Political Culture and Secession in Mississippi: Masculinity, Honor, and the Antiparty Tradition, 1830–1860*, 181.

82. "Mischief of Sensation Reports," *Newark* (New Jersey) *Daily Advertiser*, January 12, 1861, in *Northern Editorials on Secession*, Vol. 2, Howard Cecil Perkins, ed. (Gloucester, Mass.: Peter Smith, 1964), 1043–1044.

83. Allen, *Jefferson Davis, Unconquerable Heart*, 267.

84. "Two Inaugurations — Two Republics — Two Presidents," *Philadelphia Morning Pennsylvanian Northern Editorials*, February 18, 1861, in *Northern Editorials on Secession*, Vol. 2, Howard Cecil Perkins, ed. (Gloucester, Mass.: Peter Smith, 1964), 609.

85. "The Great Issue and the Choice — Separation or War," *Albany Atlas and Argus*, January 12, 1861, in *Northern Editorials on Secession*, Vol. 1, Howard Cecil Perkins, ed. (Gloucester, Mass.: Peter Smith, 1964), 337.

86. Wyatt-Brown, *The Shaping of Southern Culture: Honor, Grace, and War, 1760s–1880s*, 178.

87. Lynda L. Crist, ed., *The Papers of Jefferson Davis*, Vol. 7 (Baton Rouge: Louisiana University Press, 1983), 130, 8n.

Chapter 6

1. "A Hostile Meeting," *Richmond Daily Dispatch*, August 17, 1864. http://dlxs.richmond.edu/d/ddr/ (January 18, 2008) via University of Richmond Library Digital Collections.

2. Ibid.

3. Ibid.

4. *Richmond Examiner*, August 12–16, inclusive, quoted in D.R. Anderson, ed., *Richmond College Historical Papers* (Richmond, Va.: Richmond College, 1915), Vol. 1, No. 1: 82–83.

5. "A Hostile Meeting," *Richmond Daily Dispatch*, August 17, 1864. http://dlxs.richmond.edu/d/ddr/ (January 18, 2008) via University of Richmond Library Digital Collections.

6. "The Strongest Government in the World," *Richmond Daily Dispatch*, March 2, 1861. http://dlxs.richmond.edu/d/ddr/ (January 18, 2008) via University of Richmond Library Digital Collections.

7. "Duels and Deadly Fights," *The Columbia Spy*, May 11, 1861.

8. "Examination for Duelling," *Richmond Daily Dispatch*, August 18, 1861. http://dlxs.richmond.edu/d/ddr/ (January 18, 2008) via University of Richmond Library Digital Collections.

9. Ibid.

10. Ibid.

11. Ibid.

12. "The Duelling Case Again," *Richmond Daily Dispatch*, August 19, 1864. http://dlxs.richmond.edu/d/ddr/ (January 18, 2008) via University of Richmond Library Digital Collections.

13. Ibid.

14. "The Duelling Case," *Richmond Daily Dispatch*, August 22, 1864. http://dlxs.richmond.edu/d/ddr/ (January 18, 2008) via University of Richmond Library Digital Collections.

15. Ibid.

16. "The Duelling Case Again," *Richmond Daily Dispatch*, August 29, 1864. http://dlxs.richmond.edu/d/ddr/ (January 18, 2008) via University of Richmond Library Digital Collections.

17. Ibid.

18. Ibid.

19. Ibid.

20. "The Duelling Case Continued," *Richmond Daily Dispatch*, August 30, 1864. http://dlxs.richmond.edu/d/ddr/ (January 18, 2008) via University of Richmond Library Digital Collections.

21. Ibid.

22. Ibid.

23. Ibid.

24. "Judge Meredith's Court," *Richmond Daily Dispatch,* September 3, 1864. http://dlxs.richmond.edu/d/ddr/ (January 18, 2008) via University of Richmond Library Digital Collections.

25. "The Duelling Case," *Richmond Daily Dispatch,* September 5, 1864. http://dlxs.richmond.edu/d/ddr/ (January 18, 2008) via University of Richmond Library Digital Collections.

26. "Matters in Vicksburg," *Philadelphia Press,* April 30, 1863.

27. Ibid.

28. Charles Mattox, "Heaven is a lot Like Kentucky," *Carlisle* (Ky.) *Mercury,* June 20, 2007.

29. "A Fatal Duel in Kentucky," *Norwalk* (Ohio) *Reflector,* May 27, 1862.

30. "Statement," *New York Times,* May 23, 1864.

31. "New York City," *Philadelphia Press,* May 26, 1863.

32. "General Schurz to Leslie Combs," *Philadelphia Press,* November 25, 1863.

33. Ibid.

34. Ibid.

35. "A Duel in New Jersey," *Philadelphia Press,* August 18, 1863.

36. Ibid.

37. "The South as It Is," *New York Times,* November 2, 1865.

38. Ibid.

39. "A Duelling Correspondence," *Philadelphia Press,* November 8, 1861.

40. Ibid.

41. Hazel Dicken-Garcia, *Journalistic Standards in the Nineteenth-Century America* (Madison: University of Wisconsin Press, 1989), 52.

42. "Tuesday Evening June 5," *Brooklyn Eagle,* June 5, 1860.

43. "A Duel, Almost," *Brooklyn Eagle,* October 6, 1842.

44. "The 'Rebecca' Letter," August 27, 1842, found in Roy P. Basler, Marion Dolores Pratt, and Lloyd A. Dunlap, eds., *The Collected Works of Abraham Lincoln,* 9 vols. (Springfield, Ill.: Abraham Lincoln Association; New Brunswick, N.J.: Rutgers University Press, 1953), Vol. 1: 300–2.

45. Abraham Lincoln to Elias H. Merryman, September 19, 1842, found in Roy P. Basler, Marion Dolores Pratt, and Lloyd A. Dunlap, eds., *The Collected Works of Abraham Lincoln,* 9 vols. (Springfield, Ill.: Abraham Lincoln Association; New Brunswick, N.J.: Rutgers University Press, 1953), Vol. 1: 300–2.

46. Ibid.

47. Abraham Lincoln to Joshua F. Speed, October 5, 1842, found in Roy P. Basler, Marion Dolores Pratt, and Lloyd A. Dunlap, eds., *The Collected Works of Abraham Lincoln,* 9 vols. (Springfield, Ill.: Abraham Lincoln Association; New Brunswick, N.J.: Rutgers University Press, 1953), Vol. 1: 302–3.

48. Ibid.

49. Lerone Bennett, Jr., *Forced Into Glory: Abraham Lincoln's White Dream* (Chicago: Johnson Publishing Company, 2000), 534.

50. Benjamin Quarles, *Lincoln and the Negro* (New York: Da Capo Press, 1991), 150.

51. Edward Steers, Jr., "Book Review of *Forced Into Glory: Abraham Lincoln's White Dream,*" *Springfield* (Illinois) *State-Journal Register,* June 25, 2000.

52. "Final Draft of the Emancipation Proclamation," as issued on January 1, 1863, found in Noah Brooks, ed., *The Writings of Abraham Lincoln* (New York: G.P Putnam's Sons, 1906), 315–317.

53. John Y. Simon, Harold Holzer, and Dawn Vogel, eds., *Lincoln Revisited* (Bronx, N.Y.: Fordham University Press, 2007), 215–216.

54. Lerone Bennett, Jr., *Forced Into Glory: Abraham Lincoln's White Dream,* 536.

55. Frederick Douglass, *The Life and Times of Frederick Douglass* (London: Bemrose and Sons, 1882), 309.

56. Ibid.

57. Lerone Bennett, Jr., *Forced Into Glory: Abraham Lincoln's White Dream,* 548.

58. Edward A. Pollard, *The Lost Cause: A New Southern History of the War of the Confederates* (New York: E.B. Treat, 1867), 357.

59. Jefferson Davis speech to the Confederate Congress at Richmond, January 12, 1863, quoted in Edward A. Pollard, *The Lost Cause: A New Southern History of the War of the Confederates,* 360.

60. Edward A. Pollard, *The Lost Cause: A New Southern History of the War of the Confederates,* 360.

61. Frederick Douglass, *The Life and Times of Frederick Douglass,* 349.

62. John Moncure Daniel, *The Richmond Examiner During the War or, The Writings of John M. Daniel* (New York: Printed for the Author, 1868), 209.

63. Benjamin Quarles, *Lincoln and the Negro,* 150.

64. Edward Steers, Jr., "Book Review of *Forced Into Glory: Abraham Lincoln's White Dream,*" *Springfield* (Illinois) *State-Journal Register,* June 25, 2000.

65. Lerone Bennett Jr., *Forced Into Glory: Abraham Lincoln's White Dream*, 617.

66. John Y. Simon, Harold Holzer, and Dawn Vogel, eds., *Lincoln Revisited*, 229.

67. D.R. Anderson, ed., *Richmond College Historical Papers* (Richmond, Va.: Richmond College, 1915), Vol. 1, No. 1: 77.

68. John M. Carroll and Colin F. Baxter, eds., *The American Military Tradition: From Colonial Times to Present, Second Edition* (Lanham, Md.: Rowman and Littlefield, 2006), 79.

69. Edward A. Pollard, *The Lost Cause: A New Southern History of the War of the Confederates*, 750–751.

70. "Important Decision," *Richmond Daily Dispatch*, February 8, 1865.

71. Edward A. Pollard, *The Lost Cause: A New Southern History of the War of the Confederates*, 702.

72. "H. Rives Pollard," *Harpers Weekly*, December 12, 1868.

73. "The Pollard Homicide," *New York Times*, March 7, 1869.

74. Frederick Douglass, *The Life and Times of Frederick Douglass*, 814.

75. Edward A. Pollard, *The Lost Cause: A New Southern History of the War of the Confederates*, 752. Italicized in the original.

Chapter 7

1. Dicken-Garcia, *Journalistic Standards in the Nineteenth-Century America*, 53.

2. "From the Louisville Journal," *Atlanta Constitution*, June 30, 1868.

3. Dicken-Garcia, *Journalistic Standards in the Nineteenth-Century America*, 53.

4. Ibid., 58.

5. "The Political Ethics of Dueling," *Washington Post,* July 11, 1883.

6. "Virginia," *Atlanta Constitution*, October 12, 1870.

7. C.A. Harwell Wells, "The End of the Affair? Anti-Dueling Laws and Social Norms in Antebellum America," *Vanderbilt Law Review* 54 (2001): 1840.

8. "Riddleberger on a Rampage," *Washington Post*, October 16, 1881.

9. Ibid.

10. "Virginia Methods," *New York Times*, October 18, 1881.

11. Wells, "The End of the Affair? Anti-Dueling Laws and Social Norms in Antebellum America," 1840.

12. "Duelists Out of Trouble," *New York Times*, December 22, 1881.

13. Ibid.

14. Wells, "The End of the Affair? Anti-Dueling Laws and Social Norms in Antebellum America," 1829.

15. "About to Fight a Duel," *Washington Post*, February 22, 1884.

16. "Challenge to a Duel," *Washington Post*, October 8, 1893.

17. "Editor Gets a Challenge," *Washington Post*, January 18, 1902.

18. "Another Duel in New-Orleans — One of the Parties Wounded," *New York Times*, June 7, 1869.

19. "Editors on the Field of Honor," *New York Times*, January 28, 1880.

20. "Honor Easily Satisfied," *New York Times*, May 24, 1881.

21. "An Affair of Honor," *The New York Times*, June 11, 1882.

22. "They Were After Blood," *Chicago Daily Tribune*, September 26, 1891.

23. Ibid.

24. "Forced Editor Dupre to Fight a Duel," *Chicago Daily Tribune*, June 7, 1891.

25. Bertram Wyatt-Brown, *The Shaping of Southern Culture: Honor, Grace, and War, 1760s–1880s* (Chapel Hill: University of North Carolina Press, 2001), 272.

26. "Dueling in the South," *Brooklyn Eagle*, June 23, 1881.

27. "The Cash-Shannon Duel," *New York Times*, July 17, 1880.

28. Ibid.

29. "Col. Cash, of South Carolina...," *Washington Post*, July 19, 1880.

30. Ibid.

31. "General Telegrams," *Brooklyn Eagle*, July 18, 1880.

32. "Political Ethics of Dueling," *Washington Post*, July 11, 1883.

33. "A Duel at Augusta," *Atlanta Constitution*, December 12, 1872.

34. Ibid.

35. Ibid.

36. "The Sheriff Alone Injured," *Washington Post*, May 7, 1893.

37. "A Blunder Under the Code," *Washington Post*, May 9, 1893.

38. Ibid.

39. "Virginia Duellists — Encounter in North Carolina," *New York Times*, June 14, 1869.

40. "Gone to Fight a Duel," *New York Times*, July 28, 1885.

41. "Editor Invites a Duel," *Chicago Daily Tribune*, October 29, 1895.

42. Ibid.

43. "Probable Duel Between Editors," *Chicago Daily Tribune*, January 25, 1896.

44. "Challenge to a Duel Declined," *Washington Post*, May 27, 1890.

45. "A Bloodthirsty Tacoma Editor," *Los Angeles Times*, July 12, 1892.

46. "Preparing for a Duel in Oklahoma," *Chicago Daily Tribune*, December 6, 1890.

47. "Duel Between Editors," *New York Times*, September 15, 1882.

48. "Solemnity of the Duello," *Washington Post*, September 18, 1893.

49. "A Street Encounter," *New York Times*, January 4, 1877.

50. Ibid.

51. "The May-Bennett Trouble," *New York Times*, January 7, 1877.

52. "The Bennett-May Affair," *New York Times*, January 13, 1877.

53. "Mr. Bennett Sails for Europe," *New York Times*, January 15, 1877.

54. "The Bennett-May Affair," *New York Times*, January 13, 1877.

55. "The Bennett-May Duel Turns Out...," *New York Times*, January 10, 1877.

56. "Duels Either Farcical or Tragical," *Atlanta Constitution*, July 2, 1892. The article said it was a reprint from the *New York Times*.

57. "Eager for the Duel," *Chicago Daily Tribune*, July 28, 1892.

58. "The Mayer–De Mores Duel," *Chicago Daily Tribune*, June 29, 1892.

59. "Solemnity of the Duello," *Washington Post*, September 17, 1893.

60. Ibid.

61. "Decline Of The Duel," *Washington Post*, August 25, 1889.

62. Ibid.

63. "The Usual Georgia Duel," *Washington Post*, August 30, 1885.

64. "Two Georgia Duels on the Tapis," *Washington Post*, December 30, 1886.

65. "A Duel in Georgia," *New York Times*, April 24, 1884.

66. "Warring Editors in Georgia," *New York Times*, November 6, 1897.

67. "Somebody Must Die," *Washington Post*, November 17, 1891.

68. "Feud Between Huntsville Editors," *Washington Post*, September 24, 1893.

69. "Bloodless Duel Between Editors," *New York Times*, October 22, 1895.

70. "Their Duel Only Postponed," *Washington Post*, December 17, 1894.

71. "Editor Wounded in a Duel," *Washington Post*, August 31, 1898.

72. "His Kentucky Blood is Up," *Washington Post*, February 10, 1898.

73. Ibid.

74. Wyatt-Brown, *The Shaping of Southern Culture: Honor, Grace, and War, 1760s–1880s*, 280.

75. "A Duel in the Streets," *New York Times*, May 2, 1888.

76. Ibid.

77. "The Hamilton Gambrell Case," *Atlanta Constitution*, June 1, 1887.

78. "A Duel in the Streets," *New York Times*, May 2, 1888.

79. "Definition of a Duel," *Washington Post*, January 22, 1900.

80. Ibid.

81. "Definition of a Duel," *Washington Post*, January 22, 1900.

82. "Fighting Editors," *Los Angeles Times*, September 16, 1894.

83. "Fatal Duel in Waco," *Washington Post*, April 2, 1898.

84. "Editors Wounded in Duel," *Chicago Daily Tribune*, October 11, 1899.

85. Wyatt-Brown, *The Shaping of Southern Culture: Honor, Grace, and War, 1760s–1880s*, 280.

86. "Facts About the Duello," *Washington Post*, August 24, 1897.

87. Ibid.

88. Ibid.

Chapter 8

1. Senator Zell Miller, Keynote Speech at the Republican National Convention, September 1, 2004, available from http://www.gopconvention.com/cgi-data/speeches/files/ie65aylzuai2r6ttbl9uj6s2y6q7930j.shtml (accessed on March 28, 2005).

2. Ibid.

3. Ibid.

4. Chris Matthews, *Hardball with Chris Matthews*, September 1, 2004, 6 P.M. on MSNBC, available from http://www.msnbc.msn.com/id/5891366/ (accessed on March 28, 2005).

5. Chris Matthews, *Hardball with Chris Matthews*, September 1, 2004, 11 P.M. on MSNBC, available from http://www.msnbc.msn.com/id/5892840/ (accessed on March 28, 2005).

6. Ibid.

7. Ibid.

8. David McCullough, Keynote Speech of the Ohio University undergraduate commencement ceremony, Saturday morning, June 12, 2004, Ohio University 2004 Commencement Video, videocassette.

9. Bertram Wyatt-Brown, "Honor, Shame, and Iraq in American Foreign Policy," note prepared for the Workshop on Humiliation and Violent Conflict, Columbia University, New York, November 18–19, 2004, 1,

http://www.humiliationstudies.org/docu
ments/WyattBrownNovNYConference.pdf
(accessed on March 28, 2005).

10. Richard Reeves, "Patriotism Calls Out
the Censor," *New York Times*, October 1, 2001.

11. Ari Fleischer, *Taking Heat: The President, The Press, and My Years in the White
House* (New York: William Morrow, 2005),
184–185.

12. Bill Carter, "ABC to End Politically Incorrect," *New York Times*, May 14, 2002.

13. Maureen Dowd, "Liberties; We Love
the Liberties They Hate," *New York Times*,
September 30, 2001.

14. Although the debate currently rages
about whether blogging is actually journalism, in early March 2005, FishbowlDC, a
blog published by http://www.mediabistro.
com, was granted a White House press pass,
suggesting that blogging is a legitimate form
of journalism since it was approved by the
White House Correspondence Association.
See Katharine Q. Seelye, "Media: White
House Approves Pass for Blogger," *New York
Times*, March 7, 2005.

15. Leo Morris, "The Pajamaheddin Prevail," *Fort Wayne* (Indiana) *News-Sentinel*,
September 23, 2004.

16. Hazel Dicken-Garcia, *Journalistic
Standards in Nineteenth-Century America*
(Madison: University of Wisconsin Press,
1989), 53.

17. William Safire, "The Depressed Press,"
New York Times, January 17, 2005.

18. Joe Conanson, "Gannon: The Early
Years," Salon.com, February 18, 2005, http://
www.salon.com/opinion/conason/2005/02/
18/gannon/index.html (accessed on March 28,
2005).

19. Ibid.

20. Ibid.

21. Frank Rich, "All The President's Newsmen," *New York Times*, January 16, 2005. According to Rich, Garcia and Ryan "starred in
bogus reports ('In Washington, I'm Karen
Ryan reporting,' went the script) pretending
to 'sort through the details' of the administration's Medicare prescription-drug plan in
2004. Such 'reports,' some of which found
their way into news packages distributed to
local stations by CNN, appeared in more than
50 news broadcasts around the country and
have now been deemed illegal 'covert propaganda' by the Government Accountability
Office."

22. Howard Kurtz, "Political Perspectives
With Tunnel Vision," *Washington Post*, February 7, 2005.

23. Chris Lydon, "Blogging, Journalism

and Credibility: Battleground and Common
Ground," conference held January 21–22,
2005, at Harvard University (Day one, A.M.),
http://cyber.law.harvard.edu:8080/webcred/
wp-content/WEBCREDtransday1am.htm
(accessed on March 28, 2005).

24. Ibid.

25. Anthony Bianco et al., "The Future of
the *New York Times*," *Business Week*, January
17, 2005, 64.

26. Ibid.

27. Judith Donath, "Blogging, Journalism
and Credibility: Battleground and Common
Ground," conference held January 21–22,
2005, at Harvard University (Day one, P.M.),
http://cyber.law.harvard.edu:8080/webcred/
wp-content/WEBCREDtransday1pm.htm
(accessed on March 28, 2005).

28. Ibid.

29. Ibid.

30. Ibid.

31. Katherine Q. Seelye et al., "Bloggers as
News Media Trophy Hunters," *New York
Times*, February 14, 2005.

32. Ibid. Bertram Wyatt-Brown, *The
Shaping of Southern Culture* suggests that lynch
mobs are a manifestation of honor ethics. See
Bertram Wyatt-Brown, *The Shaping of Southern Culture: Honor, Grace, and War, 1760s–
1880s* (Chapel Hill: University of North Carolina Press, 2001), 283.

33. Erika Chavez, "Battle of the Blogs,"
Sacbee.com, 2:15 A.M. PDT, October 13,
2004, http://www.sacbee.com/content/poli
tics/v-print/story/11073470p-11990278c.html
(accessed on March 28, 2005).

34. Bianco et al., "The Future of the New
York Times," 64.

35. Dicken-Garcia, *Journalistic Standards
in Nineteenth-Century America*, 44.

36. Eric Boehlert, "Tearing Down the
Press," Salon.com, March 2, 2005, http://
www.salon.com/news/feature/2005/03/02/
media/index.html (accessed on March 28,
2005).

37. Jonathan D. Glater, "Liberal Bloggers
Reaching Out to Major Media," *New York
Times*, March 14, 2005.

38. Wyatt-Brown, *The Shaping of Southern
Culture: Honor, Grace, and War, 1760s–1880s*,
63.

39. Joan Walsh, "Who Killed Dan
Rather?" Salon.com, March 9, 2005, http://
archive.salon.com/opinion/feature/2005/03/
09/rather/ (accessed on March 28, 2005).

40. Dan Fost, "Bay Judge Weighs Rights of
Bloggers: Journalists' Shield Claimed in Re-
sponse to Apple's Lawsuit," *San Francisco
Chronicle*, March 8, 2005.

41. Dicken-Garcia, *Journalistic Standards in the Nineteenth-Century America*, 48–49.

42. Fox Butterfield, *All God's Children: The Bosket Family and the American Tradition of Violence* (New York: HarperCollins, 1996), 328–329.

43. Ibid., 243.

44. Ibid., 63.

45. Philip Katcher, *Flags of the Civil War* (Botley, Oxford [UK]: Osprey Publishing, 2000), 15–18.

46. Michael Cooper, "Confederate Flag Takes Center Stage Once Again," *New York Times*, January 13, 2008.

47. Ibid.

48. Ibid.

49. Ibid.

50. Jim Kuhnhenn, "Confederate Flag Ad Praises Huckabee," *Boston Globe*, January 18, 2008.

51. "APAC spreads the word on McCain and Romney in South Carolina," radio ad available for download on the Website of Americans for the Preservation of American Culture, http://preservingamericanculture.com/2008/jan/ (accessed on March 17, 2008).

52. "Flags That Have Flown Over Georgia: The History of the Georgia State Flag," Office of Georgia Secretary of State Website, http://sos.georgia.gov/ (accessed on March 17, 2008).

53. Katcher, *Flags of the Civil War*, 8.

54. "The State Flag," South Carolina Legislature Online, http://www.scstatehouse.net/studentpage/flag.htm (accessed on March 17, 2008).

55. Sourindro Mohun Tagore, *The Orders of Knighthood, British and Foreign, With a Brief Review of the Titles of Rank and Merit in Ancient Hindustan* (Calcutta: Catholic Orphan Press, 1884), 161–163.

56. "National Briefing, Southwest: Arizona: Sikh is Shot," *New York Times*, May 22, 2003.

57. Robert Philips Greg, Esq., *On the Meaning and Origin of the Fylfot and Swastika* (Westminster: Nichols and Sons, 1884), 66.

58. Agence France-Presse, "World Briefing, Europe; Denmark: Papers Reprint Muhammad Cartoon," *New York Times*, February 14, 2008.

59. Ibid.

60. Ibid.

61. Emran Qureshi, "The Islam the Riots Drowned Out," *New York Times*, February 12, 2008.

62. Rukmini Callimachi, "Muslim Nations: Defame Islam, Get Sued?" *San Jose Mercury News*, March 14, 2008.

63. Ibid.

64. Wyatt-Brown, *Honor, Shame, and Iraq in American Foreign Policy*, 1.

65. Ibid.

66. "Threats and Responses; An Iraqi Offer: Duels Not War," *New York Times*, October 2, 2002.

67. McCullough, Keynote Speech of the Ohio University undergraduate commencement ceremony, videocassette.

68. David Hackett Fischer, *Albion's Seed: Four British Folkways in America* (New York: Oxford University Press, 1989), 834–841. According to Fischer, the other two were Martin Van Buren and John F. Kennedy.

Bibliography

"About to Fight a Duel." *Washinton Post*, February 22, 1884

"Abraham Lincoln to Elias H. Merryman." September 19, 1842. *The Collected Works of Abraham Lincoln*, vol. 1. Edited by Roy P. Basler, Marion Dolores Pratt, and Lloyd A. Dunlap. 9 volumes. Springfield, Ill.: Abraham Lincoln Association; New Brunswick, N.J.: Rutgers University Press, 1953.

"Abraham Lincoln to Joshua F. Speed." October 5, 1842. *The Collected Works of Abraham Lincoln*, vol. 1. Edited by Roy P. Basler, Marion Dolores Pratt, and Lloyd A. Dunlap. 9 volumes. Springfield, Ill.: Abraham Lincoln Association; New Brunswick, N.J.: Rutgers University Press, 1953.

"An Affair of Honor." *New York Times*, June 11, 1882.

"An Affair of Honor." *Virginia* (Nev.) *Evening Bulletin*, August 1, 1863.

"The Affairs of Edward Gilbert.—Correspondence." *Weekly Alta California*, August 21, 1852.

Agence France-Presse. "World Briefing, Europe; Denmark: Papers Reprint Muhammad Cartoon." *New York Times*, February 14, 2008.

Allen, Felicity. *Jefferson Davis: Unconquerable Heart*. Columbia and London: University of Missouri Press, 1999.

"American Politics—A Sad Picture." *Augusta* (Ga.) *Chronicle*, October 20, 1859.

Anderson, D.R., ed. *Richmond Historical Papers*. Richmond, Va.: Richmond College, 1915, 1: 1.

"Another Duel in New-Orleans—One of the Parties Wounded." *New York Times*, June 7, 1869.

"Another Vicarious Duel." *New York Times*, October 7, 1856.

"APAC spreads the word on McCain and Romney in South Carolina." Radio ad available for download on the Website of Americans for the Preservation of American Culture. http://preservingamericanculture.com/2008/jan/ (accessed on March 17, 2008).

"Appealing to the Code." *New York Times*, June 22, 1883.

"The Argus." *Argus of Western America* (Ky.), October 28, 1829.

Ashmead, Henry Graham. *History of Delaware County, Pennsylvania*. Philadelphia: L.H. Everts, 1884.

"An Averted Duel." *New York Herald*, June 23, 1883.

Baldick, Robert. *The Duel: A History of Dueling*. London, New York: Spring 1965.

Barnes, George C. *Denver, the Man: The Life, Letters and Public Papers of the Lawyer, Soldier and Statesman*. Strasburg, Va.: Shenandoah Publishing House, 1949.

"Beirne Wounds Elam." *New York Daily Tribune*, July 1, 1883.

"Beirne's Driver Arrested as Witness." *New York Daily Tribune*, July 1, 1883.

Bennett, Lerone, Jr. *Forced Into Glory: Abraham Lincoln's White Dream*. Chicago: Johnson Publishing Company, 2000.

"The Bennett-May Affair." *New York Times*, January 13, 1877.

"The Bennett-May duel turns out...." *New York Times*, January 10, 1877.

Bianco, Anthony, et al. "The Future of the New York Times." *Business Week*, January 17, 2005.

"Bloodless Duel Between Editors." *New York Times*, October 22, 1895.

"Bloodthirsty Babies." *New York Times*, June 24, 1883.

"A Bloodthirsty Tacoma Editor." *Los Angeles Times*, July 12, 1892.

"The Bloody Code." *New York Times*, October 3, 1856.

"Bloody Recontre." *Brooklyn Eagle*, February 28, 1846.

"A Blunder Under the Code." *Washington Post*, May 9, 1893.

Boehlert, Eric. "Tearing Down the Press." Salon.com, March 2, 2005, http://www.salon.com/news/feature/2005/03/02/media/index.html (March 28, 2005).

Brigham, Clarence S. *History and Bibliography of American Newspapers 1690–1820*. Worcester, Mass.: American Antiquarian Society, 1947.

"Brooks and Sumner." *Spartanburg* (S.C.) *Spartan*, May 29, 1856.

Burstein, Andrew. *The Passions of Andrew Jackson*. New York: Alfred A. Knopf, 2003.

Butterfield, Fox. *All God's Children: The Bosket Family and the American Tradition of Violence*. New York: HarperCollins, 1996.

"By the Last Mails." *Columbian Centinel*, October 2, 1802.

"By the Mails." *Columbian Centinel*, March 2, 1808.

"By Yesterday's Mails." *Columbian Centinel*, September 24, 1800.

"The California Duel." *New York Times*, October 13, 1859.

Callimachi, Rukmini. "Muslim Nations: Defame Islam, Get Sued?" *San Jose Mercury News*, March 14, 2008.

Carr, Albert H.Z. *The World and William Walker*. New York: Harper and Row, 1963.

Carroll, John M., and Colin F. Baxter, eds. *The American Military Tradition: From Colonial Times to Present, Second Edition*. Lanham, Md.: Rowman and Littlefield, 2006.

Carter, Bill. "ABC to End *Politically Incorrect*." *New York Times*, May 14, 2002.

"The Cash-Shannon Duel." *New York Times*, July 17, 1880.

"Cause and Effect." *The New Orleans Bee*, February 9, 1860. In *Southern Editorials on Secession*, ed. Dwight Lowell Dumond. Gloucester, Mass.: Peter Smith, 1964.

"Challenge to a Duel." *Washington Post*, October 8, 1893.

"Challenge to a Duel Declined." *Washington Post*, May 27, 1890.

"The Charleston Duel." *New York Times*, October 9, 1856.

Chavez, Erika. "Battle of the Blogs." Sacbee.com, 2:15 A.M. PDT, October 13, 2004, http://www.sacbee.com/content/politics/v-print/story/11073470p-11990278c.html (accessed on March 28, 2005).

Chernow, Ron. *Alexander Hamilton*. New York: Penguin Press, 2004.

"The Cilley Duel." *Brooklyn Eagle*, April 27, 1843.

Cochran, Hamilton. *Noted American Duels and Hostile Encounters*. Philadelphia and New York: Chilton Books, 1963.

Cockrell, Monroe F. "Those Duelling Editors of Vicksburg, 1841–1860." Unpublished Manuscript in the Mississippi Department of Archives and History, S/F "Dueling."

"Col. Cash, of South Carolina...." *Washington Post*, July 19, 1880.

"Comfortable." *Brooklyn Eagle*, November 18, 1843.

"Communication." *Richmond Enquirer*, March 8.

Conanson, Joe. "Gannon: The Early Years." Salon.com, February 18, 2005. http://www.salon.com/opinion/conason/2005/02/18/gannon/index.html (accessed on March 28, 2005).

"Conflict of Authorities." *Brooklyn Eagle*, December 13, 1844.

"Congress." *Brooklyn Eagle*, May 25, 1850.

"Congress." *Springfield* (Mass.) *Republican*, March 10, 1838.

"Connecticut Courant." *Connecticut Courant*, February 15, 1825.

Cooper, Michael. "Confederate Flag Takes Center Stage Once Again," *New York Times*, January 13, 2008.

Crist, Lynda L., ed. *The Papers of Jefferson Davis*, Vol. 7. Baton Rouge: Louisiana University Press, 1983.

"The Cry of Disunion." *Richmond Enquirer*, July 10, 1860. In *Northern Editorials on Secession*, Vol. 1, Howard Cecil Perkins, ed. Gloucester, Mass.: Peter Smith, 1964.

Dabney, Virginius. *Pistols and Pointed Pens*. Chapel Hill, N.C.: Algonquin Books, 1987.

Daniel, John Moncure. *The Richmond Examiner During the War or, The Writings of John M. Daniel*. New York: Printed for the Author, 1868.

"Death of Robert Tevis, Esq." *Sacramento* (Calif.) *Union*, July 17, 1855.

"Decline of the Duel." *Washington Post*, August 25, 1889.

"Definition of a Duel." *Washington Post*, January 22, 1900.

"Denouement." *Richmond Enquirer*, February 12, 1825.

Dicken-Garcia, Hazel. *Journalistic Standards in the Nineteenth-Century America*. Madison: University of Wisconsin Press, 1989.

"The Disastrous Duel." *Richmond Enquirer*, March 3, 1838.

Donath, Judith. "Blogging, Journalism and Credibility: Battleground and Common Ground." Conference held January 21–22,

2005, at Harvard University (Day one, P.M.). http://cyber.law.harvard.edu:8080/webcred/wp-content/WEBCREDtrans day1pm.htm (accessed on March 28, 2005).

Dooley, Patricia L. *Taking Their Political Place: Journalists and the Making of an Occupation.* Westport, Conn.: Greenwood Press, 1997.

Douglass, Frederick. *The Life and Times of Frederick Douglass,* London: Bemrose and Sons, 1882.

Dowd, Maureen. "Liberties: We Love the Liberties They Hate." *New York Times,* September 30, 2001.

"Duel." *Alta California,* January 13, 1851.

"A Duel." *Richmond Enquirer,* November 23, 1827.

"The Duel." *Brooklyn Eagle,* June 27, 1843.

"The Duel." *Columbian Centinel,* March, 12 1808.

"The Duel." *The Mississippian,* April 26, 1839. Transcript in the Mississippi Department of Archives and History, S/F "William H. McCardle."

"The Duel." *Richmond Enquirer,* April 14, 1826.

"A Duel, Almost." *Brooklyn Eagle,* October 6, 1842.

"A Duel at Augusta." *Atlanta Constitution,* December 12, 1872.

"Duel Between Editors." *New York Times,* September 15, 1882.

"The Duel Fought at Last." *New York Times,* July 1, 1883.

"A Duel in Georgia." *New York Times,* April 24, 1884.

"A Duel in New Jersey." *Philadelphia Press,* August 18, 1863.

"A Duel in the Streets." *New York Times,* May 2, 1888.

"The Duel Near Richmond." *Brooklyn Eagle,* November 7, 1856.

"Dueling." *Sacramento* (Calif.) *Union,* July 18, 1855.

"Dueling in the South." *Brooklyn Eagle,* June 23, 1881.

"Duelists Out of Trouble." *New York Times,* December 22, 1881.

"The Duelling Case." *Richmond Daily Dispatch,* August 22, 1864. http://dlxs.rich mond.edu/d/ddr/ (January 18, 2008) via University of Richmond Library Digital Collections.

"The Duelling Case." *Richmond Daily Dispatch,* September 5, 1864. http://dlxs.rich mond.edu/d/ddr/ (January 18, 2008) via University of Richmond Library Digital Collections.

"The Duelling Case Again." *Richmond Daily Dispatch,* August 19, 1864. http://dlxs.rich

mond.edu/d/ddr/ (January 18, 2008) via University of Richmond Library Digital Collections.

"The Duelling Case Continued." *Richmond Daily Dispatch,* August 30, 1864. http:// dlxs.richmond.edu/d/ddr/ (January 18, 2008) via University of Richmond Library Digital Collections.

"A Duelling Correspondence." *Philadelphia Press,* November 8, 1861.

"Duelling in California." *Brooklyn Eagle,* July 12, 1853.

"The Duellists." *Alta California,* January 16, 1851.

"Duellists Still Apart." *New York Times,* June 26, 1883.

"Duels and Deadly Fights." *The Columbia Spy,* May 11, 1861.

"Duels Either Farcical or Tragical." *Atlanta Constitution,* July 2, 1892. Reprint from the *New York Times.*

"Eager for the Duel." *Chicago Daily Tribune,* July 28, 1892.

Eaton, Clement. *The Growth of Southern Civilization, 1790–1860.* New York: Harper, 1961.

"Editor Gets a Challenge." *Washington Post,* January 18, 1902.

"Editor Invites a Duel." *Chicago Daily Tribune,* October 29, 1895.

"Editor Wounded in a Duel." *Washington Post,* August 31, 1898.

"Editors on the Field of Honor." *New York Times,* January 28, 1880.

"Editors Wounded in Duel." *Chicago Daily Tribune,* October 11, 1899.

"The Effects of Assaulting Editors." *Brooklyn Eagle,* May 25, 1844.

"Elam's Wound Very Serious." *New York Daily Tribune,* July 3, 1883.

"Emancipation Proclamation (final draft)." As issued on January 1, 1863, in Noah Brooks, ed., *The Writings of Abraham Lincoln.* New York: G.P Putnam's Sons, 1906.

Emery, Michael, and Edwin Emery. *The Press and America: An Interpretive History of the Mass Media.* Englewood Cliffs, N.J.: Prentice Hall, 1992.

"Eulogy on the Life and Character of Andrew Jackson." *Vicksburg Sentinel and Expositor,* July 15, 1845. In *The Papers of Jefferson Davis,* Vol. 2, ed. James T. McIntosh. Baton Rouge: Louisiana University Press, 1974.

"Examination for Duelling." *Richmond Daily Dispatch,* August 18, 1864. http://dlxs.rich mond.edu/d/ddr/ (January 18, 2008) via University of Richmond Library Digital Collections.

"Extract of a letter...." *New York Evening Post,* September 21, 1802.

"Extract of a Letter from Our Correspondent." *New York Evening Post,* March 7, 1808

"Extract of a Letter from Washington, April 11." *Richmond Enquirer,* April 18, 1826.

"Facts About the Duello." *Washington Post,* August 24, 1897.

"Fatal Affray." *Vicksburg* (Miss.) *Tri-Weekly Whig,* September 16, 1848.

"Fatal Duel." *Brooklyn Eagle,* March 14, 1844.

"The Fatal Duel." *Alta California,* July 19, 1855.

"The Fatal Duel at Charleston." *New York Times,* October 8, 1856.

"A Fatal Duel in Kentucky." *Norwalk* (Ohio) *Reflector,* May 27, 1862.

"Fatal Duel in Waco." *Washington Post,* April 2, 1898.

Fess, Simeon D. *The History of Political Theory and Party Organization in the United States.* Boston: Ginn and Company, 1910.

"Feud Between Huntsville Editors." *Washington Post,* September 24, 1893.

"The Field of Honor." *New York Herald,* July 1, 1883.

"Fighting Editors." *Los Angeles Times,* September 16, 1894.

"Fighting Editors, The." *New York Times,* July 2, 1883, 1.

"Flags That Have Flown Over Georgia: The History of the Georgia State Flag." Office of Georgia Secretary of State Website. http://sos.georgia.gov/ (accessed on March 17, 2008).

Fleischer, Ari. *Taking Heat: The President, The Press, And My Years in the White House.* New York: William Morrow, 2005.

Fleming, Thomas. *Duel: Alexander Hamilton, Aaron Burr and the Future of America.* New York: Basic Books, 1999.

Folkerts, Jean, and Dwight L. Teeter, Jr. *Voices of a Nation: A History of Media in the United States.* New York: Macmillan, 1989.

"The Following letter...." *The Mississippian,* April 22, 1842. Transcript found in the Mississippi Department of Archives and History, S/F "James S. Fall."

Foote, Henry S. *Casket of Reminiscences.* Washington, D.C.: Chronicle Publishing Company, 1874.

"The Force Policy." *The* (Lexington) *Kentucky Statesman,* December 25, 1860. In *Southern Editorials On Secession.* Edited by Dwight Lowell Dumond. Gloucester, Mass.: Peter Smith, 1964.

"Forced Editor Dupre to Fight a Duel." *Chicago Daily Tribune,* June 7, 1891.

Fost, Dan. "Bay Judge Weighs Rights of Bloggers: Journalists' Shield Claimed in Response to Apple's Lawsuit." *San Francisco Chronicle,* March 8, 2005.

"Frank P. Blair." *Philadelphia Press,* October 3, 1860.

Freeman, Joanne B. *Affairs of Honor: National Politics in the New Republic.* New Haven, Conn.: Yale University Press, 2001.

"From the Kentucky Gazette of Sept. 18, 1829." *Argus of Western America* (Ky.), October 28, 1829.

"From the Louisville Journal." *Atlanta Constitution,* June 30, 1868.

"From the N.Y. Evening Post, Oct. 17." *Richmond Enquirer,* October 25, 1859.

"From the New York American: The Late Duel at Washington." *Springfield* (Mass.) *Republican,* March 24, 1838.

"From the Newbern Gazette of Sept. 10." *American Citizen,* September 27, 1804.

"From the *Raleigh Register.*" *National Intelligencer,* September 24, 1804.

"From the St. Louis Beacon." *Richmond Enquirer,* September 23, 1831.

"From the St. Louis Beacon." *Washington Globe,* September 16, 1831.

"From the St. Louis Beacon of August 27." *Richmond Enquirer,* September 13, 1831.

"Funeral Ceremonies of Saturday." *Vicksburg Sentinel and Expositor,* July 8, 1845.

Garrett, William Robertson, and Robert Ambrose Halley. *The History of North America, Vol. 14: The Civil War from a Southern Standpoint.* Philadelphia: George Barrie and Sons, 1905.

"General Hamilton's Death." *American Citizen,* July 23, 1804.

"General Schurz to Leslie Combs." *Philadelphia Press,* November 25, 1863.

"General Telegrams." *Brooklyn Eagle,* July 18, 1880.

"Geo. J. Trotter, Esq." *Argus of Western America* (Ky.), November 18, 1829.

Gienapp, William E. *The Origins of the Republican Party, 1852–1856.* New York, Oxford: Oxford University Press, 1987.

Glater, Jonathan D. "Liberal Bloggers Reaching Out to Major Media." *New York Times,* March 14, 2005.

"Gone to Fight a Duel." *New York Times,* July 28, 1885.

"The Great Battle." *Chicago Daily Democrat,* November 5, 1860. In *Northern Editorials on Secession,* Vol. 1, Howard Cecil Perkins, ed. Gloucester, Mass.: Peter Smith, 1964.

"The Great Issue and the Choice — Separation or War." *Albany Atlas and Argus,* January 12, 1861. In *Northern Editorials on Secession,*

Vol. 1, Howard Cecil Perkins, ed. Gloucester, Mass.: Peter Smith, 1964.

Greg, Robert Philips. *On the Meaning and Origin of the Fylfot and Swastika.* Westminster: Nichols and Sons, 1884.

Gregory, Winifred, ed. *American Newspapers, 1821–1936: A Union List of Files Available in the United States and Canada.* New York: H.W. Wilson, 1937.

"H. Rives Pollard." *Harpers Weekly,* December 12, 1868.

"Hamilton Gambrell Case." *Atlanta Consitution,* June 1, 1887.

"His Kentucky Blood is Up." *Washington Post,* February 10, 1898.

Holland, Barbara. "Bang! Bang! You're Dead." *Smithsonian Magazine,* October 1997, 122.

_____. "Gentlemen's Blood: A History of Dueling from Swords at Dawn to Pistols at Dusk." New York and London: Bloomsbury, 2003.

"Honor Easily Satisfied." *New York Times,* May 24, 1881.

"A Hostile Meeting." *Richmond Daily Dispatch,* August 17, 1864. http://dlxs.richmond.edu/d/ddr/ (January 18, 2008) via University of Richmond Library Digital Collections.

"House of Representatives." *Washington Globe,* February 26, 1838.

"House of Representatives: Monday, Feb. 12, 1838." *Congressional Globe,* February 19, 1838.

Huston, James L. *Stephen A. Douglas and the Dilemmas of Democratic Equality.* Lanham, Md.: Rowman and Littlefield, 2006.

"The Impending Fight." *New York Herald,* June 26, 1883.

"Important Decision." *Richmond Daily Dispatch,* February 8, 1865. http://dlxs.richmond.edu/d/ddr/ (January 18, 2008) via University of Richmond Library Digital Collections.

"Important News from California." *New York Times,* October 10, 1859.

"It is with deep regret...." *Richmond Enquirer.* April 15, 1808.

"Jefferson Davis Speech to the Confederate Congress at Richmond, January 12, 1863." Quoted in Edward A. Pollard, *The Lost Cause: A New Southern History of the War of the Confederates.* New York: E.B. Treat, 1867.

Johns Hopkins University. *The Johns Hopkins University Studies in Historical and Political Science.* Baltimore, Md.: John Hopkins University Press, 1914, Vol. 32.

"Judge Meredith's Court." *Richmond Daily Dispatch,* September 3, 1864. http://dlxs.

richmond.edu/d/ddr/ (January 18, 2008) via University of Richmond Library Digital Collections.

Katcher, Philip. *Flags of the Civil War.* Botley, Oxford (U.K.): Osprey Publishing, 2000.

Kuhnhenn, Jim. "Confederate Flag Ad Praises Huckabee," *Boston Globe,* January 18, 2008.

Kurtz, Howard. "Political Perspectives with Tunnel Vision." *Washington Post,* February 7, 2005.

"The Late Duel." *Congressional Globe,* July 9, 1838.

"The Late Fashionable Murder —." *Springfield* (Mass.) *Republican.* March 3, 1838.

"The Late Robert Tevis." *Sacramento* (Calif.) *Union,* July 21, 1855.

"The Late Savage Duel." *Columbian Centinel,* February 24, 1819.

"Latest Southern Duel." *New York Daily Tribune,* June 26, 1883.

"Letter from Sarah Helen Whitman, Providence, ALS, to James Ingram," February 27, 1874. In John Henry Ingram's Edgar Allan Poe Collection in the University of Virginia Special Collections.

"Letter from Washington says...." *New York Evening Post,* February 12, 1819.

"The Licentiousness of Party." *Lancaster* (Pa.) *Daily Evening Express,* January 17, 1861. In *Northern Editorials on Secession,* Vol. 2, Howard Cecil Perkins, ed. Gloucester, Mass.: Peter Smith, 1964.

Lincoln, Abraham. "Speech in Springfield, Illinois, June 26, 1857." In *The Complete Works of Abraham Lincoln,* vol. 2. Edited by. James G. Nicolay and John Hay. New York: Francis D. Tandy, 1905.

Lydon, Chris. "Blogging, Journalism and Credibility: Battleground and Common Ground." Conference held January 21–22, 2005 at Harvard University (Day one, A.M.). http://cyber.law.harvard.edu:8080/webcred/wp-content/WEBCREDtransday1am.htm (accessed on March 28, 2005).

"Matters in Vicksburg." *Philadelphia Press,* April 30, 1863.

Matthews, Chris. *Hardball with Chris Matthews.* September 1, 2004, 11 P.M., on MSNBC. http://www.msnbc.msn.com/id/5892840/ (accessed on March 28, 2005).

_____. *Hardball with Chris Matthews.* September 1, 2004, 6 P.M., on MSNBC. http://www.msnbc.msn.com/id/5891366/ (accessed on March 28, 2005).

Mattox, Charles. "Heaven Is a lot Like Kentucky," *Carlisle* (Kentucky) *Mercury,* June 20, 2007.

"The May-Bennett Trouble." *New York Times,* January 7, 1877.

"The Mayer–De Mores Duel." *Chicago Daily Tribune*, June 29, 1892.

"Mayor Wood...." *Brooklyn Eagle*, January 8, 1861.

McCullough, David. Keynote Speech of the Ohio University Undergraduate Commencement Ceremony. Saturday, June 12, 2004. Ohio University 2004 Commencement Video.

Mears, Walter R. "A Brief History of AP." In Reporters of the Associated Press, *Breaking News: How the Associated Press Has Covered War, Peace, and Everything Else*. New York: Princeton Architectural Press, 2007.

"Melancholy Event." *Richmond Enquirer*, February 11, 1819.

Miller, Senator Zell. Keynote Speech at the Republican National Convention. September 1, 2004. http://www.gopconvention.com/cgi-data/speeches/files/ie65ay1zuai2r6ttb19uj6s2y6q7930j.shtml (accessed on March 28, 2005).

"Mischief of Sensation Reports." *Newark* (New Jersey) *Daily Advertiser*, January 12, 1861. In *Northern Editorials on Secession*, Vol. 2, Howard Cecil Perkins, ed. Gloucester, Mass.: Peter Smith, 1964.

"Mr. Bennett Sails for Europe." *New York Times*, January 15, 1877.

"Mr. Buchanan and Fortnet." *Augusta* (Ga.)*Chronicle*, October 16, 1859.

"Mr. Clay on Duelling." *Brooklyn Eagle*, August 26, 1844.

"Mr. Elam's Condition Critical." *New York Times*, July 3, 1883.

"Mr. Pryor, of the Richmond *Enquirer*...." *Brooklyn Eagle*, October 8, 1856.

"Monday, September 27." *New York Evening Post*, September 27.

"Monument to Mr. Pettis." *United States Telegraph*, September 10, 1831.

Morris, Leo. "The Pajamaheddin Prevail." *Fort Wayne* (Indiana) *News-Sentinel*, September 23, 2004.

Mott, Frank L. *American Journalism: A History, 1690–1960*. New York: Macmillan, 1962.

"Muzzling the Press." *Alta California*, January 14, 1851.

"Nashville, June 7." *New York Evening Post*, July 7, 1806.

"Nashville, May 24, 1806." *American Citizen*, July 14, 1806.

Nevins, Allan. *The Evening Post*. New York: Boni and Liveright, 1922.

"New Orleans, March 4." *New York Evening Post*, March 29, 1808.

"The News by the Illinois." *New York Times*, July 12, 1853.

"News of the Morning." *New York Daily Tribune*, July 1, 1883.

"Newspaper Provocations." *New York World*, November 28, 1860. In *Northern Editorials on Secession*, Vol. 2, Howard Cecil Perkins, ed. Gloucester, Mass.: Peter Smith, 1964.

"New York City." *American Citizen*, March 8, 1808.

"New York City." *Philadelphia Press*, May 26, 1863.

"New-York Evening Post." *New York Evening Post*, July 12, 1804.

"New-York Evening Post." *New York Evening Post*, July 24, 1804.

"New-York Evening Post." *New York Evening Post*, August 20, 1804.

Nye, Robert. *Masculinity and Male Codes of Honor in Modern France*. Berkeley: University of California Press, 1998.

Olsen, Christopher. *Political Culture and Secession in Mississippi: Masculinity, Honor, and the Antiparty Tradition, 1830–1860*. New York: Oxford University Press, 2000.

"The Political Aspects of Killing Broderick." *New York Times*, October 13, 1859.

"The Political Ethics of Dueling." *Washington Post*, July 11, 1883.

"Political Murder." *New York Times*, October 10, 1859.

Pollard, Edward A. *The Lost Cause: A New Southern History of the War of the Confederates*. New York: E.B. Treat, 1867.

"The Pollard Homicide." *New York Times*, March 7, 1869.

"A Possible Consequence of the Duel." *New York Daily Tribune*, July 2, 1883.

"Preparing for a Duel in Oklahoma." *Chicago Daily Tribune*, December 6, 1890.

"Probable Duel Between Editors." *Chicago Daily Tribune*, January 25, 1896.

Quarles, Benjamin. *Lincoln and the Negro*. New York: Da Capo Press, 1991.

Quinn, Arthur. *The Rivals: William Gwin, David Broderick, and the Birth of California*. New York: Crown Publishers, 1994.

Qureshi, Emran. "The Islam the Riots Drowned Out." *New York Times*, February 12, 2008.

"'Rebecca' Letter." August 27, 1842. In *The Collected Works of Abraham Lincoln*, vol. 1Edited by Roy P. Basler, Marion Dolores Pratt, and Lloyd A. Dunlap. 9 vols. Springfield, Ill.: Abraham Lincoln Association; New Brunswick, N.J.: Rutgers University Press, 1953.

Reeves, Richard. "Patriotism Calls Out the Censor." *New York Times*, October 1, 2001.

Remini, Robert V. *Andrew Jackson and the Course of American Freedom: 1822–1832*.

Baltimore and London: Johns Hopkins University Press, 1981.

_____. *Andrew Jackson and the Course of American Freedom: 1833–1845.* Baltimore and London: Johns Hopkins University Press, 1984.

"Republican Convention." *New York Times,* February 26, 1856.

"Republicanism in Missouri." *New York Times,* May 26, 1860.

Rich, Frank. "All the President's Newsmen." *New York Times,* January 16, 2005.

"The Richmond Duelists." *New York Times,* June 28, 1883.

"Riddleberger on a Rampage." *Washington Post,* October 16, 1881.

Sabine, Lorenzo. *Notes on Duels and Duelling.* Boston: Crosby, Nichols, and Company, 1859.

Safire, William. "The Depressed Press." *New York Times,* January 17, 2005.

"Scenes of the Senate." *Vermont Gazette,* May 9, 1825.

"Searching for Bierne and Elam." *New York Daily Tribune,* June 24, 1883.

Seelye Katharine Q., et al. "Bloggers as News Media Trophy Hunters." *New York Times,* February 14, 2005.

_____. "Media: White House Approves Pass for Blogger." *New York Times,* March 7, 2005.

Seitz, Don C. *Famous American Duels.* New York: Thomas Y. Crowell, 1929.

"The Sheriff Alone Injured." *Washington Post,* May 7, 1893.

"Sikh is Shot." National Briefing, Southwest Arizona. *New York Times,* May 22, 2003.

Simon, John Y., Harold Holzer, and Dawn Vogel, eds., *Lincoln Revisited.* Bronx, N.Y.: Fordham University Press, 2007.

Sloan, Harry L. *Liberty of Power: The Politics of Jacksonian American.* New York: Hill and Wang, 2001.

Sloan, William David, and James G. Stovall, eds.; James D. Startt, associate ed. *The Media in America: A History.* Worthington, Ohio: Publishing Horizons, 1989.

Smith, Elbert B. *Francis Preston Blair.* New York: The Free Press, 1980.

"Society of Lexington, Ky." *Argus of Western America* (Ky.), October 28, 1829.

"Solemnity of the Duello." *Washington Post,* September 17, 1893.

"Solemnity of the Duello." *Washington Post,* September 18, 1893.

"Some Notes on James Franklin Hagan." In the Mississippi Department of Archives and History, S/F "James Hagan."

"Somebody Must Die." *Washington Post,* November 17, 1891.

"The South as It Is." *New York Times,* November 2, 1865.

"Southern Outrages." *Daily Chicago Times,* December 14, 1860. In *Northern Editorials on Secession,* Vol. 2, Howard Cecil Perkins, ed. Gloucester, Mass.: Peter Smith, 1964.

"The Southron." June 14, 1843. Transcript in the Mississippi Department of Archives and History, S/F "James Hagan."

"The Speech of Senator Douglas." *Brooklyn Eagle,* July 13, 1858.

Spierenburg, Peter, ed. *Men and Violence: Gender Honor, and Rituals in Modern Europe and America.* Columbus: Ohio State University Press, 1998.

"The State Flag." *South Carolina Legislature Online.* http://www.scstatehouse.net/studentpage/flag.htm. (accessed on March 17, 2008).

"Statement." *New York Times,* May 23, 1864.

"A Statement of Facts." *Lexington* (Ky.) *Gazette,* March 20, 1829.

Steers, Edward, Jr. "Book Review of *Forced Into Glory: Abraham Lincoln's White Dream,*" *Springfield* (Illinois) *State-Journal Register,* June 25, 2000.

Stevens, William Oliver. *Pistol at Ten Paces.* Boston, Houghton Mifflin, 1940.

Steward, Dick. *Duels and the Roots of Violence in Missouri.* Colombia and London: University of Missouri Press, 2000.

"A Street Encounter." *New York Times,* January 4, 1877.

"The Strongest Government in the World." *Richmond Daily Dispatch,* March 2, 1864. http://dlxs.richmond.edu/d/ddr/ (January 18, 2008) via University of Richmond Library Digital Collections.

"Submit to the Constitution, But Resist the First Attempt to Enforce the Principles of the Republican Party." *The* (Lexington) *Kentucky Statesman,* November 13, 1860. In *Southern Editorials on Secession,* ed. Dwight Lowell Dumond. Gloucester, Mass.: Peter Smith, 1964.

Sumner, Charles. "The Crime Against Kansas." In *The Life of Charles Sumner: With Choice Specimens of His Eloquence, a Delineation of his Oratorical Character, and His Great Speech on Kansas,* D.A. Harsha, New York: Dayton and Burdick, 1856.

Tagore, Sourindro Mohun. *The Orders of Knighthood, British and Foreign, with a Brief Review of the Titles of Rank and Merit in Ancient Hindusthan.* Calcutta: Catholic Orphan Press, 1884.

Tebbel, John. *Compact History of the American*

Newspaper. New York, Hawthorn Books, 1963.

"Tennessee." *Richmond Enquirer,* July 1, 1806.

"Testimonials of Respect for the Memory of General Jackson." *Vicksburg Sentinel,* June 23, 1845.

"That Duel." *New York Daily Tribune,* June 27, 1883.

"Their Duel Only Postponed." *Washington Post,* December 17, 1894.

"They Were After Blood." *Chicago Daily Tribune,* September 26, 1891.

"Threats and Responses; An Iraqi Offer: Duels Not War." *New York Times,* October 2, 2002.

"To the Editor Of the Argus." *Argus of Western America* (Ky.), October 28, 1829.

"Tract No. 1." *Brooklyn Eagle,* March 15, 1844.

"A True Bill for Murder." *Brooklyn Eagle,* June 20, 1844.

Truman, Major Ben C., Steven Randolph Wood, ed. *Duelling in America.* San Diego: Joseph Tabler Books, 1992.

"Tuesday Evening June 5." *Brooklyn Eagle,* June 5, 1860.

"Two Georgia Duels on the Tapis." *Washington Post,* December 30, 1886.

"Unfortunate Recontre and Loss of Life." *Norfolk* (Va.) *Beacon,* March 31, 1843.

"The Usual Georgia Duel." *Washington Post,* August 30, 1885.

"Various painful...." *Vicksburg* (Miss.) *Tri-Weekly Whig,* September 19, 1848.

"The Vicksburg Sentinel." In the Mississippi Department of Archives and History, S/F "Dueling."

Vicksburg Tri-Weekly Whig, June 26, July 1, 1845. In *The Papers of Jefferson Davis,* Vol. 2, ed. James T. McIntosh. Baton Rouge: Louisiana University Press, 1974, n264.

"Virginia." *Atlanta Constitution,* October 12, 1870.

"Virginia Duellists — Encounter in North Carolina." *New York Times,* June 14, 1869.

"Virginia Methods." *New York Times,* October 18, 1881.

Von Holst, Hermann. *The Constitutional and Political History of the United States: 1859–1861; Harper's Ferry to Lincoln's Inauguration.* Chicago: Callaghan and Company, 1892.

Vorenberg, Michael. "Lincoln and Politics of Black Colonization." In *For a Vast Future*

Also: Essays from the Journal of the Abraham Lincoln Association, Thomas F. Schwarz, ed. New York: Fordham University Press, 1999.

Walsh, Joan. "Who Killed Dan Rather?" Salon.com. March 9, 2005. http://archive.salon.com/opinion/feature/2005/03/09/rather/ (March 28, 2005).

"Warring Editors in Georgia." *New York Times,* November 6, 1897.

"Washington City." *National Intelligencer,* March 14, 1808.

"Washington City." *National Intelligencer,* September 22, 1802.

"Washington, Jan. 25, 1825." *Vermont Gazette,* February 15, 1825.

"We Grieve to Learn that Henry W. Conway...." *Richmond Enquirer,* December 6, 1827.

Webb, James. "Pistols for Two: Coffee for One." In *American Heritage,* February 1975.

Wells, C.A. Harwell. "The End of the Affair? Anti-Dueling Laws and Social Norms in Antebellum America." *Vanderbilt Law Review,* 54, 2001, 1813–1846.

Williams, David C. *David C. Broderick: A Political Portrait.* San Marino, Calif.: Huntington Library, 1969.

"Williamsburg (Virginia)." *Pennsylvania Packet,* July 1, 1777.

Wilmer, Lambert A. *Our Press Gang; or, A Complete Exposition of the Corruptions and Crimes of the American Newspapers.* Philadelphia: J.T. Lloyd; London: S. Low, Son and Co., 1859.

Woodberry, George. *The Life of Edgar Allan Poe.* 2 vol. Boston and New York: Houghton Mifflin, 1909.

Wyatt-Brown, Bertram. *Honor, Shame, and Iraq in American Foreign Policy.* Note prepared for the Workshop on Humiliation and Violent Conflict, Columbia University, New York, November 18–19, 2004, 1. http://www.humiliationstudies.org/documents/WyattBrownNovNYConference.pdf (March 28, 2005).

_____. *The Shaping of Southern Culture: Honor, Grace, and War, 1760s–1880s.* Chapel Hill.: University of North Carolina Press, 2001.

_____. *Southern Honor: Ethics and Behavior in the Old South.* New York: Oxford University Press, 1982.

Index

www.ingramcontent.com/pod-product-compliance
Lightning Source LLC
Chambersburg PA
CBHW031132270326
41929CB00011B/1597